BOY SMARTS

MENTORING BOYS FOR SUCCESS AT SCHOOL

Boys are worth it!

Barry

BARRY MACDONALD B.Ed, M.A., R.C.C.

Visit the author's website at www.MentoringBoys.com

For my mother:
Because you believed in me I learned to believe in myself.

Mentoring Press
A division of Sagepoint Consulting Inc.
Ocean Park PO Box 45053
Surrey, BC V4A 9L1
Canada

Email at: boysmarts@mentoringboys.com

Library and Archives Canada Cataloguing in Publication

MacDonald, Barry, 1959-
Boy smarts : mentoring boys for success at school / Barry A. MacDonald.

Includes bibliographical references and index.
ISBN 0-9738787-0-3
1. Boys--Education. 2. Boys--Psychology. 3. Academic achievement--Sex differences. 4. Sex differences in education.
I. Title.

LC1390.M32 2005   371.823   C2005-904908-1

BOY SMARTS

MENTORING BOYS FOR SUCCESS AT SCHOOL

"You MUST read this book if you are raising or teaching boys. Boy Smarts is simply the BEST there is on this subject." – *Dr. Linda Albert, author, Cooperative Discipline*

• • • • •

"MacDonald writes with a human voice that speaks from trusted experience, astuteness, and addresses the concerns I have had at home, as well as with male students in the university setting. Everyone needs this book – even if you don't have boys – your girls will encounter the challenges identified in Boy Smarts." – *Monica Scott, Career Centre Coordinator, University of Toronto*

• • • • •

"This vanguard book is passionate, balanced, and bold. MacDonald offers the inside story and amazing guidance to teach, parent, and coach boys. This book is a must read for anyone serious about leading boys to become strong, caring, and principled men." – *Ken Berry, 1980 and 1988 Olympian (Team Canada Hockey), NHL Left Winger, President, Kootenay Gold Inc.*

• • • • •

"I can tell you for a fact that this book is great! I was failing school, fighting, and at the principal's office all the time until Mr. MacDonald coached me, and my mom and teachers. Because of him and his support my life began to turn around. It is now 3 years later and I'm getting solid B's and I'm the receiver on my football team. We just won the BC championships!" – *Robbie M., Grade 11 Student*

• • • • •

"Boy Smarts integrates and condenses complex theory into practical relevance that is succinct, salient, and strategic. It is thought provoking and just plain useful. I highly recommend it!" – *Dr. Russell King, Dean, Adler School of Professional Psychology*

BOY SMARTS

MENTORING BOYS FOR SUCCESS AT SCHOOL

BOYS ARE HALF OUR FUTURE

Children are the living messages we send to a time that we will not see.
Neil Postman

• • • • •

What I saw as anxiety was interpreted as defiance and arrogance.

As an educator and Registered Clinical Counsellor working with students who are struggling and are *at-risk* for more than the past 20 years, I have seen many boys who are floundering miserably in our public school system. I see that boys are more fragile than they appear to be. I also see that they are often misread. I remember, for example, one ten year-old, who responded to a principal's questioning by fidgeting, tapping his foot, and looking away. What I saw as anxiety was interpreted as defiance and arrogance. Boys' reticence or shyness is mistaken for a lack of feeling. Their active learning patterns may be seen as threatening, and the boys themselves seem to become their labels: ADHD – attention deficit and hyperactivity disorder, or BD – behaviour disordered. Their physical forms of bonding are perceived as aggression. We can be overly quick to write them off as unteachable. As one mother said, "The teacher kept saying his lack of attention and misbehaviour was stopping him from learning, but no one really understood how to teach him."

COUNTLESS meetings with parents, school administrators, counsellors, and teachers regarding the plight of boys who are at risk of underachieving, or worse, dropping out of school, have taught me first hand about the frustrations and deep concerns for our boys who are struggling in school.

• • • • •

We are told

that boys are in

academic, social,

and emotional

danger, and are

more likely to be

in trouble with the

law than girls are.

When we read headlines announcing their inferior academic achievement and high dropout rates, we shake our heads, wondering how on earth boys will ever make it in this world. We are told that boys are in academic, social, and emotional danger, and are more likely to be in trouble with the law than girls are. Canadian statistical data from 1997 found that among youth charged with a crime, 78% were male while 22% were female and 50% of those males charged were 16 or 17 years of age. Among those charged with theft under $5000, 27% of males received a custody order while 53% were granted probation. In contrast, 17% of females were held in custody while 60% were put on probation. The American data tells an even more dismal story. Males are at increased risk for a plethora of social problems: at increased risk for substance abuse, anti-social behaviour and even suicide. Canada and the U.S. lag far behind all Western democracies in the study of boys' welfare despite the fact that indicators of their declining status have been observable for many years.

MANY SCHOOLS BECAME MORE CONCERNED WITH IDENTIFYING POTENTIAL BULLIES THAN WITH MEETING THE LEARNING NEEDS OF BOYS.

We are told that boys are emotionally impaired, that they are prone to violence despite the fact that youth violence is at a 20 year low. In the wake of school shootings in the United States and Canada, a media-induced frenzy generated more heat than light regarding the needs of boys. Televised images from Columbine, Colorado, and Taber, Alberta have become indelible images of our nightmares with close up footage of terrified students seeking safety, cut-away photographs of the victims, and yearbook mug shots of the alleged male killers.

POPULAR culture showed boys as trigger-happy and prone to violence, creating a crisis mentality that has led many North American educators to overreact to playground *rough-and-tumble play,* which became marked as bullying behaviour. Many schools became more concerned with identifying potential bullies than with meeting the learning needs of boys. Responding to the needs of all children connected with harassment–the bully, the bullied, and bystander–is essential. Zero tolerance is just futile.

• • • • •

Girls are outperforming boys in reading and writing in all western countries and in all Canadian provinces.

Many thoughtful people are worried about the plight of boys in schools and society. Girls are outperforming boys in reading and writing in all western countries and in all Canadian provinces. *The Progress in International Reading Literacy Study* assessment conducted in 2001, for example, revealed that Grade 4 girls performed better than boys in all thirty-four countries where the assessment was administered, including Canada and the U.S. The assessment administered by the *Education Quality and Accountability Office* to students in Grades 3 and 6 show that boys did not perform as well as girls in reading and writing. The American Congress requested a report from The National Center for Educational

BOYS ARE LAGGING BEHIND GIRLS IN GENDER EQUITY.

Statistics titled, *Trends in Educational Equality of Girls and Women* and claims that females have consistently out performed males in reading and writing; that they are more active than males in community service activities; that they are more likely than men to persist and attain degrees; that they generally receive a greater earnings advantage from post-secondary education than men, and so forth. Many other studies from other countries tell a similar story of boys lagging significantly behind girls in gender equity.

I would caution us, however, not to over-generalize about causal links between gender and achievement in our schools. Unchallenged, media-touted statistical tendencies and perceived trends can create unnecessary anxiety and lead to damaging labels and expectations for specific boys' lives. Our boys are not statistics. The swaggering boy with the blue hair, eyebrow piercing, baggy jeans, and perhaps a tattoo is trying to make sense of the world in his own way.

• • • • •

Positive change

begins by

capitalizing on

strengths and

past success.

OF COURSE, we must be careful not to swing away from our concern about girls' achievement to a *binary trap* whereby gains made by girls are assumed to equate to losses by boys and the problems caused by gender stereotyping. While stressing the importance of understanding the complex issues around boys' and girls' achievement in school, *Failing Boys: Issues in Gender and Achievement,* published by the University of London in 1998, aimed to move beyond alarmist descriptions and proposed solutions and toward a more thoughtful analysis as to why boys' underachievement has suddenly become an object of concern.

UNCHALLENGED, MEDIA-TOUTED STATISTICAL TENDENCIES AND PERCEIVED TRENDS CAN CREATE UNNECESSARY ANXIETY AND LEAD TO DAMAGING LABELS.

Parenting and teaching children – boys and girls – are great privileges and great challenges. Boys have unique gifts and talents. If we allow ourselves to learn about boys' special strengths and abilities, we can begin to imagine how we might better meet their learning needs by helping them to engage more fully in school and guiding them to develop a lifelong interest for learning. Positive change begins by capitalizing on strengths and past success. Understanding a boy's talents and how to mentor these talents is the central endeavor of this book.

Boy Smarts offers a conceptual framework of 100 practical, but not dogmatic, guidelines to help parents and teachers address the varied learning needs of boys. To avoid distracting readers with research citations and documentation, I refer readers to the bibliography for the references I have cited.

THE following is a sampling of the issues and questions I will address:

- How does a boy's brain organization differ than a girl's? *Chaper Two*

- Why are boys so independent and focused on maintaining status? *pages 46 & 74*

- How can we listen beyond a boy's bravado and veneer of indifference? *page 82*

- How can schools make learning more active and kinesthetic? *Chapter Eight*

- What role does competition play in boys' learning? *page 159*

- How can we manage a boy's aggressive tendencies without squashing his spirit? *page 180*

- What are consequences that are restorative and not punitive? *page 185*

- How can school staff avoid bandwagon thinking & develop a unique plan of action? *page 216*

THIS book is a practical, hands-on book for parents and educators. The 100 guidelines offered in *Boy Smarts* are divided equally among ten chapters. To illustrate the range of school issues that affect boys, I have included real-life narratives based on my experiences as a teacher, counsellor, and school district consultant/coordinator. I have changed the boys' names and identifying characteristics to protect identities without altering the meaning and significance of their accounts.

The recommendations for mentoring and teaching boys presented throughout this book could serve as groundwork for a school's action plan to raise boys' achievement – a manual for kick-starting a boy's ingenuity.

Boy Smarts has been a work of the heart. It is my hope that it will inspire you so that you, in turn, can help inspire the boys who are our future.

• • • • •

The recommendations for mentoring and teaching boys presented throughout this book could serve as groundwork for a school's action plan.

ACKNOWLEDGEMENTS

I HAVE stood on the shoulders of many creative and strong individuals – colleagues, friends, family, students, and parents, who have collectively made this book possible. I would like to take this opportunity to express gratitude to some of the many people who helped to make Boy Smarts progress from a workshop format into print.

FIRST, I would like to thank my lovely wife, **Therese MacDonald,** who encouraged my circuitous path to completion while delighting in my obsession. She is the best first reader and cheerleader that I could have hoped for. **Sue Ann Cairns**, my editor and a professor at Kwantlen University, outdid herself while I worked in fits and starts. She helped me to be selective and focussed; separated the wheat from the chaff; and warmly offered lucid and critical advice. I sensed from her all the while a deep passion for helping kids, educators, and parents – and boys in particular. Putting a manuscript into a design form that brings it further alive is a task for a visually gifted person. **Susan Cairns**, no relation to Sue Ann Cairns, is a maestro with computer design. Her ideas have made these words easy on the eyes. **Raymond Brown**, artist and illustrator extraordinaire, is responsible for the wonderful drawings of boys meandering throughout the book. Thank you to **John Spooner,** the ingenious photographer who created the book cover photograph. Copy-editing requires absolute persnickety-ness – **Dana Schepikoff** and **Marion McCristall** attended to these details with clarity and dedication, and I am grateful.

OVER the years I have worked with many brilliant colleagues, parents and students who have taught me that school leadership is about creating a place where people want to belong and excel at learning, whatever the age. To all of you I am most appreciative of your knowledge, candor, and creativity. In particular I want to extend my gratefulness to: Edna Nash, Linda Albert, Manfred Sonstegard, John Allan, Shen Elderton, Don Smart, Marilyn McGuire, Jim Bitter, Tim Richards, Gail Stanhope-Richards, John Spooner, Catherine Ralphs, Jim Skinner, Barbara McLeod, Dyan Burnell, Margaret Hanscom-Garrard, Donna Walker, and the Men's Inquiry Group in Calgary. In each of your unique ways, you have encouraged and inspired me to: "Seek out that particular mental attribute which makes you feel most deeply and vitally alive, along with which comes the inner voice which says – This is the real me – and when you have found that attitude, follow it." – William James

TO the innumerable students, parents, and teachers with whom I have journeyed: thank you for trusting me with your wisdom and angst, your challenges, questions, and innovations. Your willingness to live and explore at your edge of comfort fueled and sustained my commitment. I have been enriched beyond comprehension.

MAKING SENSE OF THE
GENDER **GAP**

Loving a child doesn't mean giving in to all his whims; to love him is to bring out the best in him, to teach him to love what is difficult.

Nadia Boulanger - celebrated French conductor

• • • • •

J ust outside my front door and across the street, a 10 year-old neighbourhood boy is gliding past the house on a skateboard while balancing a hockey stick in his mouth. As he balances the stick and board's movement, I marvel at his dexterity and concentration. Why, I wonder, has he embarked on this adventure? Simply for the challenge? For something interesting to do? He torques into the next driveway, seeming to relish its steepness. I watch him as he jumps off the board, swooping it and the hockey stick under one arm before running to the front door, and knocking.

In my next view of him, he is emerging from the garage, dragging a hockey net onto the driveway. With the stick in his mouth, he balances the net on the front of his skateboard. His left foot steadies the back of the skateboard and his right one provides the push power. The going is slow. The balance is precarious. In his intensely focussed concentration on this engineering feat, he looks happy. I marvel at this boy's ingenuity and ladish adventure, his ability to make the mundane task of transporting play tools stimulating and complex.

How do we as parents, as educators, as caring adults begin to recognize and celebrate this and all boys' special competence, gifts, and talents?

PARENTAL QUESTIONS **ABOUT THE GENDER GAP**

AS marked differences between girls and boys in overall school performance have emerged in the past decade, parents started asking questions. When it appeared that girls were falling behind in math and sciences, parents supported initiatives for girls and lobbied for adequate resources and professional development. However, as national and international studies about boys in school showed that boys were struggling and falling behind, parents have challenged the meaning of gender equity, and the way some *gender programs* that have focussed on girls have appeared to overlook the needs of boys. Of course, many children and adolescents struggle with learning, teaching personalities, and typical youth pressures, but the learning problems of boys have become increasingly hard to ignore.

• • • • •

The learning problems of boys have become increasingly hard to ignore.

• Boys have more behaviour problems in school.

• Boys are more likely to be implicated in bullying and harassment.

• Boys are more frequently absent from school.

• Boys are more likely to be suspended or expelled from school.

• Boys are more likely to be assigned a special behaviour category label, such as *behaviour disordered*.

• Boys are less likely than girls to go to university.

• Boys are more likely to drop out of school.

• Boys are more likely to commit suicide.

Parents want thoughtful and imaginative responses to their concerns through programs that identify the gender dimension in young people's experiences at school and that focus on helping both girls and boys to achieve their potential. They also want gender work to move beyond critique to provide hope and possibilities, so that boys and girls can learn social roles that are not characterized by domination and oppression. Parents are especially worried about what their sons are learning, and not learning, in school.

• • • • •

Parents long to

help their boys,

but feel helpless

to counteract the

power of peer

pressure and the

media.

IN my capacity as a Registered Clinical Counselor, consultant, and central office coordinator in a large urban school district I have listened to countless mothers describe their son's frustrations with school and their sadness at losing emotional connection with them. They have lamented their sons' struggles to hold back tears for fear of appearing weak. They long to help their boys, but feel helpless to counteract the power of peer pressure and the media. In a CBC Radio interview about the topic of raising boys last year, one of the mothers I invited to join our discussion spoke very passionately about being *pushed out of the nest* when her son distanced himself in his attempt to be a man. Mothers everywhere express their concern as boys arrive home from school with negative attitudes toward reading, teachers, and learning in general. They recognize their boys' capacity to create, but grieve to see the spark of enthusiasm smolder and die in school.

BETTER TO LOOK COOL THAN NERDY. BETTER TO APPEAR SLOTHFUL, ARROGANT, AND DISINTERESTED IN SCHOOL THAN TO LOOK LIKE A FAILURE, A LOSER, OR WORSE – *A SUCK-UP.*

The need to belong can drive boys to assume a hyper-masculine image and simply adopt the behaviours of those males nearby who offer a sense of place. Boys learn about masculinity, however, not only from their peers, but also from the men in their lives, particularly their fathers. Like their sons, fathers are subject to contradictory pressure placed on males to be independent and tough-minded while also being sensitive. I suspect that the anti-intellectual sentiment currently touted by trendy culture implicitly pressures boys to underachieve at school and excel in the wild, on the street.

THE EDUCATOR'S **DILEMMA**

• • • • •

Efforts to raise the

achievement of

boys must be

made without

threatening the

gains made by

girls in recent

years.

AT times the public discussion around gender and schooling has suggested that we must choose between boys' education and girls' education, that there has been enough focus on girls, and that now it is the boys' turn. This simplistic notion distracts from our shared aim. Efforts to raise the achievement of boys must be made without threatening the gains made by girls in recent years. Thoughtful educators who wish to provide equitable learning are questioning assumptions about curriculum, pedagogy, and assessment. They may even be asking provocative questions about the very nature of schooling: "What is school for?" As educators, our aim is to help all children – girls and boys – achieve their full potential. But while providing equitable opportunities for girls is a familiar topic, providing them for boys is a fairly recent, and increasingly urgent agenda.

Although gender interacts in complex ways with other social factors such as race, ethnicity, locality, and aspects of socio-economic status, to influence the educational success of children, be they boys or girls, gender disparity in school performance is reasonably clear. In the past, educators and parents used to take some consolation that while boys typically did not fare as well in humanities and languages, they excelled in the abstract world of math and science. Not any more. Data from many school districts reveal that where boys once

WHAT IS SCHOOL FOR?

out-performed girls in Calculus 12, for example, it is girls who are getting more A's. Current data additionally reveals that fewer girls are receiving failing lower grades than boys in this subject.

We must be wary of exaggerating small discrepancies in academic assessments as it has also been noted that there is more overlap between the achievement of boys and girls than difference. We must avoid scapegoating the bigger issues in education, that of under-funding.

• • • • •

Canadian and

international data

reveal that there

exists a significant

and widening

gap in the school

achievement of

boys and girls.

IN Canada, the British Columbia Teacher's Federation report, *G.I. Joe Meets Barbie, Software Engineer Meets Caregiver: Males and Females in B.C.'s Public Schools and Beyond*, readily admits that the quality of the educational program is central, but there is undeniable evidence that gender is a factor in education. A stunning amount of gender stereotyping remains in British Columbia public education system, from kindergarten through graduate school and beyond.

Canadian and international data reveal that there exists a significant and widening gap in the school achievement of boys and girls:

- Boys typically score lower than girls on standardized tests in the language arts.

- Boys are more likely than girls to be placed in special education programs.

- With the exception of sports teams, boys receive fewer awards for participation in leadership building activities.

- Girls outnumber boys in gifted programs, the honour roll, and district scholarships.

- Fewer boys go on to university. In September of 2004, 33% of Canadian first year students were male.

The most sensitive teachers who strive to meet the needs of boys in the classroom may feel the most frustrated. How, for example, can a teacher address boys' necessity for physical space and movement when cost-saving designs of newer classrooms and school building reduce the physical space in which to conduct learning? A teacher may intuit that boys need appropriate rough-and-tumble physical activity *to get the wiggles out*, but there is no space or time for daily physical education. Additional classroom supports, such as administrative or specialized learning assistance, have diminished over recent years, leaving teachers fully aware of learners' unmet needs, especially those boys in academic turmoil.

· · · · ·

Just as there is no single cause of the underachievement of boys, there is no single solution.

ADDITIONALLY, educators who desire to meet the learning needs of boys come up against the power of dysfunctional male images in popular culture. In the BC Teacher Magazine, Pat Clarke reports, "Our schools are supposed to be inclusive, but as far as this too large group of rogue males – aggressive and underachieving boys – is concerned, our schools appear to be mostly exclusive. I don't believe it is because we teachers don't try to include them. We do. However too often our efforts end in suspensions, failures, or mediocre achievement and wasted time. Something is wrong. It could be one of those social phenomena we are simply overwhelmed by a generally dysfunctional *Beavis and Butthead* male culture against which we are mere candles in the wind."

A 2002 Australian report called *Boys: Getting It Right* also focussed in the growing trend for boys to disengage from learning, misbehave, or be truant. Explanations offered included: the absence of fathers, the lack of male teachers, inappropriate curricula and teaching strategies, the feminization of curricula and assessment systems, the declining status of men and the prevalence of negative, violent or hyper-masculine stereotypes in the media. In New Zealand, the underachievement of boys at school also became a focus of much attention. In 1999, the Education Review Office released its national report, *The Achievement of Boys,* which noted many boys were failing to achieve the results of which they were capable. The report advocated addressing these barriers to achievement in elementary school since "the development of literacy and numeracy

EACH SCHOOL COMMUNITY NEEDS TO CONSIDER GENDER EQUITY IN ITS OWN CONTEXT.

during the first years of school affects the ability of students to gain full benefit from later instruction."

A common theme woven throughout these reports asserts that boys' underachievement be considered in its social context. Just as there is no single cause of the underachievement of boys, there is no single solution. In fact, each school community needs to consider gender and achievement in its own context and tailor strategies that fit their circumstances. This book aspires to contribute to the on-going and thoughtful dialogue about how to create the richest possible conditions for learning for boys, as well as girls, to achieve their full potential.

CAPITALIZING ON **BOYS' STRENGTHS**

AT the beginning of this chapter we were introduced to an ingenious 10 year-old boy who took pleasure in balancing his play tools. This movement revealed aspects of his unique personality and perhaps his tendency toward a certain learning style. If we are to guide and teach boys effectively, we need to understand boys' propensities and talents. Although each boy is unique, as a group boys tend toward:

- appreciating the structure rules provide so they can relax into the task before them

- thriving on action, movement, and adventure

- enjoying wonderful spatial and mechanical challenges

- being quick to forgive transgressions

- being energized by competition

- respecting authority

- being impulsive and ready for action

- focussing on end targets and goals

- communicating in a direct manner

Many men with whom I have conversed report that they experienced school as a waste of time – as meaningless *hoop jumping* that did not help them later. Some even say that it was only after they completed public schooling and entered into the world of work that they reclaimed their entrepreneurial spirit and ingenuity.

Most of these men worry that the challenges of today's world such as economic globalization, mass migrations, and environmental degradation escape our understanding. They worry that we have been lulled into complacency, leaving experts to solve these problems. How can schools help boys – and girls – tap into the innate intelligence, creativity, and ingenuity that is so sorely needed in the twenty-first century?

• • • • •

Many men with whom I have conversed report that they experienced school as a waste of time – as meaningless *hoop jumping* that did not help them later.

UNDERSTANDING
BOY **BIOLOGY**

After his mother Shirley died from a heroin overdose, 9 year-old Jason appeared flat and detached. When I asked him questions, he replied in monosyllables, looking away from me. Numbness is a powerful shock absorber for the soul. His mother had been his only family, and Jason had done his best during the nine years of his life to stay as close to her as possible. He had gallantly attended to her needs when she blacked out or came home battered and bruised. His dad, who had been addicted to drugs and was currently in prison, had left the family when Jason was just a baby. Needing a parent himself, he had very little interest in assuming care for Jason.

When we look at boys who do not seem responsive to our efforts, who may as teenagers already seem marked for a destiny of failure, we may be tempted to write them off. After all, we have only so much time and energy. We want to spend it where it will yield the most gratification. Consider the above story about a boy I mentored several years ago.

Jason has been dealt very difficult cards in life with his lineage containing decks of similar cards. Do these cards serve as a template for Jason's life? Do genetics, biology, and family history determine our fate? And what has gender got to do with destiny?

GENDER **QUIZ**

MANY of us have known intuitively for a long time that males and females are wired differently. Even though we must always keep in mind that many children don't fit the stereotypical patterns associated with their gender, new scientific research demonstrates that there are significant differences in the brains of males and females.

To become acquainted with some of the research and some of the general differences between boys and girls complete the following gender quiz, adapted from the groundbreaking and controversial book *Brain Sex*, by Anne Moir and David Jessel, to test your assumptions.

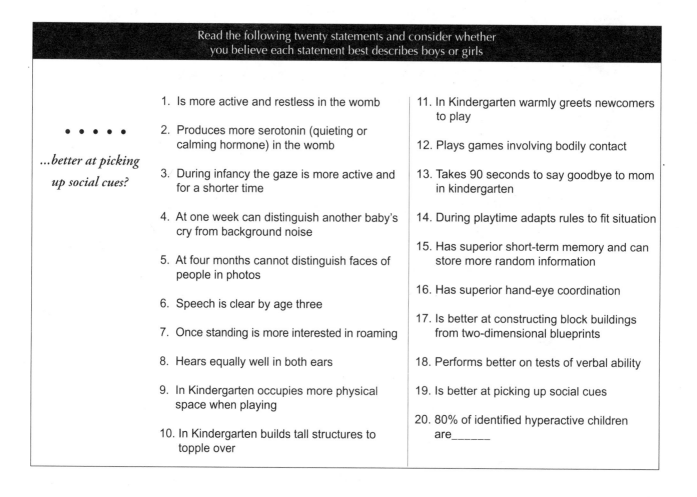

Read the following twenty statements and consider whether you believe each statement best describes boys or girls

• • • • •

...better at picking up social cues?

1. Is more active and restless in the womb

2. Produces more serotonin (quieting or calming hormone) in the womb

3. During infancy the gaze is more active and for a shorter time

4. At one week can distinguish another baby's cry from background noise

5. At four months cannot distinguish faces of people in photos

6. Speech is clear by age three

7. Once standing is more interested in roaming

8. Hears equally well in both ears

9. In Kindergarten occupies more physical space when playing

10. In Kindergarten builds tall structures to topple over

11. In Kindergarten warmly greets newcomers to play

12. Plays games involving bodily contact

13. Takes 90 seconds to say goodbye to mom in kindergarten

14. During playtime adapts rules to fit situation

15. Has superior short-term memory and can store more random information

16. Has superior hand-eye coordination

17. Is better at constructing block buildings from two-dimensional blueprints

18. Performs better on tests of verbal ability

19. Is better at picking up social cues

20. 80% of identified hyperactive children are_____

GENDER **QUIZ ANSWERS**

• • • • •

80% of
hyperactive
children are male

1.   The male fetus is more active and restless in the womb.

2.   The female fetus produces more serotonin.

3.   During infancy males gaze for shorter time and more actively.

4.   At one week females can distinguish another baby's cry from background noise.

5.   At four months males cannot distinguish faces of people in photos.

6.   Speech is clear in females by age three and four and a half years in males.

7.   Once standing males roam more frequently.

8.   Females hear equally well in both ears (right side for males).

9.   Kindergarten boys occupy more physical space when playing.

10. Boys build taller block structures that they topple over.

11. Girls in kindergarten warmly greet newcomers to play.

12. Boys' games involve bodily contact (turn-taking for girls).

13. Girls take 90 seconds to say goodbye to mom (30 for boys).

14. While boys are more rule-bound, girls adapt the rules to fit the situation.

15. Females have superior short-term memory and can store more random information than males. Males can only manage the trick when the information is organized into a format or is of specific relevance to them.

16. Boys have superior hand-eye coordination necessary for ball sports.

17. Boys find it easier to construct buildings from two-dimensional blueprints.

18. Girls perform better on tests of verbal ability.

19. Girls are better at picking up social cues.

20. 80% of identified hyperactive children are male.

QUIZ ANALYSIS   • • • • •
Males and females learn and communicate differently

AFTER several years of giving this quiz to groups of parents and teachers, I have discovered that most people already have a practical awareness of the differences typically associated with boys and girls. The book *Brain Sex* summarizes a plethora of international research on gender differences and the brain over time. It recounts, for example, how the first systematic tests of 1882 found that significant gender differences favoured men in terms of their "strength of grip, sensitivity to shrill whistle sounds, and ability to work under pressure. Women were observed to be more sensitive to pain." Beginning in the 1990's, due partly to the work of neuroscientists who have used PET (positron emission tomography) and MRI (magnetic resonance imaging) technologies to reconsider how the brain works, there is a growing acceptance that there are fundamental differences between how males and females learn and communicate.

As educators and parents, we may wonder about the practical implications of the new brain research for our children. Could biological brain differences help to explain some of the achievement gap between boys and girls in our schools?

BOYS ARE NOT STATISTICS   • • • • •
Is Jason doomed by genetics?

IF we view genetics and biology as the central determinant of our life course then Jason, the boy I described earlier, is doomed. Why bother striving to overcome obstacles if family history and a genetic blueprint have already been set in place? Why struggle to learn?

Yet how would we then explain people who have overcome great childhood adversities and then gone on to live productive lives? Why do others with similar circumstances succumb? Most importantly, how can we nurture the human qualities that allow people to overcome badly stacked odds and become contributing members of society?

Before we consider the potentially helpful application of brain research in a school setting, we should be alert to possible dangers as well.

DIFFERENCES ARE RELATIVE TENDENCIES   • • • • •
Tendencies do not deal with the individual

UNDERSTAND brain differences as relative tendencies only. Male predispositions toward certain ways of interacting with their environment are best construed as tendencies, or averages. They are statistical and mathematical means used to describe the general differences between populations. For example, knowing that the average height of an adult male is 69 inches and female is 64 inches does not help us to better understand an individual's height. These numbers do not reveal that some women are taller than men. They do not explain individual differences. Perhaps averages obscure more information than they reveal and lead us to exaggerate differences between boys and girls and thus limit our understanding of their needs. Knowing that the *average* boy finds it easier than a typical girl to construct buildings from two-dimensional blueprints does not explain why another boy has difficulty interpreting a blueprint. Statistical differences are not intended to understand individuals, but rather the leanings of the population being studied.

THE SUPERIORITY-INFERIORITY TRAP   • • • • •
Forget those age-old gender wars

McMaster University Times reported an exhaustive study of the human brain by Sandra Witelson, a Canadian neuroscientist, who found that women's and men's brains are neither better nor worse, but they are measurably different. She discerned subtle patterns that only gender seemed to explain. She also speculated that the neuron-rich layers in an area associated with perception and speech were the reason women scored much higher than males on tasks involving language and communication. The brain research of Richard Haier, as reported in *Today at UCI* (University of California, Irvine) found that while men rely on grey matter in performing mental tasks, women rely more on white matter. Grey matter is associated with information processing and white matter with communication between parts of the brain.

AVOID evaluating one type of brain as superior. Brain research that points to differences should not take us back into old tired wars about gender superiority. As leading brain and gender researcher, Ruben Gur puts it, "Men and women perform more or less equally, they just take different routes to arrive at the same answers. The fact that male and female brains do things differently may be why our species survived. It makes more evolutionary sense to have two different angles on reality." Gender differences are not evidence of superiority or inferiority, but explain how gender has organized itself across a continuum of capabilities to ensure the survival of the species.

NOT ALL BOYS ARE ALIKE   • • • • •

Will boys be boys?

AVOID overgeneralizations about boys as a group. The biological determinism argument, also known as *anatomy is destiny*, can be invoked to support facile generalizations. People may assume that certain behaviours are justified and unchangeable because *boys will be boys.* There is little consideration of the wide variety of behaviours among members of each gender or how individual males and females may relate to each other in different settings.

In our current recognition that boys are struggling within the educational system, there is a danger of portraying boys as a homogeneous group of underachievers who are victims of a female gender bias in our classrooms. Viewing boys as disadvantaged from the beginning or blaming teachers for creating feminized classrooms fuels a sense of helplessness. Thinking that there is nothing we can do to help our boys achieve may lead us to the unproductive place of leaving them alone. It is important to remember that each boy responds from his genetic blueprint in a unique and individual way that involves a complex interplay of biology, culture, and personal meaning-making.

COMING TO THE FALSE CONCLUSION THAT THE EDUCATION SYSTEM DOES NOT SERVE THE NEEDS OF BOYS MERELY BECAUSE THEY ARE BOYS, CAN BE UNPRODUCTIVE.

Just as being the eldest in a family does not automatically translate into bossy behaviour, findings about brain differences in males and females does not automatically mean all boys and all girls learn in the same way.

BRAIN RESEARCH AND POLICY • • • • •

Interpreting research for the purposes of developing policy

DO NOT use brain research findings as the basis for educational policies. Although there appears to be an innate tendency toward each gender having a preference for certain skills and capabilities, the recognition of these tendencies is not an adequate basis for educational policies. For example, we should not decide to segregate boys from girls at school because statistical information tells us that they learn differently. However, research findings related to gender brain differences can inform our thinking about how we may guide boys in school and at home.

How can we use and not abuse information about gender differences to help raise boys' educational achievement levels? Consider the following ten guidelines.

GUIDELINE 1
GENDER IS EXPRESSED ALONG A CONTINUUM

WE express our gender in everything we do—in our mannerisms, our way of speaking, and the roles we assume in social interactions. The old Mother Goose nursery rhyme illustrates an outdated understanding of boys and girls as different species from different worlds.

What are little boys made of?

Frogs and snails and puppy dog tails.

What are little girls made of?

Sugar and spice and everything nice.

The binary gender construct, where the world is sharply divided between boys and girls, men and women, limits our understanding of people. Some boys are more aggressive and demanding like *Rambo* while others are more sensitive. In reality, gender exists along a continuum from extremely feminine at one end and extremely masculine at the other with many shadings of gendered states in between.

GUIDELINE 1
GENDER IS EXPRESSED ALONG A CONTINUUM *CONT'D*

THE statistical differences between genders can be illustrated in a diagram. The center points of each bell curve identify the average tendency for each gender. You will notice that there is more variance within a gender than between genders. In the middle section of this continuum are expressions of gender that are both masculine and feminine. This boy may be less inclined to enjoy rough-and-tumble team sports but be more interested in developing relationships. It is interesting that developing male embryos are technically female until the age of six or seven weeks, at which point they are bathed in testosterone. This hormonal bath alters the brain's structure in many ways and orients the embryo's brain design along the gender continuum, *Rambo, Barbie,* or somewhere in between. It is important to note that boys and girls do not choose their brain design or position along the continuum or that sexual orientation can differ at any point along the line.

· · · · ·

There is more variance within a gender than between genders.

Certainly there are numerous behaviours common to both sexes, and a degree of *overlap* in the display of other actions traditionally associated with a certain gender. Personal variations on the common gender themes occur because all of us are individuals affected by many forces. If we lived in a world that respected unique expressions of gender, we would be able to move back and forth along the whole continuum of human behaviour.

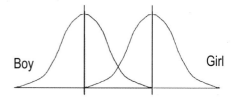

At schools, we are challenged to provide activities that appeal to boys across the whole continuum of gender. Not all boys want to become hockey stars. Not all boys dislike reading. Not all boys seek thrills and physical challenges. Rather than assume boys benefit from more rough and tumble activities, we could provide a range of activities for boys reflecting their varied needs—for reflection as well as for rambunctious play. It is important to remember that many boys need quieter activities such as chess, model building, and reading clubs.

BOYS NEED MOVEMENT

· · · · ·

Movement

is central to

multi-sensory

stimulation and

mimics real-world

interactions.

I RECENTLY spoke to a disheartened mother regarding her son's classroom experience. "My son complains of being bored a lot at school and is often bursting out of his skin when he gets home." As I listened to her frustration with his lack of motivation toward learning at school she questioned me: "Is school really just about sit down, shut up and write this down?" Another parent, a father of a boy in Kindergarten, expressed a keen awareness of his son's active learning style: "He's quite good at sticking to a task, but it has to be something with movement and something that has a purpose. For Johnny, it's usually something mechanical, like building something or making something in the sand pit. I can already see that sitting still at a school desk and working on a worksheet will be painful for him. I guess we'll have to find a way to force him to sit still but I don't know how to accomplish this without taking something away from his personality."

Brain research into gender differences helps us understand why many boys are bothered when classroom activities don't allow for enough movement during lessons. Movement is central to multi-sensory stimulation

IS SCHOOL REALLY JUST ABOUT SIT DOWN, SHUT UP AND WRITE THIS DOWN?

and mimics real-world interactions. Movement also helps boys to stimulate their brains. It allows boys to process information and to make sense of stressful circumstances. Boredom is a stressful state of mind for many boys. In the early 1990's, Francine Shapiro hypothesized that negative emotions can interfere with processing or making sense of information. She posits that a relatively minor event, such as being teased by peers or disparaged by a parent, may also not be adequately processed.

GUIDELINE 2
BOYS NEED MOVEMENT *CONT'D*

• • • • •

When boys fidget

they are actually

facilitating the

processing of

information.

MOVEMENT does more than get the wiggles out. Boys also use movement to kick-start their corpus callosums, the bundle of nerve fibers that connect the right and left sides of the brain, to maintain alertness. The corpus callosum is the message exchange centre in the brain that provides a pathway for information to travel back and forth between the hemispheres of the brain. It is typically 20% larger in females, allowing for increased cross-communication between brain hemispheres that is required for reading and scholastic activities.

Movement, any kind of movement, bilaterally stimulates the brain and assists the corpus callosum to transfer messages between the hemispheres, assisting resolution. Boys need movement like bike tires need air. I remember how, when I was a young boy and in trouble, my mother would take me aside for a reprimand. I would fidget, moving from side to side. She would ask me stand still. I would stop transferring my weight from leg to leg and begin twitching my fingers. Of course she would tell me to hold still again. I would avoid eye contact and she would demand it. Despite my very best attempt to be motionless, my body would begin to vibrate. It turns out that I was not alone and many boys react similarly. Movement seems to help boys process information.

BOYS ALSO USE MOVEMENT TO KICK-START THEIR CORPUS CALLOSUMS.

Since movement helps boys to process information by increasing blood flow to the brain, teachers should use movement activity breaks as well as chances to move during class learning for all ages. They can use activity centres or group rotations to keep the boys stimulated rather than pinned to their chairs. Boys who need to move can be encouraged to fidget, doodle and move in a manner that does not disrupt others' learning.

Guideline 3
TESTOSTRONE NEEDS TO BE CHANNELED

THE JURY is in. Scientific research shows that boys are wired for launching projectiles, roaring like dinosaurs, and knocking down towers of blocks. Boys tend to manage their social world by striving for dominance while girls tend to build alliances and inter-dependence. Girls usually bond first and ask questions later. Boys are more likely to approach social interactions aggressively. Girls emphasize cooperation while boys emphasize competition. Is testosterone, the male growth hormone, responsible for boys' attraction to rough-and-tumble, their restlessness and inattentiveness, their relatively low threshold for frustration, and their lower school achievement?

· · · · ·

Scientific research shows that boys are wired for launching projectiles, roaring like dinosaurs, and knocking down towers of blocks.

While estrogen is the hormone that gives females a sense of well being, high levels of testosterone account for general increased irritability and impulsiveness among males. It appears that the higher the level of testosterone, the greater the boisterousness of the boy.

However, if testosterone levels dip too low, they may become grumpy, nervous, bad-tempered, or worse, develop IMS, *irritable male syndrome*, according to a recently published British journal *New Scientist*. It appears that a sudden drop in testosterone could play havoc and turn confident *Luke Skywalkers* into withdrawn grumps.

WE NEED TO APPRECIATE THE ACTIVE PHYSICALITY OF BOYS IN A WAY THAT IS NOT ANTI-FEMALE.

Testosterone is often associated with the traits of hyperactivity and impulsiveness but beliefs expressed in the old Greek proverb: *Of all the animals, the boy is the most unmanageable* only marginalizes boys with their elevated energy levels and accompanying competitiveness. Rather than being reprimanded or medicated for energetic behaviour, many boys need activities into which they can channel their rambunctiousness. Despite the influence of testosterone on boys' behaviours, it is not the cause of lower school achievement. The effect of testosterone on a boy's behaviour is exacerbated by the way he is raised and taught. We need to appreciate the active physicality of boys in a way that is not anti-female.

GUIDELINE 4
PROVIDE ABSTRACT & SPATIAL REASONING OPPORTUNITIES

THE REVIEW of studies on spatial and abstract reasoning offered in *Brain Sex* concludes that males have superior spatial and abstract reasoning competencies. Spatial reasoning refers to the ability to picture things, their shape, position, and proportion, in the mind's eye. From age six and onwards boys will generally out-perform girls in areas of mathematics involving abstract concepts of space, relationships, and theory. "At the very highest level of mathematical excellence, according to the biggest survey ever conducted, the very best boys totally eclipse the very best girls." The ability to see patterns and abstract relationships explains the male dominance at the game of chess or map reading.

Engineers, architects

and race car drivers

are each required

to manipulate 3-D

objects to perform

their jobs.

MALES KNOW WITHIN A 100TH OF SECOND
WHO ARRIVED AT FOUR-WAY STOP FIRST.

Spatial reasoning, a skill crucial to understanding three-dimensional objects or drawings or appreciating higher levels of mathematics, involves the ability to think and reason through the transformation of mental pictures. Engineers, architects, and race car drivers are each required to mentally manipulate 3-D objects to perform their jobs. I personally know of an auto-mechanic who possesses similar talents that I suspect would be of interest to N.A.S.A. When the going gets tough in his local garage, and it is too expensive for his mechanics to continue working on a vehicle, he takes it for homework – in his mind's eye. With eyes closed he deconstructs the car and determines the solution. Very few of us could ever hope to possess his gift or knack to turn objects in space and see them from another perspective. Some of us can barely keep track of widgets with our eyes open! Many boys however, have superior spatial skills resulting from the opportunities afforded by video and computer games.

GUIDELINE 4
PROVIDE ABSTRACT AND SPATIAL REASONING OPPORTUNITIES CONT'D

Brain Sex also describes a study of spatial capability where both boys and girls were given city street maps and, without rotating the map, asked to describe whether they would be turning left or right at particular crossways as they mentally made their way along a pre-determined route. Females were more likely to turn the map around to physically match the direction in which they were travelling.

Males were more likely to make the spatial adjustments in their mind's eye. Males also consistently outperform females when asked to mentally rotate images to determine if they are the same or different.

> THE MALE BRAIN CRAVES BUTTONS, MOTORS, MOVING PARTS AND FLASHING LIGHTS.

Researchers at Yale University conducted a study to determine if there were any gender differences in the success rates of men and women setting up a VCR on first attempt. They concluded that while 68% of males were triumphant, only 16% of females were successful. Unfortunately the study did not report how many males damaged the VCR because they refused to read the instructions! I suspect that the same would apply to television *channel surfing*. Most females complain that the males in their company simply change the channel too quickly before they have the opportunity to see what is on the screen. Heightened spatial abilities among males might explain why they are more likely than females to ascertain within hundredths of a second who arrived first at the four-way traffic stop sign and why men loathe the visual impediment of driving behind large trucks.

PROVIDE ABSTRACT AND SPATIAL REASONING OPPORTUNITIES CONT'D

BECAUSE of this male knack for all things spatial boys are attracted to anything with buttons, motors or moving parts, makes sounds, has flashing lights, or smacks of technical wizardry. While girls tend to occupy their playtime with relational games and turn taking, boys seem to prefer toys like *Duplo* and *Lego*, along with other engineer-like spatial challenges. It also accounts for a predominance of males working in the computer gaming industry. Every time I present this information to parents and teachers I inquire as to the number of females present who like to play computer games. In a room of two or three hundred, I may get a half dozen raised arms.

• • • • •

Researchers at Yale University found that 68% of males were able to set up a VCR on their first try.

The male brain is better suited for symbols, abstractions, diagrams, pictures, and objects moving through space than static printed words. If classroom teachers are to respond to a male bias for spatial stimulation, they need to design activities that involve opportunities for spatial and abstract reasoning. In fact, the National Council of Teachers of Mathematics (2000) recommends that equal time be given to geometry and traditional computation in elementary mathematics lessons. They advocate a balanced approach where students be given equal time to explore measurement, pre-algebra and graphing, as well as computation. The research by Casey, Nuttall & Pezaris (2001) and others have shown that as girls perform less well on spatial tasks involving mental transformations or rotations, they hypothesize that increased spatial activities in the classroom not only appeal to boys, but also assist girls to advance their learning.

Both boys and girls benefit by developing their analytical strategies for solving spatial and abstract problems. Building models, mind-mapping, and graphic organizers are powerful and productive strategies to analyze information. Other ways to activate the visual cortex include: 1) changing environments; 2) opening the blinds and windows to allow for outdoor viewing; 3) seek alternatives to fluorescent lighting; and, 4) frequently change the classroom layout and contents around. Providing more opportunities for spatial and abstract reasoning will help sustain the interest and motivation of boys.

GUIDELINE 5
OFFER RATIONAL INSTRUCTIONS

• • • • •

Give a boy one

task and he

will do it well.

Give him several

and his eyes will

glaze over.

BRAIN lateralization theory hypothesizes that certain functions are located more in one hemisphere of the brain than the other. While it was initially believed that the left hemisphere is specialized for a number of cognitive processes, and the right hemisphere is predominantly involved in processing emotion, we now understand that both hemispheres process emotion, but each hemisphere is specialized for particular types of emotion. The left hemisphere is dominant for positive emotions and the right for negative emotions (Davidson, 1992; Gur, 1994).

It appears that the male brain is more centralized or compartmentalized than the female brain. Brain scans demonstrate that while females use both sides of their brain to solve a spatial problem, while males primarily use their right hemisphere. This also explains how left hemisphere brain damage produces greater impairment in males than females who typically use both sides of their brain to perform many tasks.

Give a boy one task and he can carry it through. Give him three and his eyes will probably glaze over. His thought processes are suffering serious information overload. Little wonder that when he is then accused of not listening he becomes stubborn and recalcitrant as he tries to deal with the inequality of our demands. A brain that is more compartmentalized performs better when presented with one activity at a time. This is also commonly observed in men who turn the radio down before reading driving instructions or look at a map. Females seem more likely to listen and read at the same time because their brains are configured for multitasking. They can typically talk on the telephone while attending to chores and supervising the kids.

For boys, the combination of fewer connecting fibers between hemispheres and a more compartmentalized brain results in the need to attend to one instruction at a time. In the classroom it is preferable that boys be presented with instructions that are logical and broken down into parts or steps so that they can attend to one task at a time.

Additionally, boys diagnosed with an Auditory Processing Disorder (APD) are normally not deaf. In fact most have excellent hearing and they just do not process what they hear. They may process part of what they hear but, without processing the rest, often the whole meaning is lost, or they perceive a totally incorrect idea of what has been said. They may be able to repeat the words back word for word, but the meaning of the message is lost, not processed. Simply repeating instructions is of no use if a boy with APD is not processing. These boys benefit from visual instructions.

GUIDELINE 6
LISTEN UP!

· · · · ·

Males listen with

only one side of

their brain.

ANOTHER brain lateralization study from the Indiana University School of Medicine found that males listen with only one side of their brain, while females use both. Most men showed exclusive activity on the left side of the brain's temporal lobe, which is known to be involved in processing language, while women showed activity in the left and right temporal lobes. Some women are not surprised by this research as it confirms their experience of males all along – that they are half-brained listeners! I suspect that you will not be surprised by the notion that females can express frustration when males are unable to listen to them while doing another activity, such as watching TV or reading a newspaper.

In *Brain Based Learning,* Eric Jensen notes that females hear subtle differences in voices and music more readily than males. Females perceive sound at 85 decibels to be twice as loud as males. These differences mean that females pick up vocal cues, such as tone of voice, much more readily than males. Also, females will perceive a person speaking at 85 decibels to be yelling, whereas males will consider the same person to be using a normal tone of voice. Perceptual differences may explain why females complain that males are too loud when engaged in conflict, to which males respond emphatically: "I'm not yelling!" Adults need to be vigilant to not misread a boy's loud voice and interpret it as aggression or misbehaviour.

DON'T RAMBLE – GET TO THE POINT.

Instructions for boys need to be clear and explicit. When instructions ramble or lack clarity, boys have a tendency to get lost in the instructional narrative. Boys' brains have to work harder to process verbal instructions. When I hear about a female teacher or mother's frustration regarding a boy's lack of responsiveness to guidance, it is typically because females are talking too much. It can be frustrating for many females when male teachers or fathers get immediate results when they ask their sons: "Put that in your desk and turn to page 15," or "Clean the computer station now and I will help with your flat tire." To increase the likelihood that boys will understand directions, provide succinct instructions.

GUIDELINE 7
PROVIDE TRANSITION TIME

• • • • •

Studies show that

the male brain

renews and

reorients itself

by zoning out.

APPARENTLY, the boy on your family room sofa or in the back of the classroom whose eyes are drifting toward sleep has entered a neural *rest state*. It is predominately boys who drift off without completing assigned work, who stop taking notes and fall asleep during a lecture, or who tap pencils or otherwise fidget in hopes of keeping themselves awake and learning. Studies show that the male brain renews and reorients itself by *zoning out*. It is likely that the boy in the back of the class who is daydreaming is recharging his batteries rather than misbehaving. Dr. Ruben Gur at the University of Pennsylvania conducted a study to better understand how each gender's brain responds to resting states. Brain scan imaging allowed him to determine just how much electrical activity is present when each gender is inactive and resting. The results will be of immediate relief to anyone who has been exasperated with getting the attention of their *zoned out* boy, or husband for that matter. When males are in a *rest state* 70% of electrical activity shuts down while only 10% of electrical activity shuts

A DAYDREAMING MALE MAY BE JUST RECHARGING HIS BATTERIES.

down in females. While females are paying attention when they rest, males are much less aware of stimulation or distractions in their surrounding environment. Practically speaking, males need more down-time in class and at home to recharge their circuitry. They also may need more time to make a successful transition from a rest state into another activity. Demanding that boys shift gears too quickly may invite resistance, as they seem to need more time to refocus. Pay careful attention to transitions – beginnings and endings – that alert the brain to pay attention and change. Start each lesson or concept with a hook to focus awareness. Keep boys on their toes with novel closure.

GUIDELINE 8
FORTIFY SOCIAL GUIDANCE

• • • • •

There is no society

on earth where

males are

typically the

primary

caregivers.

THE LIMBIC system is the emotional center of the brain. Brain science tells us that girls' focus on relational bonding is due to the fact that they have limbic systems that are twice as large as the typical boy's. When a girl gets upset there is approximately eight times more blood flow through her limbic system, causing her reaction to be more pronounced and dramatic. Boys, on the other hand have less oxytocin, the primary human bonding hormone in the limbic system, and require more time to process emotional stimulation. Although modern times have shown that men can be at home and effectively respond to children's needs, *Brain Sex* points out that there is no society on earth where males are typically the primary caregivers.

Girls tend to size up and cope with social situations better than boys, who often have to learn social decorum, such as tact and sensitivity, the hard way. It is for this reason that we must take care and time to teach appropriate social behaviour. They have to learn to be good listeners, to *put up* rather than *put others down*, to cooperate, and to see things from another's perspective. With loving guidance boys are more likely to become patient and empathic.

TAKING CLASSROOM TIME TO CONSIDER RELATIONSHIP DILEMMAS HELPS BOYS TO BECOME SOCIALLY CONSCIOUS AND ETHICALLY AWARE.

More importantly, we need to remember that all children learn best through role modeling. When establishing environments that facilitate respectful and constructive interactions adults *walk the talk*. We need to improve our ability to respond to breaches of discipline with calmness and quiet firmness. When a boy is acting aggressively, we want to respond calmly toward misbehaviour and avoid stepping into a boy's conflict or anger cycle. Taking classroom time to consider relationship dilemmas helps boys to become socially conscious and ethically aware.

GUIDELINE 9
HELP BOYS LEARN EMOTIONAL LITERACY

THE MALE brain typically secretes 20% – 40% less serotonin than a female brain. Serotonin is the *feel good* chemical neurotransmitter that influences emotion, attention, and behaviour. It affects our mood by calming and pacifying us. Higher levels of serotonin are associated with fearfulness, low self-confidence, and obsessive-compulsive behaviours. Lower levels are correlated with impulsive aggression, depression, and even suicide (Jensen, 1998). If testosterone is the gasoline that powers the male brain, serotonin maintains a safe driving speed and helps to steer. High serotonin levels can cause girls to become ultra-emotional, or anxious. Low serotonin levels can cause boys to have increased impulsivity and undiagnosed depression. Boys need help maintaining a safe driving speed so they can best steer around life's challenges.

• • • • •

Serotonin is the

feel good chemical

neurotransmitter

that influences

emotion, attention,

and behaviour.

Early in life many males learn to devalue their feelings, especially those of sadness and hurt. Back a girl into a corner or a stressful situation and she might begin crying to express her frustration. Back a boy into a corner and he'll likely come out swinging with bravado. His real emotion goes underground and his presenting aggression is often misunderstood.

When a boy impulsively slams the locker door at school, he might really be saying that he is hurt or feeling rejected. When he arrives

IF TESTOSTERONE IS THE GASOLINE THAT POWERS THE MALE BRAIN, THEN SEROTONIN IS THE OIL THAT KEEPS THE ENGINE IN GOOD WORKING ORDER.

home after school and proclaims: "My teachers sucks!" he might really be saying: "I'm feeling sad about what happened in class today." Emotions affect behaviour because they create distinct mind-body states. Feeling optimistic affects how one learns. Instead of following the old adage "get control of the class, then teach," we have learned from brain science that we need to "engage emotions to increase learning." With boys this means to look beyond the emotional bravado and hear what is not being said. Boys need guidance to process their emotional states so they can get on with the task of learning.

CHAPTER TWO

DON'T MISTAKE HIGH ENERGY FOR ADHD

RECENTLY a mother of two very energetic boys visited my office with her concern: "It was recommended that boys sometimes need medication to help settle them down so they can learn properly. Don't they just need to move more?" Another parent reported: "My son appears to be terribly bored and is not doing that well in school. He has trouble sitting in one spot for long periods of time and gets up and moves around the classroom more than the teachers like. Someone said he might have ADHD?"

• • • • •

ADD and ADHD are marked largely by impulsivity and the inability to pay attention.

Any thoughtful discussion about the learning needs of boys must consider the controversies around Attention Deficit Disorder (ADD) and Attention Deficit and Hyperactivity Disorder (ADHD). ADD and ADHD are marked largely by impulsivity and the inability to pay attention. ADHD is also marked by hyperactivity, although ADD could actually manifest as lethargy, (the zoning out I wrote about earlier). Students with ADD or ADHD have difficulties with organization, staying on task, and following through. They are also forgetful. Even if they do their homework, they may forget to turn it in. Some consider ADD and ADHD to be neurobiological, while others see it as an artificially manufactured syndrome. Whatever we think about its etiology, it is something that we, who are concerned about the academic performance of boys cannot ignore.

THE USE OF STIMULANT DRUGS TO MANAGE BEHAVIOUR IS AT EPIDEMIC LEVELS INTERNATIONALLY.

The Vancouver Sun, December 4, 1997, reported that Dr. Thomas Millar, author of *The Myth of Attention Deficit Disorder,* found that prescriptions for Ritalin in British Columbia soared 430% in a four-year period between 1993 and 1997. At the same time the American Drug Enforcement Administration reported a 600% increase between 1994 and 1999. Millar's article goes on to claim "...the process by which ADHD is diagnosed is as flawed as the invented category. That process starts with teachers checking items on a list, then telling the parents about ADD/ADHD and what magic Ritalin has worked in their classroom." Millar criticizes the way that the process of diagnosis of ADD and treatment by prescription de-emphasizes the parental role. He strongly urges parents to get on with the challenging task of learning how to provide leadership for high-spirited children who are difficult to parent.

GUIDELINE **10**
DON'T MISTAKE HIGH ENERGY FOR ADHD *CONT'D*

IT turns out that Millar is not alone. In 2001 The World Health Organization declared the use of stimulant drugs to manage behaviour to be at epidemic levels internationally. We must ask whether spontaneity, inquisitiveness, imagination, boundless enthusiasm, and emotionality are being discouraged to create calmer, quieter, more controlled environments. Michael Gurian, an American therapist, educator, and author of several books about boys, claims that nearly two-thirds of those diagnosed with ADD or ADHD have probably been misdiagnosed.

• • • • •

Do stimulant drugs actually help boys perform better academically – or do they merely make the boys and the classroom environment easier to manage in a traditional way?

Parents become alarmed when they learn that drugs prescribed for ADHD are central nervous system stimulants and share many of the pharmacological effects of amphetamine, methamphetamine, and cocaine. Does *Ritalin* and its variants actually help boys perform better academically – or does it merely make the boys and the classroom environment easier to manage in a traditional way? Although the interests of the larger group may be served, I have heard parents say anecdotally that their son's marks do not necessarily go up. Despite mixed reports about effectiveness of medication to actually boosting academic performance, I suspect that teachers and parents may be so relieved to have more docile boys that stimulant drugs have a certain halo effect.

MANY THINK THAT DRUGS SHOULD NOT NECESSARILY BE THE FIRST OPTION IN THE TREATMENT OF ADD OR ADHD.

Surely the medical community cannot be completely off base with ADD/ADHD and the associated prescribing medications. Medical doctors explain that the neurobiological condition of ADD or ADHD does exist. They also have empirical evidence to support the effectiveness of chemical intervention. Additionally, recent brain science confers that a boy's brain produces less serotonin and so some doctors seek to provide substitute chemicals to make up the deficit. They claim that many boys diagnosed with ADHD and ADD would, without medication, pose a problem to themselves, their family, and community.

GUIDELINE 10
DON'T MISTAKE HIGH ENERGY FOR ADHD *CONT'D*

HYPOTHETICALLY speaking, let's reverse the situation. Let's say a bunch of medical doctors got together and decided that about 20% of women were overly emotional and lacked the ability to think objectively. They also discovered that these women had higher levels of estrogen. Would we give these women medication to reduce their estrogen levels?

• • • • •

Often children who struggle with attention problems respond favourably to consistent and structured environments.

Given the current hardship ADD and ADHD behaviours cause for many families, educators should avoid offering medical advice and instead encourage parents to seek the counsel of their family doctor along with other professionals qualified to comment. Teachers can, however, take steps to help children who show ADD and ADHD behaviours through a few adaptations such as breaking large tasks down into smaller ones, making expectations and instructions clear and succinct and demystifying study and organizational skills by making them very explicit.

My survey of the literature associated with ADD and ADHD has found that drugs should not necessarily be the first option in the treatment of behaviour characterized as such. Often children who struggle with attention problems respond favourably to consistent and structured environments. The medical literature additionally indicates that drugs should only be used in combination with other therapies such as counselling intervention. Counselling support can be especially helpful with boys who are struggling with unresolved

WOULD WE GIVE WOMEN MEDICATION TO REDUCE THEIR ESTROGEN LEVELS?

trauma that can later present itself as ADHD. Sometimes, rather than counselling boys to become more attentive and focussed I advocate that parents seek consultation to learn about additional ways to support their son's behaviour.

Regardless of the diagnosis, both teachers and parents still need to maintain a positive and understanding connection with a boy exhibiting attention difficulties while also providing a clear and structured environment with ample opportunity for movement and active learning. Most importantly, we need to embrace a boy's high-spirited nature and not see him as abnormal or defective.

GUIDELINE **10**
DON'T MISTAKE HIGH ENERGY FOR ADHD *CONT'D*

• • • • •

The most precious

gifts we can give

our boys are love

– and time.

THE diagnosis of ADD and ADHD does not exist from a Chinese medicine perspective. Instead, the individual is viewed as having an *unsettled heart*. The book, *Raising Boys* tells a wonderful story about a father who was told that his son had Attention Deficit Disorder. In the trucking industry such a term rarely crossed his path at work, but being intuitive, and wanting to help his son with the diagnosis, the father concluded that it meant his son was not getting enough attention. He was determined to help his son by making sure that he got plenty of it. After school the father made great efforts to pick up his son and include him on his last trucking run. They got to know each other better as they discussed their lives and interests. The spatial stimulation and constant movement of their journeying together seemed to free them to discuss previously hot issues. During the holidays they would spend even longer periods of time chatting as they crisscrossed the country. Several months passed before the teacher informed the father that the ADD problem had completely disappeared.

This story makes me wonder if understanding and moral guidance is the real help for ADD for some boys. Perhaps a question we need to consider if we are to respond to a boy's attention problems is: "What are the needs of the boy and his particular learning circumstances?" While some boys need activity to facilitate learning, some boys need more reassurance to feel valued and appreciated, and some boys need both.

The most precious gifts we can give our boys are love – and time.

THE CULTURE OF
MASCULINITY & SCHOOLS

Standing for right when it is unpopular is a true test of moral character.
Margaret Chase-Smith

• • • • •

The dominant

culture does not

offer a static view

of masculinity,

but one that is

influenced by

historical,

economic, and

political changes.

Historians and anthropologists have shown that there is no one stable ideal of masculinity to be found everywhere. Different cultures, at different times, construct masculinity differently. For instance, some cultures make heroes of soldiers, and regard the willingness to engage in violence as the ultimate test of masculinity. Others look down on soldiers, and regard participation in violence as contemptible. The social and cultural prestige of soldiers rises and falls even within a particular country at different historical junctures. Consider the different ways in which the dominant North American culture viewed their soldiers who fought in World War II, in Vietnam, and in Iraq, for example. Traditional cultures often see homosexuality as incompatible with true masculinity. Others view same-sex relationships as a typical developmental stage in a man's life. In Canada, current political, legal, and civil controversies over same-sex marriages reflect rapidly changing cultural views within our lifetime. The dominant culture does not offer a static view of masculinity, but one that is influenced by historical, economic, and political changes.

Similarly, a boy's understanding of gender is dynamic. It is not strictly determined by cultural and biological factors, but can change over time with experience and reflection. It is true that boys' images of masculinity are influenced by the media, as well as by their school, church, and family. However, boys also interpret and express masculinity in individual ways. They adopt different masculinity practices, depending on their circumstances, beliefs, and interpretations. Rambo does not always rule.

RAMBO DOES NOT ALWAYS RULE
Masculinity takes many different forms

· · · · ·

A boy's perception

of his place in his

world affects his

motivation and

achievement.

SOMETIMES parents and teachers indicate that although questions about how gender is constructed are interesting, they really just want to find out how to raise boys' achievement. But learning and achievement do not occur in a vacuum. A boy's perception of his place in his world affects his motivation and achievement.

In my work as a school consultant, I am often asked to join discussions about how to support boys who are alienated from school or who have dropped out. I recall how one particular boy was unable to navigate the culture of masculinity at school.

Jim's decision to quit school was not sudden. The signs of his fading interest in school were obvious the last few years, but what could be done? It was in Grade 10 that he stopped all effort and didn't even bother to show up. Frustrated teachers and administrators spoke of his bright and artistic intelligence while others complained that he was too sensitive for his own good and what he needed was to toughen up. At one school meeting someone even questioned whether he might be gay.

Upon interviewing Jim, I learned that he was bored at school. Mindless 'busywork' exhausted him. "Hoop-jumping is alright if your brain is turned off or you're tired and just don't want to think," he said. He found school irrelevant, and no longer cared at all about pleasing his teachers or his parents.

Jim knew he was definitely not cool. Jim had long detached from schoolmates, who referred to him as 'the geek.' His passion for life and learning had fizzled. He didn't see a place at school for him—not for his ideas, his sensitivities, nor his quirky ways.

What happens to boys like Jim who find themselves out of sync with popular culture and lose interest in school as a result? This chapter will begin with a brief exploration of changes in the cultural understanding of masculinity, consider its potential implications for boys growing up, and later identify practical guidelines as to how we can help boys make sense of the different images of masculinity to which they are exposed.

BOYS THEN AND NOW
Those were the days

• • • • •

There were

no parents to

supervise us, tell

us the rules,

or drive us

to *the game*.

I REMEMBER how, when I was a boy in the sixties, I felt a sense of optimism as I watched Neil Armstrong take his first steps on the moon. I remember a pleasant sense of community as several of us huddled around the first neighbourhood colour TV watching Saturday morning cartoons. We ate at home, rarely in restaurants. There was one bathroom, so we had to be creative and collaborative. We assumed that wearing hand-me-downs was a natural part of life. Our playtime was rich with make-believe. There were no parents to supervise us, tell us the rules, or drive us to *the game*. My all-time favourite game was kick-the-can with whom ever was available on the streets and back-alleys of our neighbourhood. We knew who lived in every house on the block and had the opportunity to exchange greetings when the parents parked their cars out on the street after work.

In the 1960's we did not have millions of children unable to concentrate in the classroom requiring stimulant drugs to focus. The traditional classroom was expected to be a quiet, well-ordered environment. Desks were arranged so that all students could make eye contact with the teacher, see the demonstrations, and read instructions. Students were not permitted to distract or disrupt others.

IN THE 60'S CHILDREN HAD MORE FREEDOM TO PLAY AND EXPLORE.

Time was spent learning such disciplines as penmanship and rote memorization of the times tables. We had a short recess in the morning, a full hour for lunch, and a short recess in the afternoon.

Fast-forward to 2005 in North America. Children have more stuff than ever before. Many kids expect to have a TV and computer in their bedroom, as well as their own bathroom. They wouldn't dream of wearing an older cousin's hand-me-downs. Despite the materialism of today, many people behave as though they are thirsty in the rain. Adults make the kids' lunches, later deliver the forgotten lunches to school, clean their rooms, and even complete homework assignments. They are often over-involved in most aspects of a youngster's life.

BOYS THEN AND NOW *CONT'D*

· · · · ·

The media

glamorizes

laziness and

rudeness.

IN the sixties we didn't think leaping over muddy streams could be a problem. We just got dirty. But today designer kids play differently. A study conducted by a clothing detergent company who likely noticed a decrease in its sales reported that one third of children admitted to actively avoiding outdoor play because they didn't want to scuff their designer running shoes or dirty their cherished clothes (The Scotsman, April 27, 2005).

Today's popular culture often seems pumped on steroids, filled with meaningless excitation, overwhelming angst, and frenetic speed. According to film critic Michael Medved, in the early sixties the TV camera lingered on one scene an average of 45 seconds, whereas today the average is a maximum of 3 to 5 seconds per scene. Before Kindergarten even starts, boys come to school after having watched thousands of hours of flashing cartoons and shows that jump from one scene to the next in rapid succession. The media glamorizes laziness and rudeness. It also sells violence, dehumanized sex, and materialism on a daily basis to our boys. It portrays a false perfectionism and an exciting extremism that can rarely be attained in life even to our very young. The *Ottawa Citizen, May 6, 2003,* recently reported a British study that found one in four toddlers utter a brand name as their first recognizable word.

Messages from their families, peers, and the media seduce, complicate, and confuse boys as they struggle to make sense of what their masculinity means in the world.

THE VENEER OF COOL
The stress of fitting in

· · · · ·

Boys can and do

worry about

many things.

MANY boys become overwhelmed by anxiety when any of the following are added to this mix of cultural influences: neglect, abuse, mental illness, trauma, poverty, abandonment, violence, harsh peer and/or family relationships, or learning disabilities. Boys can and do worry about many things. They may worry about their changing bodies, and whether their penis is big enough. They may worry about how to respond to an offer of oral sex, which some youth argue is not real sex at all. They may worry about receiving homophobic taunts such as *fagboy*, or racist taunts, such as *raghead* if they belong to a non-dominant ethno-cultural tradition. They may worry their parents will break up.

JADED SOPHISTICATION MAY BE A COVER UP FOR FEAR AND ANXIETY.

Ultimately they worry about not fitting in.

A boy's anxieties over such matters are not particularly obvious. Popular culture has taught them to act cool at all times. Not surprisingly, in our classrooms boys cover their anxieties with a convincing veneer of jaded sophistication. It would be easy to conclude that since these boys look all right, they must be all right. However, their apparent jadedness is often a mask for worry and fear.

It is not surprising that many of these boys give up at school. Jim, the boy I introduced earlier, was bright and bored. He also felt very anxious about having no place at his school among the males who seemed so cool, so invulnerable. Trying to figure out how to respond to constricting cultural messages about masculinity was simply too much. For him it was better to retreat into his own complex inner world at home.

UNHEALTHY CONSTRUCTS OF MASCULINITY

DOZENS of unhealthy messages regarding masculinity bombard boys to varying degrees on a daily basis. How boys interpret these messages depends on their life circumstances and personal resiliency. Look through the following list, developed by Michael Obsatz, and consider which of these were present for you, your brothers, or other young boys around you as you were growing up.

• • • • •

Tough it out

at all costs.

Maintain a strong macho image, even if circumstances suggest you relax	Act tough
	Be in control
Prove manhood by taking risks, even if foolish	Dominate others
Sexualize affection - all touch is sexual touch	Devalue what is feminine in yourself and others
Dehumanize sex	Be emotionally detached
Don't be a virgin	Tough it out at all costs
Don't be vulnerable	Don't take care of your body
Don't cry	Win at all costs
Don't express fear	Abuse your body
Don't ask for help, guidance, or directions	More is better - money, sex, food, alcohol
Don't trust anyone	Bigger is better
Be disposable - be willing to die for your country	You had better prove your manhood
	You are what you achieve or accomplish
Pretend to know even when you don't	

There is no scorecard for answers here, but you are invited to reflect on the way in which these traits can damage males of all ages. Men tell me that these stereotypical ideas can sometimes drive their behaviour too.

Many adults express concern when I describe my conversations with boys about incidents or behaviours that have provoked the concern of adults. I often find they talk with pride about troubling behaviour. At one such meeting boys talked openly about alcohol, hangovers, passing out, fights, drunk driving, and casual sex, but this behaviour did not appear to worry them. Instead, they seemed more concerned about the amount of alcohol they could consume.

IN a cultural climate that associates masculinity with bravado, lassitude, or the overripe masculinity seen on *Beavis and Butthead* or *The Trailer Park Boys* called *machismo,* we can work consciously to help our boys construct healthier images of masculinity.

Having healthier images of masculinity can, in turn, help improve boys' learning and achievement. In response to requests from educators and parents, I offer guidelines 11 through 20 to assist you in meeting the varied needs of boys at home and school.

GUIDELINE 11
TEACH MEDIA ANALYSIS

• • • • •

Alert boys to the fact

that the media may

be bullying them

into making their

choices.

WE live in a media-saturated culture where its images are difficult to avoid. A recent study conducted by the Canadian Teachers' Federation of almost 6000 Canadian children between Grades 3 and 10 found that of the 50% of youth who have a TV in their bedrooms another 50% admit to watching unsuitable movies – movies that emphasize gratuitous violence and sex. Grade 3 and 4 students were supervised while they played computer less than half the time. *Grand Theft Auto,* an ultra violent and sexually explicit adult video game that was banned from Australia and New Zealand, was identified as the most popular video game among Grade 7 boys.

Rather than eliminate computers, television and other media from our homes and classrooms, boys benefit when we teach them about how their sense of identity is being shaped by the media. Since boys don't like to be pushed around, they will become more mobilized and alert to the media when they discover that they are being bullied into their so-called consumer choices. A 2001 study called *Young Canadians in a Wired World* revealed that adults rarely discuss *net surfing* with youth. Seventy per cent of the young people surveyed said their parents rarely or never ask them about the sites they visit. How are boys to make sense of the media's influence if we rarely discuss it? Parents and teachers can help boys learn how to think critically about messages from the popular entertainment culture.

GUIDELINE 11
TEACH MEDIA ANALYSIS *CONT'D*

• • • • •

Sex ads can pop

up at any time on the

Internet - even when

boys are innocently

doing research

for a homework

assignment.

WE should also be concerned about the ways in which easily accessible, extreme Internet pornography can affect a boy's developing sexuality and view of females. Even when kids are not really looking for sexually extreme images, these pop up when they check their email, and routinely delete spam. When boys are researching homework on the Internet, there can be many distractions. An average Internet porn site can generate as many sexual images, often linked with violence, as an entire issue of *Hustler*. As adult pornography has moved from the restricted shelves to accessible Internet downloads, boys don't have to sneak a peak any more. Pornography is ubiquitous in the digital age. Today's youth are part of a generation who grew up with the Internet and received the spam email ads for the Paris Hilton sex tapes along with numerous other *reality* broadcasts. We have not begun to explore the long-term implications of early exposure to extreme pornography that includes degrading sadomasochistic images of women.

Filtering software is certainly an option for parents and classroom teachers of younger boys. But it doesn't take long for boys to become adept at turning off the filtering software. The best defense for boys is critical thinking skills about pornography, hate, and violence gained through frank and open discussions.

The *Media Awareness Network* offers resources and support for everyone interested in media and information literacy for young people. The Canadian website is **www.media-aware-ness.ca.** Its latest teaching resource, *Allies and Aliens: A Mission in Critical Thinking,* offers Grade 7 and 8 students an interactive module where they are sent on a mission from Planet Earth and challenged to recognize and assess misinformation, prejudice, and racism on the Galactic Web. It is designed to increase students' ability to recognize bias, prejudice, and hate propaganda on the Internet and in other media. An extensive teacher's guide accompanies it.

PORNOGRAPHY IS UBIQUITOUS IN THE DIGITAL AGE.

GUIDELINE 11
TEACH MEDIA ANALYSIS *CONT'D*

Jo Cool or Jo Fool? is another online lesson in Web literacy for students in Grades 6 to 8. It is comprised of two flash animation modules: *Jo Cool/Jo Fool CyberTour* and *Jo Cool/Jo Fool CyberQuiz.* Youth get to visit Web sites and decide whether or not they're making smart choices.

It may also be of interest for teachers and parents to note that *Advertising Standards Canada*, a national industry association committed to ensuring the integrity and viability of advertising through self-regulation, has created the following guidelines to influence the way men and women are portrayed in ads. These guidelines may also be useful to teachers and parents looking for non-sexist ethical standards when discussing the media with children.

• • • • •

Advertising Standards Canda has created a set of guidelines to influence the way men and women are portrayed in ads.

• **Authority**
Advertisers must treat men and women equally in roles of authority.

• **Decision-making**
Advertisers must show women and men as equal decision-makers for all types of purchases.

• **Sexuality**
Advertisers are not supposed to sexually exploit men or women when promoting their products.

• **Violence**
Advertisers are not supposed to show men threatening women or women threatening men.

• **Diversity**
Advertisers must show that men and women of all ages can participate in a wide variety of activities, both in the home and outside the home.

• **Language**
Advertisers must avoid language that misrepresents, offends, or excludes women or men.

GUIDELINE 12
FIGHT HOMOPHOBIA

· · · · ·

Being called a

fag or *homo* is

the worst form of

verbal harassment

according to 90% of

boys surveyed.

HOMOPHOBIA is the fear of homosexuality. Unlike other phobias, such as the fear of snakes, spiders, or crowds, homophobia is not a psychological condition but a socially conditioned fear. It is a fear created and cultivated primarily by the society in which we live. Homophobic verbal harassment is rife in secondary schools and boys are most at-risk.

Several years ago I had the opportunity to better understand its prevalence in the elementary school setting while assisting in the preparation of a system-wide Grade Seven Boys' Conference. I surveyed hundreds of boys on a wide variety of matters, and one particular question about what sort of verbal harassment troubled them most intrigued me: "What is the worst thing that a boy could be called in Grade 7 ?" Approximately 90% of the responses were homophobic in nature and identified harassing taunts such as *fag* or *homo*. The remaining 10% of responses referred to lack of intelligence, such as *stupid, moron,* or *idiot*. It is to be expected that boys will struggle with developmental psychosexual anxieties, but where do boys go to discuss this common anxiety when a homophobic culture does not make it easy or even safe to openly discuss this form of harassment? You can certainly hear a pin drop when I raise this topic at my parenting and teacher workshops. Clearly, it is not discussed in many of our homes and schools. If parents and teachers don't tackle this issue, who will? Are we not leaving boys to seek answers from the media or other uninformed youth?

HOMPHOBIA IS A FEAR CREATED AND PERPETUATED BY THE SOCIETY IN WHICH WE LIVE. IT IS MORE A FORM OF SOCIAL DISCRIMINATION THAN A PSYCHOLOGICAL CONDITION.

GUIDELINE 12
FIGHT HOMOPHOBIA *CONT'D*

Why are gay or

bisexual men met

with such fear and

loathing by some

heteorsexual men?

THE groundwork already exists in most schools which actively promote responsibility, respect, and civility. Many school districts either already have or are considering an anti-harassment policy that includes sexuality. Schools recognize that sexuality is as much a part of identity as ethnicity. Education to counteract homophobia and heterosexism needs to be part of *education for life* in which people can develop their self-identities fully and confidently, valuing who they are, and recognizing the equal value of others. Anti-bullying policies need to be much more explicit about including lesbians, gay, bisexual, and trans-gendered people. They need to challenge the way that a dominant heterosexist perspective can oppress children.

Norman Dean Radican is a popular Australian health educator for men and special adviser on gay and bisexual issues. He sees homophobia as a socially and institutionally conditioned fear. "The problem is that the labels define us too narrowly and are often based on stereo-types and inaccurate assumptions. The truth is that our lives, our realities, our sexualities, our behaviours, our thoughts and feelings and even our politics can be, and often are, fluid and variable and are not easily defined by a single, simple label."

Radican encourages people to consider why men who are gay and bisexual are viewed with such fear and loathing. "In order for men to indiscriminately take on the fear and hatred of a group of men they do not know, they must somehow be seen collectively as a threat. The next question, of course, is why gay and bisexual men could possibly be seen as a threat to other, heterosexual men." He argues that often when heterosexual men feel threatened, it becomes important to keep gay and bisexual men in their place, on the lowest rungs of the masculine hierarchy of power. "One way of achieving this is to create an extreme, general-ized fear and hatred of those men who are different. This hatred is also extended to any men, regardless of their sexuality, who don't live up to the *normal* standard."

GUIDELINE 12
FIGHT HOMOPHOBIA *CONT'D*

RADICAN further challenges men to consider that the perceived gay threat may very well in fact be the fear of their own desire for closeness with other men. "Homophobia could act as a mechanism to help contain heterosexual men's desires to be close, to be intimate and to connect with other men." But the desire for closeness need not be sexual closeness. He encourages men to challenge the irrational fears and limiting myths of homophobia so that they can become more conscious of the ideas and behaviours that are passed on to boys.

• • • • •

A recent Ipsos-

Reid poll found

47% of Americans

believe same-sex

marriage is *wrong*

and should never

be lawful, while only

26% of Canadians

feel the same

way– *Vancouver*

Sun, July 3, 2005.

A couple of years ago Greg, a 19 year-old male, requested a meeting with me separate from his family members. Previously, I had several consultation sessions with his family regarding his younger sister. During my initial meeting with Greg we discussed many things, but it was not until our next meeting that he asked for some advice about how to let his father know that he was gay. My previous experience of his family gave me the impression that his father would be receptive. Greg, however, indicated that he had reason to believe his father would be very upset, even humiliated. Upon enquiring for evidence, Greg told a story about the previous summer when his family was vacationing at the lake and he overheard his dad

OUR SCHOOLS SET THE CRITERIA FOR SUCCESS AND FAILURE, SOCIALLY AS WELL AS ACADEMICALLY.

listening to his uncles laughing at a gay joke. He emphasized that although his father didn't offer any gay jokes himself, he laughed. Boys look for clues from fathers and the significant men in their life as they determine what is and what is not acceptable behaviour.

Along with families, our schools construct much of boys' social and cultural environment and are intimately connected with many of their fears and anxieties. Our schools set the criteria for success and failure, socially as well as academically, and create a world in which individuals are accepted or rejected on an almost daily basis. While I recognize that discussions about homophobia may be uncomfortable amidst conflicting community opinions, we must forge partnerships to provide the guidance and support boys so desperately need. At the very least educators and parents are charged to provide harassment free schools and communities where both boys and girls may develop their self-concept without unnecessary stress and anxiety.

GUIDELINE 13
MODEL RESPECT FOR WOMEN

Both men and women can feel oppressed by stereotypes.

PARENTS and teachers recognize that macho versions of masculinity damage boys as well as girls. As recently at 1968 "…female Olympic competitors were often asked to parade naked in front of board examiners. Breasts and vagina were all one needed to certify one's gender" (Fausto-Sterling). Not surprisingly, men and women complained that this procedure was degrading and has since been changed. Males and females are both oppressed by stereotypical ideas that women are weak and men are strong, or that men make decisions while women make coffee.

If we want boys to develop a more caring image of masculinity, we need to show respect for women, including female teachers, and the particular strengths and qualities that women possess. When boys see their fathers and men at school showing respect toward mothers and female teachers, then they will in turn be more likely to treat women and girls with similar regard. Both at home and at school, women must share in positions of power and not be seen exclusively as the nurturers while men are expected to be the power-brokers. It is essential for both men and women to have active roles in their sons' lives. Boys benefit when they observe attitudes of respect between men and women.

• • • • •

GUIDELINE 14
CONTEND WITH THE BOY-CODE

OVER the years, as a school-based counsellor, many fathers have confided in me that they didn't really care about the school rules when it came to their son's reputation and would tell their boys to come out swinging if ever hit first or backed into a corner. Boys who want to become *real men* fear appearing as *wimps* in the eyes of their fathers.

Studies show that in the hospital parents of newborns see their boys as hardier, stronger, and more alert. When a mother plays with her boy, she is typically more cautious than fathers, who tend to be adventurous and physical with their boys. As boys grow older, parents also tend to expect them to achieve more and be more independent and more competitive than girls. Young boys are given more freedom than girls to express themselves and are taught to figure things out for themselves. Boys' independence is prized.

GUIDELINE 14
CONTEND WITH THE BOY-CODE *CONT'D*

GENDER socialization claims that bigger than life figures like Rambo – John Wayne or James Dean when I was growing up – have taught boys that being tough, dominant, ready to fight or have sex at the drop of a hat is what manhood is all about. This particular code of masculinity, which has been a dominant force in western male culture for a long time, glorifies war and marginalizes males who are going *soft*. In a prominent book profiling the lives of men behind the Vietnam War, David Halberstam reminds the reader that the thing President Lyndon Johnson feared most was

• • • • •

Be tough, be

strong, don't cry.

Be a MAN!

THE SO-CALLED BOY-CODE IS SUBJECT TO PROFOUND MISINTERPRETATION.

that his manhood might be inadequate. "A strong man does not succumb to the cultural stereotypes of a socially toxic society that defines manhood in terms of aggression, power and material acquisition," says James Garbarino, author of the popular book *Lost Boys: Why Our Sons Turn Violent and How We Can Save Them.*

Starting at a very young age our society can channel boys into a sort of cultural straitjacket that molds mind and enforces behaviour by confining emotional expressiveness. "Don't cry or you'll be a sissy," I remember hearing adults tell boys in my neighbourhood. William Pollack, renowned author of *Real Boys,* argues that our culture supports a boy-code that celebrates emotional detachment among males and can also prevent those most under its influence from achieving their academic potential. The boy-code requires boys to appear brave, show little emotion, not to tattletale, and never to cry. The boy-code can be summed up with three phrases: *1) Be tough and strong; 2) Don't show your emotions;* and *3) Don't be a girl.* Often, if they are to avoid humiliation and rejection, boys must embrace the boy-code for themselves and enforce it in others. Even though some people argue that the stoic boy-code has certain constructive values related to honour, such as to avoid picking on little kids, hitting girls, or kicking a guy when he's down or his back is turned, I would argue that it is possible for boys to be honourable while also cultivating their capacity for intimacy and deep connection.

GUIDELINE 14
CONTEND WITH THE BOY-CODE *CONT'D*

IF boys accept that these rules for attaining manhood are in fact valid, they may feel forced to choose between following the code and subjecting themselves to rigidity, loneliness, and potential physical and emotional health problems; or to reject the boy-code and risk continual reminders that they are inadequate as males. In my experience as a counsellor working with couples, who often come to me in the midst of a messy and complicated problem marriage, I have learned that for some men the *boy-code* later becomes the *divorce-code*. Women in unhappy relationships complain that these men simply don't seem capable of real intimacy or tolerating strong emotions. These men often pursue extra-marital affairs to prove their virility and masculinity.

So what can teachers and parents do to help boys relax the boy-code and achieve their potential? Encouraging boys to be more fully human means giving them time and space. We can give boys space to talk while avoiding being too chatty or pushy. We can provide boys with time for undivided attention. We can avoid pushing boys into premature independence and let him know that real boys and men do cry and experience loss. Most importantly, we can express care and love as openly as we would to girls. I will explore more on how to talk with boys in the chapter on mentoring boys.

PROVIDE A BALANCE OF ACTIVITIES FOR BOYS.

While competitive sports can provide outlets for boys' energy and opportunities for boys to build a sense of belonging and cooperation through teamwork, an overemphasis on sports can be limiting. Some models of masculinity that show adult men fighting in hockey games and other sports are glamorized by the media, and suggest to boys that violence is acceptable. Sometimes the emphasis on toughness and winning promoted by the media and even by school sports can tempt males to maltreat their bodies, using steroids, for example, or ignoring injuries, as shown in the movie *Friday Night Lights*. Boys respond to expectations and cultural pressures placed on them. If we reinforce toughness at the expense of gentleness, boys will respond to that. Boys need both. We can value their capacity for warm-hearted affection and open-minded generosity as well as their competitive play and their energetic physicality.

We should provide a balance of activities for boys to participate in so that they can see reflected back at them a broad range of possibilities for what it means to be male.

* * * * *

We can give boys space to talk while avoiding being too chatty or pushy.

GUIDELINE 15
AVOID REACTING TO PLAYGROUND RUMBLE

PLAY is essential to the development of self-confidence. Through spontaneous play a boy learns about problem solving, negotiating, and how to get along with others. It is natural that boys will cross the line of appropriateness at times, but accepting boys as they are also means accepting their rough-and-tumble behaviour on the playground.

• • • • •

Good natured

teasing or

bantering may be

misintrpreted as

bullying.

While codes of safety around playground behaviour are necessary, school regulations of recent years typically constrict and oppose non-threatening playground behaviour. Boys who are very energetic during their recess break and participate in ritualistic play fighting, along with pushing and shoving, are often reprimanded for violating a zero tolerance fighting policy. Even boys who participate in good-natured teasing of others can be viewed as anti-social under this policy, despite our culture's long history of this bonding ritual – even in our workplace staffrooms. During recess many of our boys' good-natured cajoling or bantering can be inappropriately judged as bullying.

It seems odd to me that we promote and demand instructional modifications that allow for disability and cultural differences, yet we do not make allowances for gender differences on the playground. Rather than pathologize rambunctious play or playground rumble as bullying, we need to become more responsive and provide opportunities for boys to express themselves in the many and varied ways they

ZERO TOLERANCE FOR AGGRESSIVE BEHAVIOUR AND FIGHTING MAY LEAD TO GENDER DISCRIMINATION, RESTRICTING BOYS IN THEIR NATURAL BEHAVIOURS.

are capable of. Rather than outlaw snowball throwing, for example, we need to provide rules and supervision, teaching our boys how to throw snow in a manner that keeps everyone safe. Besides, all the rules in the world won't give rise to cooperation and integrity.

GUIDELINE 15
AVOID REACTING TO PLAYGROUND RUMBLE *CONT'D*

A FAMILY once visited my office after their son in Grade 5 was reprimanded for throwing rocks at a car. Upon listening to their story I learned that earlier in the week the playground balls were removed because the children – primarily boys – were not returning them on time. This was viewed as an appropriate consequence, but only led to more problems. You see, in search of something interesting to do, the boy used the nearby road sign as target practice with some small pebbles. One thing led to another, as when a car soon drove by, it became the recipient of a pebble's rebound. Witnesses were identified and parents were called. The family was referred for counselling.

Avoid the temptation to classify boys as potential jail inmates simply because they participate in vigorous physical play. Both boys and girls need adults to provide activities on the playground that permit energetic play. It is somewhat more common that boys just need to push and pull.

• • • • •

GUIDELINE 16
AVOID SHAMING BOYS

Males are not supposed to be victims. Are they?

WHEN I was in Grade 5 the medical doctor tried to give me a needle in my bottom-side. I was afraid and told him that I wouldn't allow it. I recall him telling me that I should be a *big boy* and take the medicine. After all, other *big boys* were able to take it. I still wouldn't take it. My mother was called in and invited to hold me down. I fought them both off and left the doctor's office without receiving the needle, but I didn't anticipate the feelings of shame that would follow.

Some say that shame can be a healthy human emotion. Can it? How? What good is it? Or can it can create unnecessary guilt, confusion, and self-doubt? Sexual abuse can create shame in its most extreme form.

GUIDELINE 16
AVOID SHAMING BOYS *CONT'D*

• • • • •

Rape of men or

boys is the most

underreported

and unaddressed

violent crime.

Over the years as a therapist I noticed that men more often than not downplayed or discounted the effects of their experience of childhood sexual abuse. It represents perhaps the strongest form of shame that can be experienced by males. It is especially difficult for men to discuss this sort of abuse when it occurs during their adolescent years or later because they feel responsible. "The rape of men in our communities is perhaps the most underreported and unaddressed violent crime. The intense shame and stigma attached to adult male rape arguably exceeds that of the rape of women, which has become a widely acknowledged and public issue only within the last 20 years," says Michael Scarce in his book on male sexual abuse.

I do not assume any predetermined effect from sexual abuse, but rather listen and am interested in how men overcome adversity and manage the shame. Wendy Maltz, author of *The Sexual Healing Journey: A Guide for Survivors of Sexual Abuse* reports "male survivors often have an especially difficult time revealing their abuse histories. One male survivor recounted his experience: …"the very hardest part of recovery for me was coming out and saying that I am a sexually abused person. I didn't know until two years ago that men and boys could be raped. We're not supposed to be victims."

THE INCIDENCE OF SUICIDE IS FOUR TO SIX TIMES GREATER IN MALES THAN FEMALES.

The cultural landscape that previously shushed male sexual abuse changed several years ago when our national hockey players publicly acknowledged the powerful and shaming effects that childhood sexual abuse had on them. All of a sudden it was permitted to openly discuss the profound effects, but most importantly, men began to talk. Although we have begun to break this particular barrier of silence, research shows that shame is still often behind suicide among adolescent males. While girls exhibit more depression and thoughts of suicide, adolescent males have a much lower image of themselves as students than do girls, and depending on their age, commit suicide at four to six times the rate of girls.

GUIDELINE 16
AVOID SHAMING BOYS *CONT'D*

• • • • •

Boys consistently

report that they

experience

shame when

publicly scolded or

reprimanded.

DESPITE boys' apparent indifference, they can struggle with emotional turmoil. It can be easy to misread a boy's shame when he glares at you with a look of anger. Anger is often one of the few emotions that many boys will allow. Look beyond the glare and consider the emotion beneath the surface. Instead of rubbing a boy's nose in his misbehaviour, make your expectations clear and help him to develop the courage to make mistakes. Shame only undermines confidence and typically leads to resentment. Having boys sit outside the principal's office when conflict erupts does not always accomplish the goals that school staffs intend. With the exception of safety issues, often times student bystanders only learn about what forms of behaviour the teacher is unable to deal with. Boys who are willing to

LOOK BEYOND THE ANGRY GLARE AND CONSIDER
THE EMOTION BENEATH THE SURFACE.

risk the shame of being put on display for *bad behaviour* often raise their status as they demonstrate to other boys their flagrant disregard for authority. Creating unrealistic behavioural contracts are also counterproductive. Boys accept the logic but feel controlled and rebel. Boys consistently report that they experience shame when publicly scolded or reprimanded. Boys will often put up with what they cannot immediately change and later seek revenge. Often, their feelings of shame and of feeling over-powered only goes underground and transforms into passive power to avoid future shame.

Also, avoid holding the entire class responsible for the behaviour of a few as this only creates widespread resentment and not guilt in a few as intended. Finally, don't blame students for your own shortcomings as a teacher or parent. Unrealistic expectations, erratic pacing, poor planning, and unclear instructions are our responsibilities.

GUIDELINE 17
PRACTISE INCLUSIVENESS WITH BOYS FROM LOW INCOME FAMILIES

• • • • •

Gifted programs

are often designed

around middle-

class values and

tend to exclude

boys from lower

income families.

TOM MCINTYRE, recipient of the *Golden Web Award* from The Guidance Channel for **www.behavioradvisor.com**, a noted authority on kids who are disadvantaged, reports that it is typical for boys from lower socio-economic classes to be at higher risk for a diagnosis of serious emotional disturbance. Perhaps this is because they typically display the most extreme levels of stereotypical male behaviour and more often engage in confrontational behaviour to gain acceptance into groups, develop friendships, and establish their place in the friendship dominance hierarchy. It has also been suggested that Caucasian middle class females, who comprise the majority of the teaching force, may have value-reflecting behaviours that conflict strongly with those of lower socioeconomic male and minority students. These different values may cause some teachers to misinterpret behaviours that are tolerable in the youngsters' homes or neighbourhoods as being aggressive, inappropriate, or otherwise intolerable in a classroom setting. This conflict of value orientations may make general educators prone to referring these students for discipline, learning assistance, and behavioural services.

Despite gifted minds being equally distributed across the socio-economic stratosphere there is often less support for gifted students among the poor. Under the guise of fairness, school districts can omit students who come from poor school communities from gifted programs while increasing the numbers in other special education programs, such as be-

POVERTY IS A DEBILITATING FORCE AMONG BOYS – THE UNDERLYING CAUSE OF A NUMBER OF PROBLEMS AT SCHOOL AND AT HOME.

havioural support. Gifted boys who live in poverty do not come to school with middle class experiences and values, and thus supports must be adjusted for them to further develop their inquiring minds.

GUIDELINE 17
PRACTISE INCLUSIVENESS WITH BOYS FROM LOW INCOME FAMILIES *CONT'D*

POVERTY is often a primary underlying factor for boys who leave home early. Unfortunately, this can lead them to alcoholism, drug abuse, and an incomplete education. How many teachers have considered what it is like for a boy to be lured into the sex trade in search of relief from the anguish of poverty? Prostituting oneself for drugs is a common stereotype. At least in the sex trade money initially appears available for clothes and food until the growing shame is masked with drugs and the stereotype becomes a reality.

Boys benefit when school communities are sensitive to family income and provide pre-school initiatives, meal programs, clothing swap opportunities, bulk shopping, communal cooking, after school activities, and special cultural events. Most importantly, boys benefit when we look beyond their circumstances of poverty and support the genius within so that a boy may develop to his fullest potential.

• • • • •

GUIDELINE 18
SUPPORT BOYS FROM NON-DOMINANT ETHNO-CULTURAL TRADITIONS

AMONG American school children, boys who are black consistently underachieve. With respect to early school leavers, between 25% and 30% of America's youth fail to graduate from high school with a regular diploma. That figure climbs to over 50% for black male students in many U.S. cities. The story is even worse for Native American children.

In Canada, those youth who are less likely to complete secondary school are Aboriginal students, certain other ethnic students, along with male students who have a litany of poor academic performance. According to the Special Chiefs' Conference on Education, Aboriginal Canadian youth are twice as likely as other youth to leave school before graduating. Both country's histories of racism have left people in cycles of poverty and underachievement.

GUIDELINE 18
SUPPORT BOYS FROM NON-DOMINANT ETHNO-CULTURAL TRADITIONS *CONT'D*

• • • • •

Despite our greatest efforts to avoid racist thinking, we need to acknowledge our propensity for doing so.

A MALE counsellor recently reported to me a hallway scene all too familiar to him in his community with a high percentage of youth who are Aboriginal. He witnessed a female teacher reprimanding a boy of Aboriginal ancestry. She appeared agitated. The boy avoided eye contact and was quiet throughout her lecture. Later, she explained to the counsellor that she saw the boy as *passive-aggressive* because he had no eye contact and didn't answer her questions quickly enough. He explained to her some cultural differences and she was shaken by her unintended racism. She apologized to the boy and appreciated the counsellor's courage to speak with her.

In my travels I am frequently shocked when I hear school staff explain that Aboriginal students underachieve because they are lazy or that they likely have Fetal-Alcohol Syndrome or Fetal-Alcohol Effect. Although FAS and

SYSTEMIC RACISM IS ANOTHER CAUSE OF UNDER-ACHIEVEMENT AMONG BOYS FROM MINORITY GROUPS.

FAE are recognizable risks for Aboriginals whose parents and grandparents have often suffered displacement, residential school abuse, poverty, and other ills, we must not make racist assumptions. When the unique aspects of Aboriginal culture and other cultural groups are respected, boys are better able to learn and achieve. We need to be sensitive to cultural differences and adapt our approaches.

GUIDELINE 18

SUPPORT BOYS FROM NON-DOMINANT ETHNO-CULTURAL TRADITIONS *CONT'D*

• • • • •

When the

unique aspects

of a culture are

respected and

understood, boys

are better able to

learn and achieve.

I RECALL being invited to present an evening workshop on homework to parents and was informed that expectations for attendance were low as almost 50% of the community was Aboriginal. When I suggested that we should have two workshops, one at school and the other at the Band Office I was again surprised to learn that "…it had never been done before and it likely wouldn't work." I insisted and later found myself at the Band Office with several parents who had previously never attended any meetings at their child's school. We spent the majority of the time discussing our lives, most of which had nothing to do with homework. Compared to the banter that often fills many parenting workshops, there were many periods of comfortable silence. With only fifteen minutes left – on my time anyway – the Band Chief asked me what I thought about homework. The ensuing discussion was rich with complexity and concern. They observed and listened intently before questioning. Eye contact was minimal. I especially appreciated how a period of thoughtful silence followed when a new idea was ever so softly expressed. At no point was a family or individual singled out. Metaphors were frequently used. It reconfirmed my previous experiences of reaching outside my cultural context.

CAUCASIAN TEACHERS WOULD DO WELL TO UNDERSTAND THE TEACHING AND LEARNING DIFFERENCES WITHIN THE ABORIGINAL CULTURE.

Teachers of European ancestry may be inclined to negatively evaluate the overall learning and communicative styles of non-dominant ethno-cultural boys. Despite our greatest efforts to avoid racist thinking we need to acknowledge our propensity to do so. It is simply too deeply rooted in our cultural traditions.

GUIDELINE 19
SUPPORT BOYS WITH ALTERNATIVE SEXUAL ORIENTATION

ADOLESCENT boys who are gay, bisexual, and or transgendered follow a developmental path that is both similar to and quite different from that followed by adolescents who are heterosexual. All teenagers face certain developmental challenges, such as developing social skills, thinking about career choices, and fitting into a peer group. Boys who are not heterosexual must also cope with prejudiced, discriminatory, and violent behaviour and messages in their families, schools, and communities. Such behaviour and messages negatively affect their health and education. These students are more likely than heterosexual students to report feeling isolated and often miss school due to fear. It is this isolation and lack of support that partially accounts for higher rates of emotional distress, suicide attempts, risky sexual behaviour, and substance use. The promotion of *Reparative Therapy* adds insult to injury and is likely to exacerbate the risk of harassment and fear. The majority of professional and religious associations have publicly disputed the claim that homosexuality is a mental disorder and that this therapy can eliminate it. The online fact sheet offered by the American Psychological Association has more details.

• • • • •

When adults

suggest that

homosexuality is

a mental condition

that can be

cured, feelings

of stress are only

compounded.

Probably the single greatest fear boys face is rejection by their family and friends. It is this deep-seated fear that places gay adolescents in the highest risk category for suicide and depression. A boy's secret about being gay can eat away at his developing personal identity and self esteem. Also, many boys who are gay often begin to believe that somehow they deserve this fate – that underneath it all they must actually be a bad person. Instead of harassment, they need access to a supportive community for their developing sense of identity – typically other gay teenagers. Gay-straight Alliance support groups in our schools and communities can be integral parts of a community of support to help boys who are gay find their place in society. Such groups additionally communicate the message in our schools that everyone is worthy of respect, regardless of gender, race, class, or sexual orientation.

GUIDELINE 19
SUPPORT BOYS WITH ALTERNATIVE SEXUAL ORIENTATION *CONT'D*

BOYS who are gay especially need acceptance and love from their parents. Parents can make use of organizations like P-Flag, (Parents and Friends of Lesbians and Gays), to help them overcome their own confusion and homophobic thinking. Boys who are gay typically do not expect immediate acceptance but they do need a parent's attention and understanding so that they can mature and focus on more important matters like becoming courageous, caring, and ethical men. All students deserve an opportunity for learning and healthy development in a safe and supportive environment, including youth who are lesbian, gay, bisexual, and transgendered.

• • • • •

GUIDELINE 20
TEACH HEALTHY MASCULINITY

THE MEDIA, books, and talk shows spend a lot of time criticizing the boy-code and what is commonly considered to be unhealthy masculinity. It seems to me that boys, and girls for the matter, could benefit if we took the time to teach about healthy masculinity. The alternative to Rambo's manliness is a more encouraging and constructive one where a boy matures into manhood from the inside out in a community of concern. This authentic process, learning about oneself, and then loving what one learns would make boys into healthier men – both emotionally and physically. Men who achieved authentic manhood would not be easy to manipulate, dominate, or control. A man would know who he is, what he stands for, and what his life is about. He would not need to abuse substances or push people around to prove masculinity. Instead, he would focus on contributing to those around him and address the pressing social needs of our time. His interest would be socially motivated – to look out for and help others.

GUIDELINE 20
TEACH HEALTHY MASCULINITY *CONT'D*

If we change the 'p' in paternity to 'm', we have maternity. Then we could discuss the qualities of healthy womanhood. And guess what? Healthy manhood and womanhood involve the same character traits. And, believe it or not, men will not turn into women, and women will not turn into men. Healthy manhood and womanhood would create a culture with less pain, less loss, and instead more joy and more interconnectedness. We can teach both boys and girls these traits of gender health through role modeling and mentoring.

RECENTLY, I received a list identifying healthy masculinity traits from a father attending a presentation I gave in Vancouver, BC. I later discovered that Dr. Michael Obsatz developed the following list as a constructive guideline for personal reflection and also as a teaching tool so that boys at home and school may discuss openly what healthy masculinity looks and acts like (www.angeresources.com/shamebased.html).

PURPOSE
Knowing one's purpose gives one's life meaning and direction. Whole manhood requires commitment and goal-setting.

POWER FOR AND WITH, NOT OVER
Real power is power for others, to help others, and sharing power with others. It involves faith in oneself, assertiveness, and compassion.

PASSION
Passion is being alive, with vitality, energy, sensuality, healthy sexual energy. It involves cherishing as well as grieving, and allowing oneself to fully connect emotionally.

PATERNITY
Paternity involves helping others, children and animals, and mentoring and stewarding the earth.

PIETY
Piety is about wonder, gratitude, reverence, humility, and spiritual connectedness.

PERSISTENCE
Persistence includes endurance, resilience, responsibility, and follow-through.

PRESENCE
Presence means being open, not judging, accepting others, and paying attention.

PATIENCE
Patience means delaying gratification, impulse control, and being slow to anger.

PARDON
Pardon means forgiveness and kindness.

PARTNERSHIP
Partnership includes collaboration, community building, and negotiation, and compromise.

PLIABILITY
Pliability is flexibility, openness to change, and willingness to see other points of view.

PLAYFULNESS
Playfulness is laughter, joy, and lightheartedness.

PEACEMAKING
Peacemaking includes justice-seeking, non-violent alternatives, and mediation.

POLITENESS
Politeness means having courtesy and manners.

PERSPECTIVE
Perspective is being able to see the larger picture.

CHAPTER FOUR

UNDERSTANDING A BOY'S
MOTIVATION TO **LEARN**

*People attain worth and dignity by the multitude of decisions they make
from day to day. These decisions sometimes require courage.*
Rollo May

• • • • •

As boys get

older many

begin to

associate

learning with

drudgery.

Parents rarely complain that a zippy preschool boy lacks motivation. Young boys are propelled by curiosity, eager to explore their environment, interact with it, and make sense of it. Unfortunately, as boys get older, many begin to associate learning with drudgery. They invent multiple excuses to avoid schoolwork. In high school, some start skipping regularly and are pushed out or drop out. Parents wonder sadly why their once bright-eyed, eager boys have become so apathetic, cavalier, or even hostile toward learning. I remember a story of a boy which may seem familiar to you.

Fifteen year-old Justin was just barely scraping by in school. His parents and teachers were stymied and frustrated by his low school achievement. Most days he preferred to hang out at the local skateboard park with his friends rather than attend class regularly. He would not study or hand in assignments on time. His parents were at their wits' end, having tried every way they could think of to motivate him to be successful in his studies. He was also slacking off at home, not doing his chores, and creating conflict when pushed. The only thing that they could count on was his appetite. Justin found school boring, said his teachers were idiots, and he didn't seem too crazy about his family either. They viewed his behaviour as irresponsible, defiant and threatening to his academic success, which may limit future possibilities if he didn't 'pull up his socks'.

Sound familiar? What would you say is going on here?

• • • • •

Being a

brainiac was

not considered

COOL among

Justin's peers.

CLEARLY, as Justin needs to assert his growing desire for autonomy, the tensions between Justin and the adults in his life are part of the inevitable tension of those push and pull adolescent years. In addition, while Justin's parents and teachers see his present behaviour as irresponsible, and worry that it will limit his future opportunities, Justin does not take this long range view. He needs to be physically active, and is totally focused on living in the moment.

In addition, Justin's main developmental need at this stage is to fit in, to be liked and accepted by his peers. As is often the case, being a *brainiac*, as he called it, is not considered cool among Justin's peer group.

But there is more to the story.

Then something really interesting happened. Justin met a learning assistance teacher who connected with him through a shared passion for hockey. He started to look forward to that one part of his school day when they would meet. She had high expectations and really pushed him to attend classes, complete assignments and prepare for tests while maintaining her authentic connection and interest in him through hockey. After a few months of hard work the earth shook – Justin got straight B's on his report card and he made the honour roll. He still hung out at the skateboard park with his friends but had made school a priority too.

Before he received the support from the learning assistant teacher, Justin felt backed into a corner and trapped in circular arguments with adults. When pressured, he'd clearly chosen the path of ease at the skateboard park rather than the struggle of learning. Given firm and friendly support, Justin discovered what he needed to be successful in both worlds. The learning assistance teacher did not force Justin to get higher letter grades. It was her clarity, caring and respect for his self-determination that influenced his success. She recognized the truth of the old proverb – *You can lead a horse to water, but you can't make it drink.*

The challenge is to re-ignite that natural curiosity and desire to learn so prevalent in young boys, but sadly missing in teenagers.

WHY do so many boys stop investing themselves in learning? How can boys start to care about learning for its own sake? And how can we help re-ignite their passion to learn, and in the process, help them raise their school achievement?

Let's begin by reflecting on how motivation typically operates in boys.

Motivation implies the desire to participate in the learning process. As the book *Punished by Rewards* argues, the carrot and stick approach to motivation, employing external bribes and rewards, does not work in the long run. A system of bribes, rewards, and punishments, which are sometimes disguised as consequences, can perhaps give short-term results. However, these kinds of reinforcements rarely lead to the development of good judgment, responsibility, and self-discipline. Tapping into intrinsic motivation of boys to learn is not the same as trying to force or demand cooperation. Boys need to develop internal motivation if they are to assume command of their lives.

THE THREE C'S OF **INTERNAL MOTIVATION** • • • • •

IN ORDER to develop internal motivation at school, at home, and in life, boys need to feel connected. They need to feel capable. And they need to feel that they count.

All humans need to feel socially connected. But while girls tend to express their need for connection directly through eye contact, hugging, and language, boys are more constrained. The rules associated with masculinity can narrow their options for connection. Just watch boys as they greet each other at the playground, the mall, or at school, and you'll probably notice a certain aloofness that somehow communicates roundabout interest. Boys don't usually stand face-to-face, preferring instead to stand shoulder to shoulder.

THE THREE C'S OF **INTERNAL MOTIVATION**

BOYS need to feel competent and capable. When a boy feels he can do things well and he learns to overcome obstacles rather than failing, his confidence grows in leaps and bounds. Almost more than anything else, boys want to know that they can take care of themselves and handle what life brings at home and school. It is when boys are not able to satisfy their need to feel capable and connected that they often resort to misbehaviour. They can get good at being bad, at living up to a label such as *difficult child*. When boys are encouraged to test their competencies in a safe atmosphere without fear of humiliation, they can learn to believe in their own ability to solve problems. Along the way they learn how to express themselves, to assume responsibility, and to develop good judgment in the service of self-discipline.

Only when we forget ourselves can we find ourselves.

IF BOYS FEEL THAT THEY CAN'T BE GOOD AT BEING GOOD, THEY OFTEN RESORT TO BEING GOOD AT BEING BAD.

Boys need to feel that their existence counts. When boys belong and feel capable, and that their contributions are valued, the resulting confidence may lay the groundwork for lifelong habits of generosity. Rather than focussing on their own insular lives, boys will be motivated to contribute toward the well being of others and the community. As Rudolf Dreikurs, renowned Adlerian family therapist, once said: *"Only when we forget ourselves can we find ourselves."*

For more information on the 3 C's of internal motivation refer to *Kids Who Can*, by Amy Lew and Betty Lou Bettner, who originally developed the concept.

BEHAVIOUR **INVOLVES CHOICE**

• • • • •

Over-analysis

can lead to

paralysis.

WHEN we try to analyze the why of boys' behaviour—especially what we regard as mis-behaviour—we can become overwhelmed by all the possible explanations. Is it ADHD that is to blame? Is it a genetic conduct disorder or even an attachment disorder? Maybe it's a perceptual-motor impairment. Is he lost in complicated grief? Did the divorce damage him? Will play therapy help? Or medication? But what about the side effects? Could it be that newly discovered disorder just publicized on the radio?

Such over-analysis can lead to paralysis. Although such considerations can sometimes lead to finding the help we need, they leave out an important ingredient of human motivation – the power to choose. The realization that behaviour is based on choice can provide us insight into boys' motivation, and strategic leverage in our responses.

The following ten guidelines follow from the premise that all boys are capable of making positive choices and becoming responsible citizens.

• • • • •

GUIDELINE 21
ADDRESS ORIGINS OF BEHAVIOUR RATHER THAN SYMPTOMS

SIBLING rivalry, birth order, temperament, family and social environment, genetics, and cultural factors all influence choices. Early childhood observation and learning leads children to develop a largely unconscious blueprint of beliefs about who they are, what they have to do to belong and to be loved, what the world is like, and what males and females are like. As children grow, they practise, test, fine tune, and act from this blueprint to help them function and move in the world. A child's behaviour, based on his unique perception, always makes perfect sense at the level of the blueprint. His behaviour represents his version of adapting to his environment and life circumstances to ensure his survival.

GUIDELINE 21
ADDRESS ORIGINS OF BEHAVIOUR RATHER THAN SYMPTOMS

CHILDREN are great observers, and sponge up experiences, but they are often poor interpreters of what they observe. Teachers, parents, and mentors who understand that children choose behaviour based on how they perceive their reality are in the best position to guide and influence boys. When they recognize this power of choice and understand that all behaviour is purposeful, they can look for what's below the behaviour for clues on how to respond. Instead of getting sidetracked by responding to the behaviour alone, they can respond to the underlying needs that motivate behaviour. Consider the following examples of what boys are thinking when they make some non-constructive choices:

- *"I may not be able to do much, but at least I am important when you notice me."*

- *"Maybe I don't do it right, but you won't make me do it."*

- *"Nobody loves me, everybody hates me. Boy, will I ever get them back and hurt them!"*

- *"No matter what I do, it doesn't measure up, so why bother?"*

For a more indepth discussion of this topic refer to *Cooperative Discipline* by Linda Albert.

• • • • •

GUIDELINE 22
RESPECT STATUS NEEDS

BOYS, like the men they imitate, are motivated by the need to maintain or sometimes regain status. Just as very few men are comfortable enough to ask for directions when they get lost, many boys will say they know how to do something when they haven't the foggiest idea. Boys sense trouble when they perceive that they may not have what it takes to handle the tasks that confront them publicly. Many will choose to withdraw rather than lose status by failing. Avoidance of failure becomes their goal.

GUIDELINE 22
RESPECT STATUS NEEDS *CONT'D*

• • • • •

Men's or boys'

emotions are

often masked by

indifference or

criticism.

CONSIDER how a man who has had an emotionally upsetting day might talk later with his golf buddies on the golf course. Unlike many females, who would disclose their feelings, preferring to attend to their emotional needs immediately and perhaps even postpone the golf game, Chuck doesn't say anything at first. He may swing at the ball a bit more aggressively. Maybe by the second fairway he'll mutter, "My boss is an idiot!" Chuck may interject the emotions of the day throughout the game, but at any point along the way he can shut it down if he perceives criticism or disinterest. Men typically do not spill out their real feelings because they fear a loss of status. Emotions can be masked with indifference or criticism.

In general, while girls' speech is affiliative, boys' talk is competitive and even adversarial. Whereas females who are conversing tend to agree, support, and empathize, males tend to question, cajole, and challenge. They are typically more aggressive, caustic, and forceful in their language than females. They often give orders, criticize others' ideas, and jostle for authority.

CONSIDERING A BOY'S PERCEPTION OF STATUS, OR LACK OF IT, HELPS US UNDERSTAND BOYS' MOTIVATION.

The male style of communication may place its users at risk for being perceived by females as disrespectful and inappropriate. Boys need to jockey for status, and build a hierarchy to feel safe. When teachers ask boys publicly if they want help, they experience a loss of status in the class. They will most commonly say no, even if they need assistance. We should inquire discreetly and be aware of a boy's reaction, as some boys are more status-sensitive than others.

GUIDELINE 23
RESPECT INDEPENDENCE WHILE TEACHING COLLABORATION

KEEPING in mind the ways in which status needs affect males, we can better understand why boys might find it difficult to find a balance between independence and interdependence, cooperation, and competition.

· · · · ·

Men strive

to maintain

sovereignty, even

when it appears

to be against their

own self-interest.

Boys learn to value independence over collaboration as they are growing up. Deborah Tannen, author of the international bestseller, *You Just Don't Understand: Women and Men in Conversation,* discusses the example of gender differences by using an example of how men and women might negotiate parking lots. Men strive to maintain sovereignty, even when it appears to be against their own self-interest. While women accept and appreciate an invitation to back out of a parking stall, men hesitate. Indeed, men will often wave courteous drivers on, especially if they are male. They do want to leave the parking stall but instead fiddle with their cell phone, seatbelt, or radio – anything to avoid being told what to do! For men an invitation from another male to back out of the parking stall can present a loss of status –a movement from a position of superiority to inferiority. The same can occur at four-way intersections when a male invites the other to proceed earlier than his turn. Again, men will wave each other on, thinking, "I decide when I will proceed, not you!" Meanwhile the young boy in the back seat is quietly absorbing these rules for being male.

PARENTING AND TEACHING INVOLVES STRIKING A DELICATE BALANCE BETWEEN SUPPORTING A BOY AND ALLOWING HIM TO GROW ON HIS OWN.

GUIDELINE 23
RESPECT INDEPENDENCE WHILE TEACHING COLLABORATION *CONT'D*

• • • • •

When boys receive

constant threats

and reminders

with no follow

through, they

often conclude

that there is no

need to change

their behaviour.

WITHOUT meaning to, our attempts to help boys may actually be an unwitting infringement upon their needs for independence and autonomy. A mother recently emailed me her concern about her young teenage son: "How can I motivate my stubborn and disinterested 13 year-old to do better in school and life? He has three failing grades on his report card. All he wants to do is play on the computer. He won't clean his room unless I stand over him. He won't do homework unless I get after him. Even yelling doesn't work anymore. Got any suggestions?"

A teacher had a similar request and struggled with boys who don't hand in their homework on time. She went on to explain how she does everything possible to make it easy for them, but no matter how much help she provides, they don't respond. She routinely even makes adjustments in due dates to avoid discouraging and confronting boys.

As it turns out, we can discourage boys by doing too much for them or by reminding them too often of what they are supposed to do. When we take a boy's lunch to school because he forgot it at home, he learns not to remember it himself. He may also conclude that we don't have faith in his ability. When boys get frequent verbal reminders about homework due dates, they don't concern themselves with keeping track. Boys can become overly dependent on us when it is actually to their benefit to be held responsible for their actions. Boys often conclude that when parents and teachers offer repeated reminders and threats with no follow through, there is no need to change their behaviour. We have to be willing to let boys experience the consequences of their actions without interruption or reminders.

GUIDELINE 23
RESPECT INDEPENDENCE WHILE TEACHING COLLABORATION *CONT'D*

WHEN boys are given too much independence too soon they can become anxious or feel out of their depth. These feelings of inadequacy can increase self-doubt and interfere with confidence building.

Boys respect clearly stated expectations when they are left to choose their responses. To motivate boys, make your expectations absolutely clear: "You are to submit your completed assignments to me by 4 pm on Tuesday, May 14th." Detail the consequences if expectations are not met: "If your assignment is submitted late, or is incomplete, you will lose 5 marks

Boys need independence to follow through on the courage of their convictions, and interdependence to have empathy for those around them.

WE HAVE TO BE WILLING TO LET BOYS EXPERIENCE THE CONSEQUENCES OF THEIR ACTIONS WITHOUT INTERRUPTION OR REMINDERS.

per day and you will not receive any marks for questions you do not complete," – then stick to it. Although there can be occasional special circumstances where leniency is appropriate, teachers and parents who don't follow through with their expectations communicate to boys that they aren't expected to be responsible.

If we want boys to become useful and contributing members of society, they need to learn that each of us relies on other people, and we are also responsible for our own actions and selves. We can help them to locate the middle ground between going it alone and going it with others, cooperation and competition. Boys need independence to follow through on the courage of their convictions, and interdependence to have empathy for those around them. William James, a turn of the century American psychologist and philosopher, said it best: "The community stagnates without the impulse of the individual. The impulse dies away without the sympathy of the community."

RECOGNIZE BIRTH ORDER INFLUENCES

• • • • •

Throughout the animal kingdom, fitting in has always ensured survival.

A CENTRAL and persistent theme of personality development is related to striving for significance and the need to belong and fit in. This need is equated with survival in our families of origin because as children we are born into the world heavily dependent on parents to meet our most basic needs and fitting in ensures survival. Adler said that striving for significance results in forward movement and is oriented to the future as one works to overcome feelings of insignificance and inferiority. A boy's early childhood feelings of inferiority lead him to create an underlying central goal that directs behaviour by seeming to promise future security and success. For example, a child may decide based on his early perceptions that in order to have a place and belong he must be strong and in charge at all times. This belief is, in fact, a fictional goal because there are many other ways for him to belong but he filters his experiences and behavioural responses through this central theme as if his very survival depends on it. This is commonly seen in adolescent males who toil at the gym to chisel their bodies into manhood, or younger boys who compete on the playground as though their very life depended on it. The depth of the inferiority feeling usually determines the strength of the goal that then becomes the root of behaviour patterns, both constructive and non-constructive.

PARENTS AND TEACHERS OFTEN MISUNDERSTAND THE BIRTH ORDER FACTOR BECAUSE THEY ASSUME A CAUSAL RELATIONSHIP BETWEEN A BOY'S BIRTH POSITION AND CERTAIN BEHAVIOURS THAT DEVELOP.

Children are usually not consciously aware of the purpose behind their behaviour, and even when they are unhappy with its results, they still pursue it despite failure or personal loss. Essentially, it becomes a flawed way of understanding how to belong in their world. Most people understand this concept when they consider the beliefs that children can acquire as a result of growing up in different birth positions within the family.

GUIDELINE 24
RECOGNIZE BIRTH ORDER INFLUENCES *CONT'D*

• • • • •

How a boy views

his place in the

family provides a

source of valuable

information as to

what motivates him.

PARENTS and teachers often misunderstand the birth order factor because they assume a causal relationship between a boy's birth position and certain behaviours that develop. Birth position sets the stage for possible characteristics to develop that are common to a specific place in the family, but they are only possibilities. What is more important is how a boy views his particular place within the family. For example, characteristics that are often ascribed to the eldest include a propensity for excess and overdoing life, responsible, bossy, serious, rigid, and righteous behaviours. Although, these descriptions could also be attributed any boy in any birth position, depending on his unique circumstances and conclusions about life, more often than not they are represented in greater numbers by the eldest. Another example would be that among lawyers there is a large representation of middle children. Typically, middle children experience the squeeze, as they are sandwiched between older and younger siblings and acutely aware

THE STEREOTYPICAL ELDEST CHILD IS BOSSY, RIGHTEOUS, PROTECTIVE AND OVER BEARING.

of issues regarding fairness and justice within the family. They know how to state their case and engage in convincing arguments.

The purpose in considering birth order is to become aware of the typical pressures placed on children in different birth positions and then consider whether or not it fits a particular child. A more productive question then becomes, "What's it like being an eldest in your family? What do you like about it and what troubles you about it?" The answers to this question will reveal the degree to which the stereotypical birth order view is relevant or irrelevant. More importantly, it can explain how a boy views his place in the family and provides a source of valuable information as to what motivates him.

GUIDELINE 24
RECOGNIZE BIRTH ORDER INFLUENCES *CONT'D*

• • • • •

Look closely at

those taxi drivers or

food servers reading

Proust while they

take your order.

IN THE CASE of the typical eldest boy, parents and teachers can often relieve pressure and encourage him to lighten up and not take life too seriously. If parents and teachers are not aware of how a boy's birth position can contribute to their developing sense of self they may inadvertently feed into discouraging patterns of belief. For example, when a teacher observes an eldest boy who takes schoolwork very seriously the teacher could unintentionally discourage the boy by pushing him even more, not realizing that he is already working to capacity. Being pushed hard is alright at times, except when it is overdone and boys give up, concluding that they can never be perfect enough. Some of the unhappiest perfectionists I have met are people who did not learn healthy limitations, became discouraged, and underachieved as a result. The classic image of the taxi driver or food server with an incomplete PhD is a case in point. I will not outline typical points of discouragement for each of the other birth positions, but instead direct you to one of the many excellent parenting books, primarily written from an Adlerian perspective.

THE PURPOSE IN CONSIDERING BIRTH ORDER IS TO BECOME AWARE OF THE TYPICAL PRESSURES PLACED ON CHILDREN IN DIFFERENT BIRTH POSITIONS.

Although school staff and parents endeavor to understand the motivation behind a boy's underachievement, rarely do they comprehend the strength of his core purpose. The point is that teachers and parents need to take the time to consider what lies beneath a boy's struggle with school achievement while recognizing that at some level it makes perfect sense to him. Our job is to consider possibilities and discover his reasons for poor achievement and work to ameliorate them.

GUIDELINE 25
PROVIDE CHOICE THROUGH VOICE

• • • • •

Practice in

understanding

and expressing

their own

preferences helps

boys to develop

responsibility.

ENCOURAGING boys to voice their preferences and views helps boys develop a stronger sense of self. Examining and evaluating choices can help boys understand they have control over certain aspects of their lives. Practice in understanding and expressing their own preferences helps boys to develop responsibility. They are in a better position to resist peer pressure and to think through the consequences of their actions.

Offering choice and listening to boys' responses invites cooperation. However, when we discount boys' choices and views, boys can become disengaged, and perhaps also increasingly hostile and unmanageable. Of course, the choices we offer need to be meaningful and age-appropriate, and they need to be real choices. We ought to avoid offering choices where none exist – this *Hobson's Choice* is an occupational hazard for many parents and educators. How do we balance the desire to get boys to make the choices we really want them to make with their need to be heard? I remember one mother telling me about her son, who was admittedly not a very compliant choice-maker, complaining when he was reminded that he signed the school behaviour contract: "What choice did I have when it was shoved in front of me and everyone was sitting around waiting for me to sign it?" Providing choice can be a charade if it is really just providing the appearance of choice.

Of course, boys need guidance for many of their choices, and they need to learn the limitations of the options that are available to them. If they have too many choices for their developmental stage, boys can be deeply conflicted, even overwhelmed.

We need to let boys air their questions and criticisms. Adults are not always right. When a boy complains about homework he may have a valid concern if the work has been poorly designed or the deadline is unreasonable. Perhaps playground rules are better suited to adult convenience rather than a boy's developing needs. When we engage in genuine dialogue with boys they learn to respectfully offer their criticisms and perspective.

Boys can learn about the responsibilities of making choices and having a voice through family and classroom meetings where they practice the skills of democratic discussion and decision-making. Boys learn that groups of people can disagree respectfully, moving toward acceptance of differences or toward consensus in a way that is pleasurable and empowering. Engaging in dialogue also enables them to process what they are learning on a deeper level.

GUIDELINE 26
LISTEN BEYOND BRAVADO

• • • • •

Boys learn

to mask their

inner world with

bravado.

STUDIES have shown that boys and men can feel things just as deeply as girls and women, but they learn in our society to shut down their emotions to varying degrees. Sometimes boys hide their emotions so well that their mothers can't even tell what they are feeling. Boys learn to mask their inner world with bravado or with clowning behaviour. They can also get sidetracked when the class responds to their *sallies* with laughter. While girls tend to sacrifice honesty for harmony, boys more commonly opt for frank and direct communication of their views. Sometimes they are too bold and direct for their own good. While their masks can obscure, they are not impenetrable.

At school a boy may express bravado when he complains, "This homework is stupid!" It can be easy to be defensive and critical and not listen to what is really being said. Perhaps they don't understand what they are being asked to do. When boys seem to be spouting off, we can consider whether they are only attempting to avoid shame. If so, we can allow them to express feelings without trying to shame them, by jumping in to correct them or by trying to solve their problems for them. When we deny a boy's feelings or don't give him the time he deserves, we feed tension that can often escalate. Even though their language is sometimes harsher than we like, we need to listen for what's underneath, perhaps simply waiting rather than saying something right away. We can also mirror the boy's frustration: "Sounds like you had a tough day."

ACTIVE LISTENING COMMUNICATES EMPATHY, RECOGNITION AND PROMOTES PROBLEM SOLVING.

Listening for underlying needs is essential if we are to tap into a boy's motivation for learning and social connection. Active listening communicates empathy, recognition and promotes problem solving.

Guideline 27
RESPECT INDIVIDUAL PERSONALITIES

· · · · ·

The story of

Pygmalion

and Galatea

illustrates how our

expectations to

sculpt others to

meet our needs can

sometimes backfire.

SINCE boys, like teachers and parents, have different personalities, it is only natural that the strategies that work with one boy may be less effective, or may even backfire, with another. When parents and teachers understand personality type, they can manage tensions better so that conflict is reduced. Recognizing one's own personality style can help adults avoid being reactive. A cartoon that I use in my workshops depicts an incredibly stressed out adult with the caption, *"I have one nerve left – and you're getting on it."* Knowing your personality and how to avoid becoming reactive helps boys to learn.

When we don't understand personality type, we can unwittingly discourage boys from developing along their natural path for their personality type. For example, when a boy with a logical bias tries to make objective decisions, he may be criticized for not attending sufficiently to others' feelings. Conversely, boys who are highly sensitive may be criticized for not being logical like their math teachers. In this manner, a boy may be discouraged from developing within his individual personality style, and instead be pushed to grow according to the opinions and views of others. In the long run this attempt to mold boys can prevent them from trusting their own decision-making process.

The following Greek legend illustrates how our expectations and attempts to mold others to meet our needs can sometimes backfire.

An impetuous young sculptor named Pygmalion found the women of Cyprus so marvelously gorgeous that he was determined to carve a statue of his ideal woman. For months he laboured with all his extraordinary skill until he had shaped the most beautiful figure ever. So exquisite indeed was his creation that Pygmalion fell passionately in love, and could be seen in his studio kissing the statue's marble lips. But soon, Pygmalion became unhappy, for the lifeless statue could not respond – the cold stone could not return the warmth of his love. He had set out to shape his perfect woman, but had succeeded only in creating his own frustration and despair.

GUIDELINE 27
RESPECT INDIVIDUAL PERSONALITIES *CONT'D*

TO VARYING degrees, we can all conduct ourselves like Pygmalion. Many of us are initially intrigued by people's different personalities, but over time we may come to see their differences as flaws. We try to change them into our ideal, what we think they should be, according to our own agendas. Like Pygmalion, we sculpt them little by little to suit ourselves. We criticize, complain, and mold with guilt and praise. We can fall into a pattern of control and coercive behaviour.

Before we begin the task of guiding boys to be more successful in school, we need to understand and appreciate how the uniqueness of each boy's personality influences his choices and motivation to learn.

• • • • •

GUIDELINE 28
RECOGNIZE STRENGTHS

WE FOSTER a child's natural curiosity about the world when we welcome their questions, encourage exploration and risk-taking, and nurture their special talents, gifts, and strengths. When parents and teachers dwell on faultfinding, shortcomings, and deficiencies, boys can lose their courage toward life. Boys with learning disabilities are usually bright students with many talents which too often remain hidden, smothered by a system that looks more at what they can't do than at what they can do. We must help these discouraged boys recognize their own capacities, abilities, and talents.

I am reminded of a Grade 5 boy who was recently diagnosed with Autism Spectrum Disorder and is fascinated with drawing characters from video games, each involving violence and high adventure. I was told that his teacher and teacher assistant disallowed his drawings in the classroom due to the school's anti-violence policy. His drawings were of excellent quality and, although there were a lot of weapons and blood, the characters seemed to live to fight again and again. He then tried to write about his inner world of action and exploration but was stopped. His parents were told that his fantasies would not be accepted in any form. He started to complain about his health and found reasons to remain at home, but his parents knew the truth.

GUIDELINE **28**
RECOGNIZE STRENGTHS *CONT'D*

THE MOST successful teachers build on the talents of their students by giving them opportunities to apply their gifts in roles that suit and stretch those talents. Boys then feel valued, useful, challenged, and well connected to the larger community, which in turn becomes stronger because of boys' diverse contributions. The result is a stronger classroom community and a stronger boy. While teachers can still recognize needs and deficiencies, they can choose to focus on strengths instead. When we believe in boys, they learn to believe in themselves, regardless of their life circumstances. The following suggestions will guide teachers in championing the strengths of the boys they teach.

• • • • •

When we believe

in boys, they

learn to believe

in themselves,

regardless of their

life circumstances.

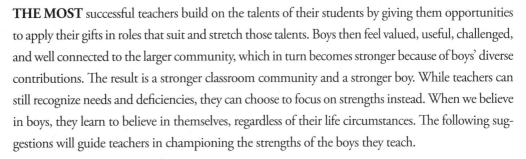

- Help boys accept and value the talents they have. Many people aren't satisfied with their own talents. Instead, they waste time envying the talents of others, trying to emulate other people's gifts while ignoring their own natural abilities. Teachers can help boys value their own gifts.

- Inspire boys to recognize the talents of others. Great teachers help their students understand how their varied talents can help achieve group and community goals. They also teach boys to spot the talents of others. The more boys recognize and celebrate other students' talents, the more they can build team strength and the skills of collaboration.

- Help boys to learn the relevance of their talents. Help boys understand just how their unique capabilities are practical and relevant. For example, a boy who has become habituated to getting attention as the class clown can use his extroverted and improvisational abilities in a class role-playing exercise. Boys need to know how to use their natural abilities.

Frequently, when I am invited to participate in family and school-based discussions about boys, I listen to the presenting concern and then ask everyone to identify a particular boy's passion and talent. Sometimes people are stymied by my request. They are accustomed to discussing the problem from every perspective (a talent universities train professionals well in). The focus on problems rarely works. Recognizing strengths and assets does not detract from confronting real problems but can provide insight into motivation, into alternate ways to generate solutions, and to create pathways of hope and recovery for boys entrenched in underachievement. If people are willing to participate in strength building, they can discover productive solutions and ideas. This emphasis has never failed me in over twenty years of working with youth, families, and school staff!

GUIDELINE 29
TRANSFORM SHAME TO HONOUR

BOYS can learn to move from shame to honour. The first step is for educators and parents to recognize that even when boys use strategies that are ultimately self-defeating such as withholding effort, cheating, procrastinating, and so forth, their goal is actually to protect their sense of self-worth and to avoid shame. This is commonly the case when boys scowl and throw away the artwork that you just offered praise about. Often, when a discouraged boy hears words of praise, he feels controlled by the words of praise, mistrusts the intention behind them, and desires to avoid the possibility of being shamed. Sometimes boys are afraid they can't live up to the praise or that the praise is not sincere. Some even think that they're being mocked.

We should never shame boys by showing contempt. The shaming language, "How could you!" should change to, "What has happened?" so as not to humiliate. Once the shame response is activated, boys clam up and disengage from conversation. The relationship also deteriorates.

When boys struggle with learning we can teach them to face challenges openly by:

- concentrating on the tasks rather than becoming distracted by fear of failure

- responding to frustration by retracing their steps to find mistakes or figuring out alternative ways of approaching a problem instead of giving up

- attributing their failures to insufficient effort, lack of information, or reliance on ineffective strategies rather than to lack of ability. It can also be productive to help boys portray effort as investment rather than risk, portray skill development as incremental, and focus on mastery

Although we have come a long way from a knight's medieval notions of honour, honesty, and valor – some would say, thankfully so – we can appeal to a boy's sense of masculine honour, not as a basis for misplaced loyalty to a gang, but in the service of building self-respect and social connectedness.

> Sometimes boys
> are afraid they
> can't live up to the
> praise or that the
> praise is
> not sincere.

GUIDELINE **30**
UNDERSTAND THAT BELIEF BECOMES DESTINY

ONCE boys start school they build on basic beliefs about themselves and their world which they acquired in earlier years. As they interpret their school experiences, they begin to move along the continuum of school success and school failure. The sources to which they attribute learning successes (effort, ability, or luck) and failures (lack of effort, ability, or luck) have important future implications for how they approach and cope with learning. Developmental stages comprise one more strand of the motivational web. For example, young boys tend to maintain high expectations for success, even in the face of repeated failure; older boys do not. Young boys tend to see effort as uniformly positive, older boys view it as a double-edged sword. For older boys, failure following high ef-

> Young boys tend to see effort as uniformly positive, older boys view it as a double-edged sword.

fort carries more negative implications in how they view their ability, than failure that results from minimal or no effort. A boy's perception about his success or failure either expands or inhibits his learning and sometimes it's easier to not try at all.

OUR CELLS ARE CONSTANTLY EAVESDROPPING ON OUR THOUGHTS AND BEING CHANGED BY THEM.

Pioneering psychologist Alfred Adler said, *"Ideas have absolutely no meaning except the meaning we give them."* He went on to develop child guidance centres based upon the notion that children's perceptions account for their experience in life. When we believe something is possible, we experience a rebirth of thinking which supports our potential for change and learning. Even more encouraging, recent advances in cellular biology, fueled by quantum physics, confirm that our thoughts can be observed on a cellular level!

GUIDELINE 30
UNDERSTAND THAT BELIEF BECOMES DESTINY *CONT'D*

ACCORDING to Bruce Lipton, a cellular biologist and author of *The Biology of Belief: Unleashing the Power of Consciousness, Matter, and Miracles*, genes and DNA alone do not control our biology. They are merely a blueprint and must be switched on by environmental signals from outside the cell. He proposes that in the multi-cellular community of our bodies, our thoughts send out a continuous broadcast, like CNN, that affects us on a cellular level.

· · · · ·

Constructive

thoughts enhance

our growth;

destructive thoughts

inhibit growth.

> MORE THAN GENETICS, MORE THAN INTELLIGENCE, MORE THAN ANY OTHER SINGLE FACTOR, IT IS THE BELIEF AND ENCOURAGEMENT OF CARING ADULTS THAT CAN HELP TO MOTIVATE BOYS TOWARD ACHIEVEMENT.

Deepak Chopra, a physician and bestselling author, explains it this way: "Our cells are constantly eavesdropping on our thoughts and being changed by them. A bout of depression can wreak havoc with the immune system; falling in love can boost it. Despair and helplessness raise the risk of heart attacks and cancer, thereby shortening life. Joy and fulfillment keep us healthy and extend life. This means that the line between biology and psychology can't really be drawn with any certainty. A remembered stress, which is only a wisp of thought, releases the same flood of destructive hormones as the stress itself."

Constructive thoughts enhance our growth; destructive thoughts inhibit growth. Because our thoughts, emotions, psyche, and physical body are intricately connected, our thinking affects us on all levels. More than ever before, teachers and parents have the opportunity to influence children to interpret and perceive environments in growth-enhancing ways.

After years of providing guidance and support as a teacher and counsellor, I have come to the conclusion that each boy has innate talents. A boy's own creativity and resilience can help him, when supportive adults offer encouragement, to find a constructive life path. More than genetics, more than intelligence, more than any other single factor, it is the belief and encouragement of caring adults that can help to motivate boys toward achievement. When respected others believe in a boy's potential, he can believe in himself, in the possibility, and reality of success.

MENTORING **BOYS**

Difficulties meet us at every turn. They are the accompaniment of life. Out of pain grow the violets of patience and sweetness. The richness of the human experience would lose something of rewarding joy if there were no limitations to overcome.

Helen Keller

. . . . .

It is important that boys find a male mentor to fully develop toward manhood.

Life for many boys is a frustrating search for the father who has not yet offered protection, nurturing, modelling, or especially acceptance. Robert Bly, a poet, a mentor of men, and author of *Iron John* says that, "When we stand physically close to our father, something is exchanged that can't be described in material terms, something that gives the son a certain confidence, an awareness, a knowledge of what it is to be male." According to Bly's notion of the route to manhood, boys must first feel their mother's love and her acceptance and then they must separate from her. Boys then learn from their primary male mentor, their father. This step poses a problem for many boys as they cannot love and leave their fathers unless a father is present and available to approve of them. The ensuing difficulty for many boys is that they then find it difficult to entrust themselves to another male mentor as their original male attachment bond has been broken. Boys, who get stuck at this point in their development, often compensate for their uncertainty about being male with a show of hyper-masculinity. They are more likely to become competitive with older boys or to become Don Juans who need to seduce females to prove their worth. It is important that boys find a male mentor to fully develop toward manhood. Boys need their masculinity blessed so that they can relax into self-acceptance.

CHAPTER FIVE

WHEN fathers are often physically and/or emotionally separated from their sons, boys often mask their loneliness with a show of indifference or bravado that makes them hard to reach. But all boys have to become men one way or another. The following story highlights the way in which a caring male teacher helped a boy in his journey toward a healthy masculinity.

· · · · ·

Boys who grow

up without fathers

often try to cover

up their loneliness

with expressions

of bravado or

indifference.

Like many boys, Jimmy – or James, as he preferred to be called by grade eight – had grown up without a father. During his early years it didn't bother him much. His mother placed him in circumstances where men could mentor him. Although she introduced him to a wide variety of extracurricular activities, James preferred the rough-and-tumble of team sports. Feedback from his coaches over the years indicated that he had 'the right stuff.'

By Grade 8 James was clearly not performing as well at school as he was on the sports field. He was very competitive and frequently found himself in the principal's office angrily awaiting discipline that he would only reject. James always

SOMETIMES A PERIOD OF FIVE MINUTES WOULD GO BY AND HE'D NOT RESPOND.

seemed to push too far. When other students recognized that the teacher was reactive and having a bad day they kept their distance. James was unable to read social cues well and would end up provoking. School staff couldn't figure out why he was so antagonistic.

In Grade 9 James announced that he wanted to quit school. When I met with him to discuss his failing grades and relational problems I was careful to be indirect and not be just another problem-focused adult telling him what to do. Instead, I listened beneath his subterfuge to learn about his world. We'd meet in the school gym and together organize the balls and other gym equipment as he filled me in about his passion, soccer. Every now and then I'd ask a carefully worded question and let it sit with him. Sometimes a period of five or so minutes would go by and he'd not respond.

When he seemed ready, I mentioned that I had some ideas about what was behind his trouble at school and why he might want to quit. I asked him if he wanted to know my thoughts. After one of many long silences filled with activity – by this time we were redesigning the gym storage room based on his notions of how to make it more efficient – our meeting time was up and he never responded to my question.

> "You're bright and good at soccer and you know it. Yet somehow you feel like you don't belong among your peers at school."

At the beginning of our next meeting, however, I knew he was ready to talk. I was late and he was already in the storage room working away. Immediately after I stepped into the room, he sat down and asked, "So what's your diagnosis. Am I really as screwed up as everybody says?" While spinning a ball and purposefully avoiding eye contact, I set about succinctly offering my hypothesis and invited him to correct me when I was off track. It went something like this: "You're bright and good at soccer and you know it. Yet somehow you feel like you don't belong among your peers at school. If you could get a soccer goal everyday it would still not be enough. You are trying hard to become a man but you don't know how many 'break-aways' you have to get to feel like you are good enough. I think you'd like to have someone guide you but feel like a little kid to ask for help."

WE FINISHED UP AND HE LEFT ASKING ABOUT WHEN WE'D MEET AGAIN.

I paused for reflection and provided time for him to redirect or correct me. I commented on how his new placement of the track-and-field equipment was ingenious and continued with my speculation: "When you escalate conflict with others and especially teachers, you are showing them that you are in charge. Initially, you feel powerful, but later you feel alone."

He said only, "Sounds like you know me better than most." We finished up and he left asking about when we'd meet again.

Eventually one thing led to another and I was able to influence him. He came to appreciate the Big Brother his mother had found for him, whom he had seen on a weekly basis for a couple of years, as a significant male mentor. He also realized that one particular male teacher in his school, the man who regularly took the time to stop by his locker to check in, actually cared about him and saw the person under the misbehaviour. When he was able to see himself in a new way, he was able to open up to new possibilities.

His passion for soccer led him to change to a school that was renowned for its intensive soccer train-ing. It required a 'B' average to participate, but James had no problem boosting his grades once his sights were clear. He also felt a deep sense of comradeship as he got to rub shoulders with his coach, the assistants, and other players throughout the school day. Life took a new and healthier direction.

• • • • •

Adult males on

television are all

too often either

ultra-competitive,

violent, or dim-

witted.

After two years I had the opportunity to catch up with James when he agreed to be inter-viewed by me when I was speaking about mentoring boys in front of a large community audience. His Big Brother mentor also came. In a matter-of-fact way, James told about the important role his Big Brother had played in his life story. When I opened up the discussion for questions from the audience, a mother wanted to know how his mentor had helped him *process* or make sense of his life difficulties, to which James replied: "We never talked about them. We talked about soccer mainly and about my future goals."

Like James, boys often find their way in life without analyzing it or openly reflecting on it as females tend to. I stressed that while boys need a mentor, as do females, males do not

MANY BOYS MISS THE ACTIVE INVOLVEMENT AND GUIDANCE OF SIGNIFICANT ADULT MALES.

typically hash over the past, but are influenced through consistent involvement and interest. When boys feel accepted by men, they can relax into their passage of manhood.

Many boys miss the active involvement and guidance of significant adult males. Men some-times think that rearing children is a job for women. *Big Brothers Big Sisters* organizations, for example, rarely have difficulties recruiting females as big sisters, but struggle to find males willing to commit their time. Many boys will pass through all of their primary edu-cation without having had a male teacher or a male mentor. Even those boys who do have fathers may have little interaction with them.

Boys typically see much more television than they see of their fathers. But adult males on television are all too often either ultra-competitive, violent, or dim-witted. There is not much to choose from, even if you have cable or satellite TV.

• • • • •

Boys may also

come to define

masculinity

through a

reaction

against

females.

ANOTHER pathway boys can follow to learn about masculinity leads them behind the school among peers. Unfortunately, these lads, who often believe that it's the most aggressive and violent male who calls the shots, can end up exemplifying overly aggressive and triumphant masculinity.

Boys may also come to define masculinity through a reaction against females. As damaging as it is for boys to use models of masculinity from the media and from peers, this one is potentially the most harmful. When primarily women surround boys, they may begin to construct masculine behaviour based on whatever is not female. The particular danger of constructing masculinity in that manner is the anti-female attitudes that are likely to develop in reaction to mothers and female teachers as adolescent boys attempt to separate, but have very limited range of behaviours that are accepted as male. Females become the targets of the boy's frustration, anger, and despair. Boys will degrade women and even become violent during this passage. Some boys never grow out of this adolescent reactivity.

SOME BOYS MAY START TO DEFINE MASCULINITY AS ANYTHING THAT IS NOT FEMALE.

By the time many boys become adolescents, they are often physically and emotionally stressed at school. They may be prone to aggressive outbursts, self-medicating with illicit substances, and entrenched in low academic achievement.

The guidelines offered in this chapter suggest ways to mentor boys on the road to a healthy and socially constructive manhood.

CHAPTER FIVE

GUIDELINE 31
MOTHERS AND FEMALE TEACHERS MATTER

BOYS of all ages, like girls, cannot be spoiled by too much healthy love and support from their mothers. Instead, boys who share a close connection to their mothers will likely become more confident, do better in school, sports, music, and later have a stronger likelihood of avoiding substance misuse, than boys who have distant relationships with their mothers. When boys come from families where they are nurtured and their needs are met they develop healthy attachments. No amount of appropriate bonding, attachment, or nurturance from a mother is harmful or leads boys to become weaklings or sissies. Boys do not need to be rushed into independence.

• • • • •

Maternal love and nurturing does NOT make a boy a sissy or a weakling.

However, they should not be unduly restrained from it either. With all the recent constructive emphasis on attachment theory, well-intentioned parents can mistake their boy's misbehaviour as a problem with attach-

A BOY'S MOTHER IS HIS CENTRAL MENTOR–THEIR RELATIONSHIP MUST REMAIN STRONG.

ment when it is actually over-parenting. I especially hear about this occurrence after concerned parents initially learn about the importance of keeping close to their kids – throughout all stages of development. Teachers and parents need to tune into the sensitivities of a particular boy while also being careful not to do things for him that he can do for himself. Experienced teachers and parents recognize that over-parenting, over-teaching, and over-protection in general can smother a boy's emerging independence. Early primary teachers, who devote amazing energy to teaching boys in creative ways, need to be sensitive and flexible during what is often a painful separation process between mother and son at the beginning of school. Humiliating boys at home or school because of their desire to remain close to their mothers can damage the relationship between them. A central mentor in a boy's life is his mother.

GUIDELINE 31
MOTHERS AND FEMALE TEACHERS MATTER *CONT'D*

· · · · ·

Mothers must not

only tolerate,but

must also wish

for and actively

support a boy's

separation

and search for

manhood.

DURING pre-puberty and adolescence, however, boys often prefer to leave the security of their mothers to stretch toward manhood. Although mothers and female teachers can model healthy female behaviour, they cannot provide boys with models of masculinity. Renowned author of *The Art of Loving*, Erich Fromm, suggests that mothers must not only tolerate, but must also wish for and actively support a boy's separation and search for manhood. Wise mothers and female teachers understand the tension that can build around separation during puberty and find ways to support boys from a greater distance. They also recognize a boy's simultaneous ambivalence about growing up and desire to remain close.

Not surprisingly, a shift from the easy communication of earlier years is difficult for many mothers and teachers as boys assume dominant male communication patterns informed by a sexist culture. During the push-and-pull conflict as

DON'T EXPECT

EYE CONTACT.

boys struggle to mature, adult females can be horrified to hear their boys demean them, even using words like *bitch* or *hoe* to show their toughness. Boys need clear boundaries so that they can learn respect for women. When women realize that the boys are trying, in misguided ways, to define themselves as males by negation of females, they can quietly tell the boy how an offensive word makes them feel and that they do not want to hear it again.

Mothers and female teachers need to continue to show their interest in boys and maintain connection without being pushy. Even simple questions like, "How was your day?" can lead to arguments. Instead, comment on your own day and ask, "Is there anything about your day that you want me to know about?" Be direct and to the point. Then leave it alone. Last night I overheard an adult male at an adjacent restaurant table emphasize his need for effective communication: "Get to the point, be brief and stop talking – just wait." Wait for boys to comment on his report card rather than interrogate. The general guideline for females mentoring boys is to choose their words wisely and be prepared to step back if he appears disinterested or uncomfortable. Some women tell me that when they are mentoring boys they remind themselves to talk less and wait more with boys. Also, do not expect expect eye contact!

CHAPTER FIVE

GUIDELINE 32
RESPOND TO FATHER HUNGER

UNLIKE agrarian and industrial times, when fathers and sons might have bonded through shared work and through father-son talks as they toiled together in the fields and factories, today there is often little energy left for fathers to connect in a meaningful way with their sons after a long working day.

Distant or negative father-son relationships are clearly linked to a host of problems among boys.

This means that boys see very limited aspects of masculinity and not the full range of male behaviour. I recollect a story of a senior male executive who came to me looking for advice on how to handle his two boys who fought on the weekends. The word weekend tipped me off as I know that sibling rivalry is rarely for the benefit of siblings but is usually an attempt to draw parents in. Why express concern about fighting on the weekend and not during the week? I learned that the father never saw his sons from Monday to Friday. He left before they got up and returned from the office after they went to bed during the

> IF FATHER HUNGER IS TOO INTENSE, A BOY MAY ASSUME THE OVER-THE-TOP MASCULINITY OF VIDEO GAMES OR TELEVISED MALE HEROES.

week. No wonder they vied for his attention early Saturday morning when he just wanted to relax and read the weekend paper. By the way, the boys did get his attention, just not the sort of attention they really needed, but attention for misbehaving is better than no attention at all.

Distant or negative father-son relationships are clearly linked to a host of problems among boys including violence and substance abuse regardless of family income. If boys are to become ethical, caring, and courageous men, they need other men to show them the way. When healthy adult males demonstrate caring, acceptance and involvement, boys are less vulnerable to the media displays of hyper-masculinity and to negative influences from aberrant peers.

GUIDELINE 32
RESPOND TO FATHER HUNGER *CONT'D*

• • • • •

An involved

father, or a single

caring adult male

in a boy's life,

can make all the

difference.

IF mentoring is absent, inadequate, or marked by excessive emotional distance, boys can develop distorted views of themselves. If father hunger is too intense, a boy may assume the over-the-top masculinity of video games or televised male heroes and never feel good enough. He may distrust other males fearing their criticism and abandonment.

Boys need significant male role models to show them how to identify and express their thoughts and feelings with safety and confidence. Boys need to see their fathers or male teachers being more open and reflective about feelings. When making presentations to men, I often suggest that while women typically express their frustrations associated with a difficult day immediately upon arriving home, and perhaps request a hug to make them feel better, men in similar circumstances tend to act stoic or angry. People laugh when I tease fathers and male mentors to instead say something like, "Hello everyone! I'm here and I'm feeling really vulnerable. I need a hug and then I want to tell you all about my worry." Remember, it is strong men who are capable of expressing strong emotions.

• • • • •

GUIDELINE 33
AUTHENTIC HEROES HELP BOYS FIND COURAGE

ESSENTIALLY, mentoring a boy means helping him to identify and appreciate ways to develop courage. Courage implies a positive, solid belief in oneself – an *I can do it* attitude toward life. Courageous people are resilient, and do not peg their self-worth to successes or failures. Rudolph Dreikurs, a prominent leader in the field of child guidance, said that courage is the ability to make mistakes without a loss of self. Courage, which can motivate boys to move toward success in school and life, is the trait of the authentic hero.

GUIDELINE 33
AUTHENTIC HEROES HELP BOYS FIND COURAGE *CONT'D*

ALTHOUGH boys can often feel inadequate, authentic heroic courage encourages them to persevere because they recognize the value of struggle and their place of value in the world of males. I can think of one particular heroic teacher who devotes himself to providing leadership and outstanding educational support to boys who have been identified as requiring behavioural intervention. The boys in his fold look up to this gregarious, tough-minded man who understands his role as mentor to troubled boys. He loves his job. Sometimes the boys in his class joke affectionately about his messy hair or the lunch that manages to find its way onto his collar. I have participated in meetings where he has challenged the principal to not suspend or abandon a particular boy. In a professional manner he advocates for them as if they were his own.

• • • • •

One thing that keeps me going as a mentor to boys is the realization that I – like other caring adults – can make a saving difference.

This teacher can make all the difference to boys like Tyler, a boy I counselled who lived in poverty with a violent older brother and a mother diagnosed with depression. He had long been without a father, and, like many boys, could not easily find language to express his inner world. I often ask boys like Tyler to use a barometer to discern variance in emotion and perspective, with 10 being the most and 0 the least level of disturbance or concern. When I asked Tyler where he would go for understanding and support, he identified and rated the three most influential people in his life: "Mom is a 10 out of 10, my brother is a 0 out of 10, and Mr. Clark is a 9 out of 10." In Tyler's world, his teacher was a hero as well as a mentor.

One thing that keeps me going as a mentor to boys is the realization that I – like other caring adults – can make a saving difference. Whether we know it at the time, whether we find out then, later, or not at all, we can plant the seeds and fully anticipate they will grow. Recently, I became aware of the significance I had in the life of a boy named David, who I worked with twelve years ago. As a district counsellor I travelled from school to school. I was the only male in this role, and found myself providing guidance and mentorship to boys struggling with underachievement and emotional difficulties. The other female members of our counselling team supported me, also somewhat relieved, I think, to pass on many of the boy referrals to me when they read of certain behaviours such as classroom masturbation, feces spread on bathroom walls, or violent chair throwing, for example.

GUIDELINE 33
AUTHENTIC HEROES HELP BOYS FIND COURAGE *CONT'D*

• • • • •

Our myths tell us

that a metaphorical

hero lives inside

each male psyche.

WITH David, as with most boys, I referred to myself as a *coach*, a *life coach* as many males view the term counselling as synonymous with crying or losing control of one's emotions. Most counsellors I know are skilled at helping people get control of their emotions to create the results they desire. David seemed most amenable to this informal approach. He was lost in a complicated grief process as his parents died and he had gone into the care of the state. He had one of the most extreme forms of social discomfort and shyness I'd encountered.

Despite our bulging stack of new referrals, my supervisor supported my continued weekly visits with him. Later, even after I left that particular assignment, I looked for opportunities to touch base with him and on occasion took him out for a bite to eat. Later yet, when he stopped going to school in Grade 10, it became harder for me to visit him at his home and we saw each other less frequently. Still, I made sure I gave him a small gift at Christmas and continued the tradition of getting together on his birthday.

ORDINARY, EVERYDAY PEOPLE CAN BE AUTHENTIC HEROES WHO GIVE BOYS THE COURAGE TO DEVELOP HEALTHY AND CONSTRUCTIVE MASCULINITY.

Despite my training and knowledge as an educator and counsellor, I never anticipated the impact I would have in his life. As David was approaching his 19th birthday, his community-based youth worker called me to discuss her efforts to help him find a job and mentioned to me how influential my involvement with David had been. I was grateful for her acknowledgement of my efforts of a dozen years ago, but I was not expecting that David himself would see me as he does. When she asked David who his father figure was, it was my name that came to him.

GUIDELINE 34
USE ACTION-TALK

AS I wrote earlier, movement helps boys learn and process information, especially when it is emotionally charged. A boy's internal processing of thought and release of feelings often involves action – sometimes seen in his fidgeting, or quick bursts of energy, like slamming a door. To teach and mentor boys effectively, we need to respect and even capitalize on this style of learning. When raising my boys and wanting to discuss an important topic, I'd suggest that we walk the dogs, which was a daily part of our chore ritual and therefore also served a practical purpose. While we walked, we talked.

• • • • •

With boys,

action-talk

promotes

closeness.

Discussion of delicate issues like sex and relationships were best saved for car rides. The movement and spatial stimulation made what I referred to as our weekly growth and maturation talks less threatening. They would both groan from the back seat and roll their eyes when I asked about what questions they might have. Nine times out of ten they didn't have any, but I got my chance to make brief comments about the typical questions and concerns a parent might have. For example, "I read in the paper that many adolescents think that oral sex is not real sex. What do you both think?" While one would groan in disgust, the other would announce that he didn't care – typical male indifference. It provided me an opportunity to comment on safety. I avoided eye contact. And I waited.

FOR MANY MALES, TALKING IS LIKE FISHING AT THE LAKE, WITH BURSTS OF EXCITEMENT AND PERIODS OF CALM.

I was rarely discouraged by a non-response, but read their silence as processing time. Of particular importance to me was that when they did have a question – they'd ask!

When you want to communicate with a boy, consider setting the scene first. Get away from familiar environments. At home, find neutral ground by completing a chore together, taking a day-trip, or a longer time away with a boy. At school, request help at the photocopier or ask the boy to retrieve something left on the ball field. Productive conversations with boys tend to come in fits and starts. Boys need space to digest what's been said. If you and a boy are doing something together, they are more relaxed than in a face-to-face encounter. For many males, talking is like fishing at the lake, with bursts of excitement and periods of calm– all while you're both engaging in a practical pursuit.

GUIDELINE 35
MOVE INTO SILENCE

• • • • •

Men debate and

women relate.

BOYS may be wary of counselling because they are afraid to talk about their feelings. They think feeling talk is unmanly and they're scared that if they allow themselves to feel and really talk about their experiences, emotions may flood them. Feeling overwhelmed can mean tears and crying.

Boys – and most men for that matter – assume that crying implies weakness. "If I said what I really feel they would call me a wimp," or "If I told my dad he'd just tell me to stand up for myself," are typical responses boys have about discussing their emotional world.

Because of gender differences in communication styles, females are often frustrated with male silence. Not surprisingly, it's confusing for women when men talk up a storm at social gatherings but have no time to discuss their personal relationship at home. When we understand that men debate and women relate, however, we can see that for some men, talk in a social setting helps them maintain status through showing what they know even

FRUSTRATED BY THE MUTENESS OF BOYS, MOTHERS AND FEMALE TEACHERS TRY TO CONNECT BY USING YET MORE WORDS.

though this style of pontificating does not impress their partners. It can be difficult for many women to depersonalize male silence which seems to negate their need to be heard and feel respected. A female teacher I know spoke for many women when she claimed that she goes *squirrelly* when the males in her life do not answer her questions or respond to her overtures to connect through conversation. She waits for a response, frustrated as the wait time drags on. Struggling to connect in the face of male silence, women will sometimes say more, say it in a different way, or say it louder. Mounting frustration can sometimes erupt into anger or sometimes even despair.

GUIDELINE 35
MOVE INTO SILENCE *CONT'D*

FRUSTRATED by the muteness of boys, mothers and female teachers try to connect by using yet more words and sometimes repeating themselves. Boys then may lose the thread of the conversation or become confused with too much narrative or verbal instruction. Emotionally they may retreat even further, *turtling* inwards.

• • • • •

Male silence does not mean indifference or lack of a desire to communicate.

Male silence does not usually mean indifference or lack of desire for contact but it can be hard for many to know how to read it. Is the boy who clams up in class afraid of making mistakes? Is he distracted by personal problems? Is he *stoned*? It can be hard for caring adults to stay with boys' silence, to move with it, to reflect on it, to accept it for a time, and to try to understand its purpose and significance. Male silence occasionally signals unhappiness and inward struggle, but more often it means that a boy is feeling comfortable and does not feel obliged to fill the air with words.

SPEAK CONCISELY, KEEP THE STORY SHORT, AND LEARN TO BE COMFORTABLE WITH SILENCE AS YOU MEET BOYS ON THEIR TURF.

Most women reluctantly accept that a boy's silence does not usually stem from a problem, but is a product of male culture and perhaps to some extent the hard wiring of the male brain.

Don't take boys' silence personally, but see it as a gender difference. Allow yourself to move into silence with the boy. You can still spend time together, saying little, but listening to the subtle cues behaviour can provide.

GUIDELINE 36
ENTER THE FORBIDDEN ZONE

• • • • •

Boys are

bombarded with

mixed messages

concerning sexual

behaviour and

drug use.

RECENTLY, I was called to discuss an incident at a secondary school where a Grade 9 boy had been caught in the male washroom with a Grade 8 girl who was providing oral sex while two other boys watched and waited their turn. You will likely not be surprised with the *BC 2003 McCreary Centre Survey* results: 7% of 13 year-olds, 21% of 15 year-olds, and 43% of 17 year-olds had sexual intercourse in the past year. It also discovered that 24% of sexually active youth use no protection or birth control methods. As some adolescents try to negotiate their sexuality while maintaining their virginity they may turn to practices such as rainbow parties, and wearing sex bracelets to advertise how far they will go. Without parent and teacher input, teens are left with the ever-powerful presence of media or peer groups to guide their sexuality. Boys are flooded with distorted messages that seek to sexualize them at increasingly earlier ages. The attitudes of today's easily accessed and brutal pornography, which makes the groundbreaking 1972 X-rated film *Deep Throat* look tame, seep insidiously into the language, fashion, and actions of our boys.

Mixed messages also exist about drug use. Nearly 50% of parents do not regularly talk to their children about drugs. Perhaps this is because many of these parents were themselves smoking the much milder pot of 20 or 30 years ago, or they were so removed from the drug scene as adolescents that they cannot relate today. Parents may lack confidence in their message and their methods to explore drug issues with their boys. To make matters worse, even those parents who are telling their boys to avoid drugs are being drowned out by a society that supports its use. Just consider the winks and nods that world-class basketball stars receive who are renowned for smoking marijuana (commonly called weed among youth). Research tells us, however, that while it is no guarantee, frank and non-judgmental talk with boys about avoiding drugs will reduce the likelihood of their using drugs to self medicate.

Although boys need plenty of private space and want to independently solve life's dilemmas, they need plenty of adult input and guidance. Don't shun the topics of sex, drugs, and other risky behaviours at home or school. Even though boy culture tends to prefer superficial bantering to serious discussion of the forbidden zone, boys need caring adults to invite them into this territory with frankness–not preachiness.

CHAPTER FIVE

GUIDELINE 37
TEACH BOYS TO PACK A PARACHUTE!

RESEARCH indicates that from birth onward, boys are more inclined than girls to engage in risk-taking and think less about consequences. For many boys the greater the risk the greater the proof of manhood, evidenced among boys who proudly show off their playground wounds and scars. In the newspapers, on TV, or even in our own neighbourhoods, we learn how this risk-taking behaviour can lead to serious, sometimes fatal, consequences. With boys between the ages of 15 and 24 dying in accidental deaths at three times the rate of girls in this age group, parents and teachers have reason to be concerned.

• • • • •

Boys are three

times more likely

to die in accidental

deaths than girls.

Our culture compounds risk-taking behaviours by sending out unhealthy signals and pressures for boys to measure their emerging sense of manhood against. Consider the high school football player being shot up with *Novocain* in order to override an injury and continue playing. It is no wonder that boys, especially healthy and adventurous thrill-seeking boys who are impulsive, are attracted to risky behaviours that can lead to deadly consequences.

IN THE PG-RATED MOVIE *SCOOBY DOO 2* A SUBTLE REFERENCE TO INHALANT ABUSE IS PASSED OFF AS COMIC RELIEF.

An example of heedless thrill seeking is dusting. *Dust Off* is a computer-cleaning agent compressed into a small, pressurized can that may be sitting in your computer desk drawer. It is the ingredient used in a dangerous and potentially lethal game that boys between the ages of 9 through 15 can play at home or in the school washroom. Inhaling the contents gives them a slight euphoric dizzy feeling for about 10 seconds. Uninformed boys think it is only cold compressed air they are inhaling, but it contains the refrigerant propellant, *R2*. It is a gas heavier than air and when inhaled fills the lungs and inhibits oxygen intake. Any time an inhalant is misused in this manner it could be fatal. It could happen the first time, the second time, or the 20th time.

GUIDELINE 37
TEACH BOYS TO PACK A PARACHUTE! *CONT'D*

• • • • •

Kids are going to

take risks as part of

their developmental

need to push the

limits and learn

about their abilities

and boundaries.

THE media is again implicated as the practice of inhaling is graphically displayed in the R-rated movie *Thirteen* – commonly rented by boys who are 13 years of age. And even in the PG-rated movie *Scooby Doo 2* a subtle reference to inhalant abuse is passed off as comic relief. Consider what happens in the teen years when drugs and alcohol are added to this mix, especially when adolescent males get behind the wheel of a powerful car and drive recklessly, perhaps even participating in drag racing.

How do adults encourage boys' adventurous spirits while minimizing the risks? Most of us can remember participating in some childhood activities that our parents would not have approved of. Kids are going to take risks as part of their developmental need to push the limits and learn about their abilities and boundaries. The very best we can do is to be aware of emerging trends among our risk-prone boys and talk openly about taking calculated risks, and encouraging boys to seek safer thrills. Let-

AS THE INUIT SAY,

"HE WHO HESITATES IS FROST!"

ting boys know we care, engaging their critical thinking and reflective skills, and ensuring that their responsibilities grow in line with their rights are all important safeguards. As boys learn to think critically about the outcomes of their choices, they develop a greater sense of responsibility. The delicate balance between risk and responsibility is the ground where boys learn about themselves, boundaries, and their capabilities.

In his defense of moderation, Aristotle argued that in many areas we suffer from excess or lack. We go too far, or not far enough. Not enough risk-taking can lead to immobility, fear, and anxiety. Too much risk-taking can lead to foolhardy endangerment. The best kind of risk-taking occurs at the right time, in the right place, and for the right reason. We need to encourage boys to pack their parachutes if they choose to skydive.

GUIDELINE 38
USE SOCRATIC DIALOGUE INSTEAD OF LECTURES

TEENAGE boys have trouble talking about their difficulties in navigating the gauntlet of peer pressure, hormonal changes, and stress to perform and be a man. How do we get them to open up?

• • • • •

Teenagers often complain that adults do not know what it's like to be young.

When older boys visit my office, they often complain about how adults just don't get what it's like to be young. I smile inwardly as I reflect on how many of us teachers and parents responded in similar ways when we were young, but of course it's easy to forget. It's easier to moralize than to remember that turbulent time when we were adolescents. Recently, a Grade 11 boy complained about his father's tunnel vision on school grades and the lack of appreciation for his social life. He knew that grades were important, but having his father pounding on grades only drove distance between them. He especially despised his teachers' and father's simplistic injunctions like, "Don't go out – stay home and do your homework." Kids learn to shut us out when we preach, "You need homework so that you will be prepared for university." Adults–fathers and male teachers in particular – can reach boys better through dialogue than through lectures.

BECAUSE TEACHERS HAVE MORE EMOTIONAL DISTANCE FROM BOYS THAN PARENTS, THEY CAN BE PARTICULARLY EFFECTIVE WITH SOCRATIC DIALOGUE.

Socratic back-and-forth dialogue stimulates independent thought without creating acrimony. When they are not so concerned with being right, and more concerned with the give and take of honest exploration, teachers and parents can help boys develop their own insights. I remember when our oldest announced that he was "sick and tired of school" and wanted to quit. Although my impulse was to say "not on your life," I recognized that he needed to decide what to do on his own. Instead, I remarked that it was an interesting suggestion. Had he thought about what he would do instead? What ensued was a thoughtful exchange about life goals during which he eventually expressed his frustrations with school. I withheld my impulse to tell him what to do but respected and trusted that he would figure it out – with guidance. We both left the conversation without conclusion and the next day he announced that he wouldn't quit but that he needed help to figure out how to work around a teacher with unreasonable expectations.

GUIDELINE 38
USE SOCRATIC DIALOGUE INSTEAD OF LECTURES *CONT'D*

I LEARNED of a similar incident in a school where a concerned teacher overheard a group of Grade 12 boys discussing the quantity of alcohol they had amassed for the upcoming weekend party. Instead of patronizingly lecturing them about being under-aged he said: "Trying booze is one thing, getting in a car with a drunk driver is another. Take it easy, guys." Meeting the boys where they are while showing faith is a powerful way of encouraging responsibility and self-reliance.

Teachers, who typically have more emotional distance from adolescents than parents, can be particularly effective with Socratic dialogue. Sometimes a brief comment in the hallway can show that you have been giving serious thought to their plight: "Lots of guys think about dropping out – what reason do you have to drop in?" A turn of phrase like this might allow boys to sense concern, and even become stimulated enough to try on a new perspective.

Dialoguing with boys about possibilities means being open, respectful, and non-blaming of individual students or groups of students. Don't react to blunt assertions, but listen for the boy's true underlying concerns. Just one warning – genuine dialogue can change your perspective too.

• • • • •

Dialoguing with boys about possibilities means being open, respectful, and non-blaming.

• • • • •

GUIDELINE 39
FACILITATE PEER MENTORING

PEERS are vital to a boy as he stretches into growing autonomy. They offer him a sense that he belongs, is liked, and likable. They validate him, share his needs, and widen his interests. At home if you reject a boy's peers you reject him. At school, if you deny the influence of peers you deny one of the greatest opportunities to facilitate leadership among older boys.

GUIDELINE 39
FACILITATE PEER MENTORING *CONT'D*

• • • • •

The experience

of a boy helping

another boy has

the potential to

exponentially

boost the self-

esteem of both.

RECENTLY, I co-produced a documentary called, *Project Resiliency: Youth Overcoming Addiction,* and spent considerable time discussing substance misuse among students. When I reflect on the insight and input of countless youth including the director, who was a recent high school graduate himself, I am struck by the power of youth to youth mentoring. In the film a 15 year-old boy who was struggling with a marijuana addiction commented: *"I've seen scare tactic videos and they're just crap. Propaganda. Youth will listen to other youth because they'll tell it straight – like it is. They won't pretend that it's easy to just say No. Adults are full of hypocrisy, isn't alcohol a drug? Then you watch a beer commercial and everybody is having fun."* I believe the reason most drug prevention films are judged as ineffective by youth is because they underestimate the clout of youth culture to mentor from within. It doesn't matter whether you call it peer tutoring, peer coaching, peer counselling, peer mediation, or peer mentoring. When boys help one another, they tap into the power of youth social order where boys learn the value of their contribution and how much they can make a difference.

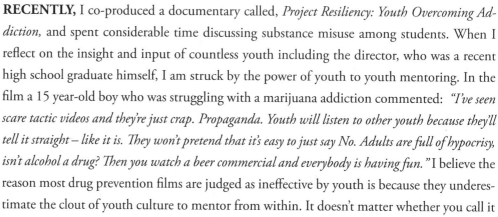

75% OF STUDENTS WITH LEARNING DISABILITIES, THE MAJORITY OF WHOM ARE TYPICALLY MALE, DISPLAY INAPPROPRIATE SOCIAL SKILLS.

Although the name of the mentoring program typically isn't important for boys, they will identify with a title that reflects their reality. Often the tag or handle emerges organically from within their experience as boys take ownership of their program. For example, while names like the *S.M.A.R.T Mentoring Program* (Student Mentors Advising Rising Talent) might be attractive to teachers and boys in certain cultural contexts, a simpler handle like *Yak-Attack* may be more realistic in another school community. Ensure that the boys have at the helm of any peer-mentoring program a wise and compassionate adult who can provide guidance. We cannot exaggerate how much the experience of a boy helping another boy can boost the self-esteem of both. While they develop a deeper and more strategic approach to problem solving and belonging, they also improve their academic achievement, feel part of the school community, and have greater confidence in their ability and potential. Mentors themselves develop their own ability for reflection, as well as facilitative and leadership skills.

GUIDELINE 39
FACILITATE PEER MENTORING *CONT'D*

• • • • •

Recent studies

suggest that

boys benefit

greatly from

peer mentoring.

THE Counselling Foundation of Canada has a Web site that identifies a research data bank on the effectiveness of peer support programs (**www.counselling.net).** One particular study by Topping & Whiteley examined whether males or females benefited the most from peer tutoring. They found that, of the 327 children and adolescents studied, the male combination produced the best results. The Council For Exceptional Children reported a study by Forness & Kavale indicating that 75% of students with learning disabilities, the majority of whom are typically male, display inappropriate social skills that set them apart from other students. Peer mentors can give feedback about essential social and behavioural expectations that an adult can't. Floundering Grade 8 and 9 males also benefit by having the opportunity to look up to a Grade 11 boy who has *been there.* I have marveled at the supportive relationships that develop – sometimes lasting even into manhood.

In *Homies: Peer Mentoring Among African-American Males*, author Warren Braden explores the gritty communication and poignant bonding that develops between boys and men from the west side of Chicago. Their social contributions and mutual support provide inspiration about the value of male mentoring in an alternative reality. Male mentors within a particular culture understand the subtle nuances, status dilemmas, and pressures that teachers from a middle-class cultural group likely could not.

While written over a dozen years ago, a couple of valuable references that have stood the test of time are: *Positive Peer Culture* by Harry Vorrath and Larry Bendtro, and, *Cool Solutions: A Complete Guide to Peer Counselling in the Elementary School,* by Debra Bailey and Marion McCristall. Extensive peer mentoring resources are also listed on Web sites **www.peer.ca, www.mentors.ca.** and **www.mentoringboys.com.**

In a resource-scarce climate, the possibility of maximizing peer culture to assist in social, educational and general development of boys becomes less of a curiosity and more of a necessity. When boys help other boys succeed, the entire school community benefits and boys learn to offer help and to reach out for the help that they so greatly need to experience success.

GUIDELINE 40
SEEK LAUGHTER AND FUN

The scientific studies conclude that when the tough get going – they laugh.

DAVID Keirsey and Marilyn Bates, authors of *Please Understand Me,* note in their report that while 56% of teachers have a temperament geared toward *work first play later,* only 38% of students share the same temperament. Conversely, where 38% of students are natural play as you work personality types only 2% of teachers fit this category. You can see where teacher and student temperaments have potential for conflict and misunderstanding. Now, here's the rub: Students eventually grow up and become parents of new young students and their temperament remains very much the same; 38% of the general population have a play as you work approach to life or sensing-perceiving bias in their personality type. This difference in temperament can create misunderstandings between teachers and parents, as parents know that success in life is not always based on achievement in school. Still, as it turns out, the task of teaching youth requires adults who are dependable, organized and have a work first play later approach. This difference in personality type is to be expected in school communities.

LAUGHTER IS INNER JOGGING.

There is paradox here that I believe is worth contemplation. Humour can help everyone to thrive amidst change, remain creative under pressure, learn more effectively, play more enthusiastically, and stay healthier in the process. It also activates the body's physiological systems, including muscular, respiratory, and cardiovascular. As Norman Cousins, the author of *Anatomy of an Illness,* said, "Laughter is inner jogging." By working less and laughing more our brains are energized, our immune system is given a boost and we become smarter.

GUIDELINE **40**
SEEK LAUGHTER AND FUN *CONT'D*

• • • • •

Conventional

wisdom has it that

laughter is, indeed,

the best medicine.

WHEN laughter fills a classroom, life-affirming chemicals pour through the body. Laughter releases opioid peptides – a group of internally produced neural transmitters – from the frontal lobe of the brain. Laughter enhances human cognitive processes, including creativity, self-actualization, and bonding. Joyful laughter also improves immune functioning in several key ways: 1) cortisol, the stress hormone, levels drop significantly – which gives the immune system a break; 2) infection-fighting immunoglobulins increase – which serve as the body's most important defense mechanisms; 3) natural killer cells, which seek out and destroy abnormal cells increase significantly; and, 4) plasma cytokine gamma interferon levels, which enhance immune system functioning, more than double.

LAUGHTER IS THE GREAT MOTIVATOR
AND RELATIONSHIP EQUALIZER.

In my numerous discussions with boys about the attributes they admire most in a teacher, I have learned that they by and large value teachers who take time to have fun and laugh with them. Laughter is the great motivator and relationship equalizer. It helps us work harder without feeling strained. Mentoring boys means that we can turn what would be mundane tasks into fun. Mentoring boys has many rewards, but it can also have stresses – I don't need to tell you that. Those who work with boys would do well to cultivate opportunities for the healing power of the best stress-reduction strategy there is: laughter, humour, and play.

ORGANIZING A CLASSROOM FOR
BOYS TO BE SUCCESSFUL

The classroom and the teacher occupy the most important part, the most important position of the human fabric.... In the schoolhouse we have the heart of the whole society.

Henry Golden

• • • • •

Even in the best

schools; the

classrooms are

organized so that

kids have to sit for

long periods

of time.

Cultural rules, routines, expectations, relationships, and rewards have a gendered history that is reflected in the organizational structures and metaphors of schooling. William Pollack, author of *Real Boys* says, "With all due respect, I don't think the boys are so difficult. I think the schools are so difficult for boys . . . Even in the best schools; they set up their classrooms so that kids have to sit for long periods of time. The average boy needs five to six recesses up to the age of 10. He's lucky if he gets one. What do we do if he wiggles in his seat before recess? We take recess away. Then, he either becomes a bad boy, and goes to the principal, or he becomes a disturbed boy and goes to a psychologist. And Lord knows I don't know which is worse for the boy."

I agree with Pollack that confining school structures are hard on boys, though my experience also suggests that the majority of schools are trying hard to meet boys where they are, and that they care about best practice teaching for boys in the classroom. We need to consider the ways in which the culture of masculinity—the question of how boys find meaning as males—influences the way we organize classrooms.

WILLIAM Glasser, the author of *Unhappy Teenagers* and *Control Theory in the Classroom*, argues that it is sometimes adults' disorganized living structures which can give rise to unruly behaviour. Why is it that in some schools it is the boy who gets sent to the office when the teacher is having a bad day, or later at home he gets sent to his room when parents are tired? I can think of a boy whose lack of even the simplest of structures, except those offered by the television, led to his continuous pushing of boundaries that were actually a search for them.

· · · · ·

The TV, always on for company, had been his babysitter, his best friend, parent, and most importantly, his life-teacher.

Bobby, an only child, was raised by an appliance. The TV, always on for company, had been his babysitter, his best friend, parent, and most importantly, his life-teacher. Even as a young lad he could recite entire programming schedules and sing the lyrics to most commercials. With the exception of school, TV was the main influence in his life. Later, as a teenager he didn't have to go 'cool-hunting'. He knew all the trends and used his early knowledge of what was hot to his advantage.

IN ORDER TO BECOME GENUINELY INDEPENDENT, BOYS REQUIRE A MEASURE OF CONSISTENCY AND PREDICTABILITY.

Despite his veneer of Hollywood confidence, Bobby had always had trouble fitting in at school. By Grade 9, however, he had discovered how to flirt, which, along with his natural good looks, helped him get a lot of favourable interest from the girls. With minimal supervision and structure at home, Bobby gave up on teachers and grades and turned his energy toward sexual conquests. His notoriety and status was growing amongst his male peers as he continued with his 'love them and leave them' tactics. His life was structured in a haphazard way as if he didn't know where the top, bottom, or sides were. All he knew was that the attention felt good – and nothing else mattered.

SOME parents and teachers might imagine that providing a stable and consistent structure is monotonous—a wearing drudgery. But boys need reasonable boundaries so that they learn to accept healthy limitations and expectations for cooperative living. For boys who are tough to reach and tough to teach, the structure of the environment at home and at school greatly affects their ability to learn and develop self-confidence. In order to become genuinely independent, they require a measure of consistency and predictability. When a boy's caregivers behave in arbitrary and neglectful ways, they undermine a child's confidence and generate emotional dependency, but when they show trust and provide consistency, the boy begins to trust himself, his judgment, and other people.

• • • • •

When a boy's

caregivers behave

in arbitrary and

neglectful ways,

they undermine a

child's confidence .

HOW DO WE KEEP CLASSROOM LIFE FUN AND UPLIFTING—NOT LABOURIOUS AND BORING – WHILE ALSO PAYING ATTENTION TO SPECIAL STUDENT NEEDS, INCLUDING THE NEEDS OF MANY BOYS?

So the perplexing question is, how can teachers set about to organize certain aspects of the classroom to enhance their responsiveness to the needs of boys? How do working teachers encourage students – boys in particular – to find joy in learning when they are having to translate complex curriculum standards into simple, workable classroom structures that embody exemplary instruction? How do teachers begin the task of organizing classrooms to be active, experiential, collaborative, and democratic, with a focus on learning, while simultaneously meeting best practice standards across subject areas and throughout the grades?

IN A society where corporate expectations of *more for less* permeates even our approach to schooling, it is difficult to assert that the cost-cutting approach of business works for our most valued resource – our children. Clearly, we are not in a position to fund all desired changes to help children in schools. However, there are low-cost or even no-cost ways that we could organize our classrooms to benefit both boys and girls. When we understand that masculine identities are not fixed, but are honed in the classroom through the daily rub of student–teacher interactions and peer group influences, and that they are continuously being developed, tested, and renegotiated, teachers can choose to organize the classroom to support learning in more effective ways.

The following time-tested guidelines are approved by boys, teachers, and parents – with girls' authorization too.

• • • • •

GUIDELINE 41
CONSIDER PHYSICAL ELEMENTS OF CLASSROOM

Educators can consider how physical elements of the classroom may facilitate or inhibit boys' learning:

- **Classroom** lighting and colour need to be reviewed so that lighting is quieter, with less glare from fluorescent lighting. More subdued lighting creates a calmer atmosphere where boys can talk about their feelings and discuss emotive and other difficult issues. Subdued lighting also results in more settled behaviour for both girls and boys and doesn't cause headaches.

- **Provide** boys with adequate space around their desks. If they are seated so that they can touch each other without getting up, they can distract each other more easily and struggle with completing quiet independent work.

GUIDELINE 41
CONSIDER PHYSICAL ELEMENTS OF CLASSROOM *CONT'D*

• **Keep** all items not in immediate use in cabinets or closets.

• **Make** areas of the room activity specific. For example, desks are for work; the large table is for group discussion; and the *thinking-desk* is dedicated to *cooling off* and thinking. This reduces confusion over what behaviour is expected at a given place and time.

• **Keep** the temperature needs on the cool side with plenty of fresh air. When possible, have windows open.

• **Remove** clutter that contributes to the feeling of chaos and disorganization.

• **Use** colour rather than black and white in displays at the front of a classroom so that boys are more likely to watch the front and retain information provided.

• **The** brain processes up to twenty thousand bits of auditory stimuli every second. In poorly designed classrooms that fail to address and reduce ambient noise – echo effects, reverberation, and other acoustical problems – boys' attention decreases.

• **Keep** everyone hydrated. Boys, who tend to be active, need to drink water regularly if they are to have optimum learning and manage stress. Because our body systems require electrical transmissions to make the brain operate efficiently, water provides the hydration necessary to conduct the body's electrical impulses. Without proper hydration, humans feel short-circuited and are less able to think clearly. Adults should also drink throughout the day to keep their own circuitry running smoothly and role-model this essential habit. Water fights aside, children should be permitted to have water bottles at their desk where they can drink frequently, even if there is a water fountain in the classroom. In older schools, water fountains are frequently down the hallway and further limit regular hydration.

• **Encourage** boys to have healthy nutritional snacks so that their bodies are fueled for active boys as they burn more slowly and provide longer lasting energy as compared with carbohydrates.

• **Make** sure boys can find shelter and shade in schoolyards and playgrounds so they can interact in a pleasant atmosphere.

• • • • •

Without proper

hydration, humans

feel short-circuited

and are less able

to think clearly.

GUIDELINE 42
SEATING HELPS BOYS HAVE A SENSE OF BELONGING

FOR boys, their turf or territory is often important. If they feel there is nowhere within the school that is theirs, they tend to regard the school as a foreign place to which they show no loyalty or belonging, potentially causing discipline problems such as vandalism and graffiti.

• • • • •

Boys need their own turf to feel comfortable in their surroundings.

Although teachers should recognize and respect friendships among boys, arrange classroom seating and the composition of project groups in ways that encourage mixing and minimize peer pressure, bullying and especially, isolation. In fact, the British document, *National School Standard to Raise Boys' Achievement*, highlights seating placement as an essential ingredient in its recommendations and claims that success hinges more on seating arrangements and chairs than you'd think. *Maintaining Sanity in the Classroom* also underscores the importance of how group structures can reinforce certain desirable attitudes and behaviours.

The authors remind us to be cognizant of the subtle patterns of interpersonal relations that ebb and flow throughout the day. Teachers and administrators must be particularly vigilant in seeking out boys who are loners in our

ARRANGE CLASSROOM SEATING TO MINIMIZE PEER PRESSURE, BULLYING AND ISOLATION.

schools, who are suffering rejection by the peer groups and who feel they are alone. Unless we help them find their place of belonging and value, boys who feel isolated, rejected by peers and frustrated with learning will be more prone to self-harm and school violence. It goes without saying that exiling a disruptive boy as a pariah in the hall outside the class, like expelling boys from the school, can exacerbate feelings of isolation and rejection that create more problems down the line.

Each class of students has its own particular chemistry formed by relationships among individuals in the class. This collective energy has a tremendous bearing on everyone's motivation to learn and on the structure and atmosphere of the classroom. Skilled teachers are sensitive to group dynamics and organize activities to best suit students' collective needs.

CHAPTER SIX

GUIDELINE 42
SEATING HELPS BOYS HAVE A SENSE OF BELONGING CONT'D

WHEN a teacher is faced with a group that does not respond to modifications, conducting a *Sociogram* can improve group dynamics by providing teachers with student perspectives on how they belong, and on how each student is viewed by peers. The results of the *Sociogram*, which are often surprising to teachers, will assist with desk placement as well as group learning composition. They can operate as a social health barometer for a classroom, as well as individual students, to clarify how they feel about and interact with each other.

> SOCIOGRAMS SERVE TO IMPROVE GROUP DYNAMICS, PROVIDING TEACHERS WITH STUDENT PERSPECTIVES.

• • • • •

The results of a Sociogram, which are often surprising to teachers, will assist with desk placement as well as group learning composition.

To gather information for the *Sociogram* ask each person to identify two students whom they would like to work with in the next group project, indicating a first and second choice. Gather this information confidentially and take about 20 minutes to record the responses on a matrix with chooser on one axis and chosen on the other. When privately analyzing the matrix, teachers should give special attention to those students who were not chosen by anyone and be certain to place them with one of their choices. Since they are likely discouraged youth, placing them with others they admire will raise their sense of belonging in the group in a special way.

As teachers work to facilitate harmonious classrooms that have less stress and more learning, noting which students are selected more frequently will help to highlight their role as potential leaders. In particular, they can help to identify students' unmet needs for belonging and therefore guide the teacher in structural decisions that boost everyone's learning potential.

GUIDELINE **43**
CONSIDER HOW POWER IS DISTRIBUTED

LIKE parents who, from the moment their child is born, do everything possible to ensure that their child has the skills and abilities to live independently of them, so a teacher, from the moment a new set of students enters his or her classroom, does everything to provide them with the skills and abilities to be confident and autonomous learners and citizens. Pampering of boys – sometimes simply because they are boys – can lead to a sense of entitlement that keeps them blind to the power of others, particularly girls. On occasion this sense of entitlement can lead to a controlling attitude or even tyranny through charm or intimidation, rebellion, or arrogance. Boys, like all human beings, need to learn to share and negotiate power.

Human interactions cannot be understood by gender alone without an analysis of the impact of privilege and access to power. Just ask any student who raises an arm exploding with ideas only to be thwarted by being overlooked. "That's the real world," you might say, but I think we can do better to provide students with meaningful opportunities to discover their personal agency along with the dynamics of power and privilege.

• • • • •

Pampering of boys, sometimes simply because they are boys, can lead to a sense of entitlement that keeps them blind to the power of others, particularly girls.

WHEN CHILDREN HAVE AN OPPORTUNITY TO PRACTISE RESPECTFUL POWER-SHARING, THEY MAKE WAY FOR A MORE PEACEFUL WORLD IN THE FUTURE.

Boys learn by doing and benefit from experiences related to sharing power.

Like an ideal community mayor, a sensitive teacher can demonstrate respect for shared power by valuing the contributions of boys and girls equally and also by sharing his or her use of power with all students. Negotiating options and choices is essential. When students are trusted participants in a process of constructing their shared environment, everyone wins. For example, students may participate in the curriculum design by helping to form a range of options, certain themes, or works of literature to focus on. Students may also contribute to the design of their assignments, within their teacher's parameters. Finally, students may have some say about how their assignments are evaluated.

GUIDELINE 44
FACILITATE STUDENT-LED CLASSROOM MEETINGS

THE outdated rule of being tough and authoritarian until Christmas so kids know who's boss creates a power imbalance that almost invites boys to challenge authority or domination. A colleague's father, who was once a principal in Detroit, put it as "Don't smile until after Christmas." We help to develop boys' sense of personal agency when we create opportunities for them to have a say in what's happening around them or participate in creating age-appropriate rules that directly affect them.

• • • • •

Some people think teachers shouldn't smile until after Christmas.

In any power structure that we operate within, we are more likely to be invested and cooperative if we have both voice and choice. Student-led classroom meetings are a microcosm for practising democratic citizenship. Through group discussion and decision-making, students can express their views and experience having their voices heard. Classroom meetings provide the opportunities for students to practice leadership, to speak and listen to others in a respectful manner, and to be invested as co-creators of any structures that emerge.

Take time during the first week of school to investigate students' views on what helps and/or sabotages learning and other aspects of classroom living. From this list, together establish classroom rules and policies. Note that in classroom meetings, efficiency is not the goal as much as inclusiveness. If kids have a say, they will learn that they don't always have to have their way.

TAKE TIME DURING THE FIRST WEEK OF SCHOOL TO INVESTIGATE STUDENTS' VIEWS ON WHAT HELPS AND OR SABOTAGES LEARNING AND OTHER ASPECTS OF CLASSROOM LIVING.

GUIDELINE 44
FACILITATE STUDENT-LED CLASSROOM MEETINGS CONT'D

THROUGH the practice of student-led classroom meetings, students develop the communication skills to express their concerns in a civil and responsible manner. If the future meeting agenda is posted on the classroom wall, students are free to post their ideas and relational concerns. I am amazed at how well students resolve conflict when they become aware that their disagreement may be discussed at the classroom meeting. For boys who might be turned off if the meeting becomes too relational, agendas should reflect a balance of activities:

- what's working well

- what's not working well

- how can we make classroom life better (teachers need to be prepared to give up preconceived notions here especially – such as homework during vacation time)

- action plans for creating interest, sustaining motivation and achieving results

The Internet and classroom management books are full of additional ideas to facilitate regular, student-led classroom meetings.

• • • • •

GUIDELINE 45
INVITE THE VIGOUR OF INQUIRY

SCHOOLS are orderly places, governed by timetables, bells, regulations, curricula, and examinations that provide fixed points of reference for the natural changeability of young people. But too much repetition, and the four grey walls of the classroom, can make boys feel hemmed in. As a classroom teacher I sometimes felt stifled and used to arrange for school-based outings on a daily basis as well as bigger weekly adventures with students. These outings helped energize me as well as the students. In conversation with boys about why they dropped out of school I have often heard them criticize the repetitiveness of classroom life and request, "switch it up, switch it up!"

GUIDELINE 45
INVITE THE VIGOUR OF INQUIRY CONT'D

BOYS learn best when they are actively involved in a process of knowledge construction rather than passively swallowing information. Make boys' involvement essential parts of the learning process through problem solving, role-playing, stimulation, and inquiry. In such a classroom, the teacher provides students with experiences that allow them to hypothesize, predict, manipulate objects, pose questions, research, investigate, imagine, and invent. The teacher's role is to facilitate this process – to become a consultant that guides inquiring minds. Whereas boys shrivel in classrooms filled with worksheets and *busy-work,* they thrive when inquiry is fundamental.

• • • • •

Classrooms organized around inquiry foster critical thinking and create motivated and independent learners.

Boys then learn to invent rather than accumulate facts, adapt and change old ideas, and rethink previous views while coming to new conclusions. Classrooms organized around inquiry foster critical thinking and create motivated and independent learners.

I HAVE OFTEN HEARD BOYS CRITICIZE THE REPETITIVENESS OF CLASSROOM LIFE AND REQUEST, "SWITCH IT UP, SWITCH IT UP!"

According to the national bestseller, *Flow: The Psychology of Optimal Experience,* author Mihaly Csikszentmihalyi indicates that inquiry necessitates a sense of competence and control. I have found that boys pursue the interests they value through literacy activities outside of the school, whether reading magazines, newspapers, or electronic text and figure out well-designed questions through the investigation that they control. Be prepared, however, as testosterone helps males to focus on a particular task with more intensity than the typical female, resulting in distortion of time and single-mindedness which can become very intense. A boy in a state of flow becomes completely focussed, and there is no space for distracting thoughts or irrelevant feelings. I recall one particular boy who was on a mission to collect information from teachers around the school. He was time conscious as he wished to complete his errand before recess when it was his turn to be the captain of the team. With intense focus he misread a teacher's hand signal and interrupted her anyway. He ended up missing recess and sitting outside of the vice-principal's office.

GUIDELINE 45
INVITE THE VIGOUR OF INQUIRY CONT'D

• • • • •

Novelty and fun

decrease stress

levels and prime

the pump for

learning.

A BOY'S hyper-focus can be extremely off-putting to females who typically possess learning styles more suited for multitasking and interruptions. Males who are in a state of deep concentration can be oblivious to outside requests and can even become targets of misinformed discipline.

Be sure to provide transition time to bring these boys out of complete concentration. I have often found that a particular piece of music, such as the theme from *2001: a Space Odyssey* helps to smooth transitions.

We might reflect on what neuroscientists have to say about learning and the brain – *prepare for snow!* This phrase metaphorically reminds us to be responsive to circumstances and opportunities as they present themselves. Teachers and the best public speakers have a knack for incorporating the unforeseen sounds within the room to create laughter while maintaining and deepening focus. I acquired one of my favourite techniques for accomplishing this goal from *Cooperative Discipline.* It's called *doing the unexpected.* When classroom focus faded into listless boredom, or threatened to dissipate into exuberant chaos, and I wanted to do something beside pleading, "CLASS!" I would have a conversation with the wall. I don't recommend this strategy with very young students, who might be confused by it, but middle and older students regularly enjoyed such antics and regained focus. Sometimes they would even request, "Mr. Mac, tell the wall something funny again."

"MR. MAC TELL THE WALL SOMETHING FUNNY AGAIN."

Stimulating breaks like these can help reinvigorate the class and create conditions for optimal learning. As brain researchers point out, novelty and fun decrease stress levels and prime the pump for learning.

While facilitating a weeklong summer institute in Ireland over a dozen years ago with approximately thirty teaching nuns on the topic of classroom organization and discipline, I learned about the value of *switching it up.*

GUIDELINE 45
INVITE THE VIGOUR OF INQUIRY CONT'D

I WAS somewhat fatigued from the previous late night discussion and Sister June offered a brain break in the middle of our morning agenda. She could see that we were fatigued and suggested that we take a few moments for *party pieces*, which involved someone offering to sing a song, tell a story, or dance a jig. I marveled at how confident participants were to perform in front of each other. Even the shyest of sisters got up to contribute her talents. Although it took a couple of minutes out of class time, the resulting energetic response propelled us forward while also building a strong sense of community. I must add that I didn't have a *party piece*, but when it was my turn, I sang a tune and they responded as though I was a visiting rock star. I was star struck with the power of taking breaks and have been advocating them ever since. For more information on brain compatible strategies read Eric Jensen's numerous books on this subject. Some teachers fear that the break will lead to misbehaviour, but boys tell me that they are necessary to the learning process – and brain researchers support the boys.

• • • • •

GUIDELINE 46
ARRANGE FOR KINESTHETIC LEARNING

NEUROSCIENTIFIC research is redefining how we approach education. By understanding how brain cells and bodily systems function best, we can organize classrooms to effectively capture attention, boost motivation, extend memory, and enhance reading, writing, spelling, math, and other academic skills for boys of all ages and all learning styles. The right side of the brain controls the left side of the body and vice versa. Our brains are better problem solvers when they use both hemispheres. You'll want to encourage boys to use both sides of their brain to maximize learning – remember the corpus callosum. Cross-lateral activities force the brain to engage both hemispheres at once.

GUIDELINE 46

ARRANGE FOR KINESTHETIC LEARNING CONT'D

- - - - -

Research shows

that retention

can be improved

when gestures

and words are

combined to learn

terms.

I HAVE often noticed that boys will unconsciously partake in cross-lateral movement to stimulate their brains. One Grade 6 boy I taught years ago negotiated with classmates to play with several micro-machines on his desktop during school time. Although I was initially concerned about his minimal eye contact I was open to the notion that it may be an integral aspect of his unique learning style – to be kinesthetic. I marveled at his cooperation with classmates as he kept the disturbance of his play to a minimum; he seemed to need movement as he reached for higher thought. One day during a demonstration lesson to a group of visiting teachers he surprised them all by providing the culminating insightful response after a questioning process that led students to deeper thought. Most observers thought he was misbehaving – but the proof was in the pudding!

CROSS-LATERAL ACTIVITIES FORCE THE BRAIN TO ENGAGE BOTH HEMISPHERES AT ONCE.

Later, he was the same boy who suggested tossing a ball to the next speaker to cultivate more classroom movement. Rarely do boys sit in their assigned seat with both feet squarely on the floor. I have noticed that even men registered in my university class squirm and wiggle.

Rub your palms together and imagine they represent neurons. Say the word neuron. Research shows that retention can be improved when gestures and words are combined to learn terms. Learning consists of growing and strengthening networks of neurons. Showing and saying the word neuron expands the new neural network by engaging the visual, auditory, tactile, and proprioceptive sensory systems. In this way, cross-lateral stimulation works as mental glue as boys learn.

It is for these reasons that I encourage adults to obtain active sitting devises for boys in school, such as the *SitFitter* – an inflatable air cushion that sits on a chair, mimics the shape and feel of a ball, and permits movement and cross-lateral brain stimulation. A good source is *Fitter First* (contact information is identified in the bibliography).

Guideline 47
Begin With the End in Mind

BOYS easily lose interest when they don't know where they are going. Often they tell me that they get lost in wordy lesson preambles and narratives. When targets are blurred, and boys don't understand up front the clear purpose and desired end result, they can feel powerless and tune out.

When we begin with the end in mind, we design learning backwards. When we have a clear destination or outcome, we can better plan how to get there. Begin with identifying desired results and then determine the criteria that will demonstrate success. For

BOYS THRIVE IN LEARNING ENVIRONMENTS WHERE THEY FEEL COMPETENT AND IN CONTROL.

more information about how to design learning experiences and instruction with purpose in mind, refer to *The End of Education*, by Neil Postman or *Understanding by Design*, by Grant Wiggins and Jay McTighe.

Giving set, explicit time frames for tasks focuses boys' work and reduces the time-wasting they are often prone to, especially during group work. Suggesting time allowances helps boys budget their time and make homework tasks seem more manageable. This also limits the extra time that girls tend to spend on homework and enables parents to get an idea of what is expected.

• • • • •

When we have a clear destination or outcome, we can better plan how to get there.

GUIDELINE 48
PICTURE SHORT-TERM GOALS

WHEN goals are clear, feedback relevant, and challenges and skills are in balance, attention becomes ordered and students more fully invested. While boys who are disruptive tend to be more motivated when they can see the big picture, they are especially focused when they can distill clearly defined mini-goals that move them toward achievement of the desired end.

A book report assignment can overwhelm boys who do not know the steps involved or how to manage their time with larger projects. This building block approach to completing larger tasks, with clearly defined deadlines that are monitored, provides valuable structure with explicit and attainable-targeted goals. This approach additionally helps boys shift from thinking, *"No, I can't"* to *"Yes, I can!"*

• • • • •

GUIDELINE 49
ENCOURAGE MISTAKES AND CALCULATED RISKS

MARTIN Luther King Jr. said, "We must constantly build dikes of courage to hold back the flood of fear." Encouragement shores up our courage and self-trust. When toddlers learn to walk, we say, "Come on" and "You can do it," never doubting the results regardless of how many falls there are along the way. Children are usually aware of their mistakes and being reminded of them repeatedly will undermine the confidence needed to keep trying. When they are not aware, it is a teacher's job to help them make the changes that are needed while continuing to focus on any progress they have made. If a boy is experiencing difficulty in one part of an assignment, remind him of positive progress in other parts of the assignment. Adults teaching boys at home and school need a focus that says, "I can always see the positive possibility in any situation." As boys come to anticipate your supportive and encouraging involvement, they become free to explore their potential while also being willing to discuss their mistakes.

GUIDELINE 49
ENCOURAGE MISTAKES AND CALCULATED RISKS CONT'D

• • • • •

Encouragement

shores up our

courage and

self-trust.

THE punishment and chastising experiences that schools sometimes used historically diminish people and limit learning. Shame and trauma around schooling can live long in the minds of discouraged learners. Boys learn best when they are free to make mistakes without fear of being humiliated. Criticism, especially in a group setting, challenges a boy's status within the group and invites behaviour or attitudes such as a show of anger or indifference that will help him regain status. When boys are afraid to try, learning stops in its tracks. Boys must feel free to risk making mistakes if they are to embrace learning.

Encouragement produces courage. When I look back at my schooling years, teachers who encouraged me–"*Atta boy*, I knew you could do that"–helped me develop the courage to learn and make mistakes. Helen Keller, a childhood hero of mine, said, "Keep your face in the sunshine and you cannot see a shadow."

• • • • •

GUIDELINE 50
CONSULT WITH BOYS

CHILDREN gain when they are encouraged to see their place in the world as contributors who can make a difference. Interviews with boys, who typically want to be independent and in charge, have made me realize how counterproductive it is to remove responsibilities from boys until they toe the line. This practice stimulates underground power-broking and passive resistance. We need to find a delicate balance with boys – providing guidance while also trusting boys with responsibility – sometimes before they have already proven that they are worthy of trust. Boys report micro management or hovering as the learning exterminator which shuts down creativity and initiative in a snap.

GUIDELINE 50
CONSULT WITH BOYS CONT'D

• • • • •

Consider the

variety of ways

boys can assume

responsibility for

school tasks.

SEARCH out ways for boys to take on responsibility and give input. Consider the variety of ways boys can assume responsibility for school tasks such as research, programming, committee membership, project publicity, or fundraising. Boys who are not ready to join committees can sometimes contribute ad hoc input with their ideas, through informal discussion or even dropping ideas in a suggestion box. Sometimes deliberately developing a strategy to create a two-way flow of information by seeking boys' opinions through forums, focus groups and surveys, sends the valuable message that their involvement is important. When appropriate, help boys learn to reach decisions by consensus.

Create opportunities for boys to develop special expertise through consultancy. Short-term consultancy is often the first step. Boys can provide leadership around specific issues or events – such as determining which day might be best to schedule Sports' Day or providing input on a new school policy. Developmental participation concerns ongoing and structured ways for boys to be involved.

BOYS REPORT MICRO MANAGEMENT OR HOVERING AS THE LEARNING EXTERMINATOR.

Youth councils are an example where boys can be part of complex systemic thinking over time.

Consulting with boys, and involving them in significant decision-making, can help them to internalize this paradox: that one condition of freedom is the ability to accept the limits that are in place for the greater good of the larger society. We need to help boys develop the human resourcefulness and leadership skills that are sorely needed in this conflict-ridden century.

IMPROVING
BOYS' LITERACY

It must be remembered that the purpose of education is not to fill the minds of students with facts... it is to teach them to think, if that is possible, and always to think for themselves.
Robert Hutchins

• • • • •

Basking in his

passion, Kevin

began to thrive.

Sometimes it seems as if boys can change dramatically in a moment, but more often change happens almost imperceptibly over time. I remember a student I taught named Kevin, who struggled with reading several years ago. After having made little progress with two previous years of learning assistance, he was now resistant to being taken out of class for learning support. It was the end of September and I was certain that he had not yet tried any writing assignments in class or other classes for that matter. The learning assistance teacher had remarked how often he seemed to be off in another world, daydreaming.

After we conferred, we decided to try having her integrate more into the regular class. She would give in-class help at the *Editing Centre* and *Author's Corner*. While others were writing, Kevin drew. I didn't pester him to write, but took the opportunity to encourage his drawing talent: "Looks like you're working hard at that." I wanted him to feel that his passion and interest in drawing were accepted. Kevin grinned, clearly enjoying his chance to express himself through drawing. Other students also took notice of my comment and began to request his artistic talents to help in presenting their projects. Basking in his passion, Kevin began to thrive.

THE LITERACY **GENDER GAP**

• • • • •

Then with an

incredulous look

questioned, "I wrote

that?" I knew that we

had struck gold.

ONCE I saw that he was comfortable with his role as the classroom artist, it seemed only logical to challenge him to write more frequently. In conversation, he was richly articulate, his oral expression certainly beyond his reading and writing levels. Soon I had one of his prized Arctic Wolf drawings – a specialty of his – on the wall behind my desk with his description below that I scribed for him. After school one day he waited until everyone had left and asked me to read the caption out loud to him. He wanted me to read it a second time. Then with an incredulous look questioned, "I wrote that?" I knew that we had struck gold.

A week later he showed up at the editor's table with another beautiful drawing and his own printing text below. I wasn't sure what he wanted and offered, "Editing advice at your service." He pointed to a passage that he had underlined. I smiled and said, "I can see you're the kind of student who cares about drawing and writing." I was about to say more but he smiled and took his paper back to his desk. Later that day he pointed to a punctuation mark and said he'd like to know if it was right. I sensed that we had to proceed cautiously.

THE ACHIEVEMENT GAP IS DRIVEN PRIMARILY BY PERFORMANCE DIFFERENCES IN LITERACY.

When I inquired about who he thought might be his best teacher for punctuation, he motioned toward a boy – an avid reader very different from Kevin with whom he'd not worked with previously.

This avid reader was delighted to be singled out to teach from his strength, and the rest is history.

The achievement level of boys is lagging considerably behind that of girls in North America and elsewhere. Stats Canada, October 2004, reported that the gap in achievement between boys and girls is widening. Between the years 1993 and 2002 the male undergraduate enrolment dropped from 47% to 42%. Another study of British children, *Girls Rock, Boys Roll: An Analysis of the Age 14-16 Gender Gap in English Schools*, which investigated data from over half a million students in over 3000 schools, echoed international concerns about the gender gap in educational attainment. This extensive study found that the achievement gap is driven primarily by performance differences in literacy.

PARENTS often wonder when they hear that best teaching practice in literacy is designed for everybody – not just boys – and question what boys' particular literacy needs are. The 2003 OFSTED report, *Yes he can: Schools Where Boys Write Well,* named three main factors associated with boys' success in writing:

1) a culture in the school and classroom where intellectual, cultural, and aesthetic accomplishment by boys as well as girls is valued

2) value placed on diversity of style and approach, succinctness as much as elaboration, and logical thought as much as expressiveness

3) emphasis placed on both boys and girls reading widely for pleasure so that they absorb a range of models for their own writing.

The following guidelines suggest some ways that teachers can help boys with their literacy needs.

• • • • •

GUIDELINE 51
TEACH MULTIPLE LITERACIES

SCHOOL librarians – the few that are still employed in schools – tell me that the idea that boys are reluctant readers is a mistaken notion. They say that boys and girls read a wide variety of books, but with one difference – most boys prefer nonfiction. It is for this reason that boys will benefit if we expand our previous definition of traditional literacy and expand it to include multiple literacies; visual and technological literacy, for example, as well as literacy with forms from the performing arts such as storytelling, music, and video.

GUIDELINE 51
TEACH MULTIPLE LITERACIES CONT'D

RECENTLY I was involved in an action research project to determine how groups of boys from Kindergarten through Grade 4 select books in the library. When we met with the boys, we learned that they didn't grasp the wisdom of the axiom "don't judge a book by its cover." Even after encouragement to explore the contents of the book, boys consistently selected books where the cover image, titles, and captions attracted them. Their selections had less to do with design, font, and colour and everything to do with appeal of the topic – boys' stuff.

• • • • •

Boys typically
prefer books about
risk-taking, about
weird or unusual
facts, about fearful
dangers overcome.

They robustly described their preference for books about risk-taking, about weird or unusual facts, about fearful dangers overcome. They were drawn to topics such as sports, sharks, skateboarding, hockey, volcanoes, and monster trucks. Even the boys who were too young to career dexterously on skateboards prized skateboarding books. Boys also valued a book offering a scientific explanation about flatulence. When asked about who else liked the topics they'd selected, most said their dad. I frequently find that boys mirror the reading tastes of their fathers.

BOYS LOVE TO HAVE FUN AND WANT FUN BOOKS THAT APPEAL TO THEIR ZANY SENSE OF HUMOUR.

When we removed the non-fiction, boys identified fiction books about similar topics and expressed a special fondness for bathroom humour, which we'll get to later. Boys love to have fun and want fun books that make them laugh and appeal to their zany sense of humour. Boys also liked books with sports or action heroes that focus more on action than emotion, or books that matched their image of themselves, or who they would like to be. Perhaps because they are so often told to behave less rambunctiously, to be more organized and compliant, boys relish books that feature characters victoriously breaking away from adult rules.

Recently, the United Nations declared, "…that a renewed and expanded vision of literacy is essential for success…that it embraces a wide range of dimensions of personal and social life and development – and that is a lifelong learning process." Boys benefit when we expand opportunities for literacy.

GUIDELINE 52
REACH OUT TO RELUCTANCE

• • • • •

Studies proclaim

that poor

early reading

achievement leads

to higher dropout

rates, lower rates

of advanced

education,

and ultimately,

longer periods of

unemployment and

reduced earnings.

SIGNIFICANT numbers of boys experience difficulties with literacy at an early age. *The Early Development Instrument* tells us that 20% of four and five year-olds do not have the language background for kindergarten success. Without intervention this problem becomes more pronounced as they proceed through schooling and along a path of more and more dismal results. In 1996 the John Howard Society of Canada reported that 68% of the people incarcerated in federal penitentiaries have limited literacy skills. Furthermore, 60% of Canadian social assistance recipients have not completed secondary school. Studies proclaim that poor early reading achievement leads to higher dropout rates, lower rates of advanced education, and ultimately, longer periods of unemployment and reduced earnings. I have noticed that if a boy becomes turned off school before Grade 4, this early

BOYS START SCHOOL WITH A CONSIDERABLE VERBAL AND PSYCHOSOCIAL DEVELOPMENTAL LAG OF UP TO 18 MONTHS BEHIND GIRLS.

disenchantment may set a pattern for his remaining school career. It can be tough to teach boys science, math, or social studies in the later years when they have a hard time reading the textbook.

The first step in helping readers who struggle is to ensure that they experience some form of success to boost their confidence levels. Involve boys in literacy experiences that build on their prior knowledge, language, and vocabulary. Focus on themes and content that are meaningful to their lives. Begin with materials boys themselves choose, and seek to understand their choice as you engage them in meaningful dialogue. Reading begins with talking – so pursue rich and varied topics of discussion.

GUIDELINE 52
REACH OUT TO RELUCTANCE CONT'D

• • • • •

Dialogue and

social interaction

support the

development of

literacy.

SOCIAL and family interaction requires the decoding of verbal and emotional cues and supports literacy development. Thus, even if they are a bit noisy and rambunctious, boys should be encouraged to play a role in family gatherings. They should not be shuttled off somewhere to play on the floor or outside, while their sisters are serving food, and interacting with family and friends, all the while honing their communication and interpersonal skills. Boys start school with a considerable verbal and psychosocial developmental lag (up to 18 months), behind girls. They often do not catch up until into their late teens—if then. Realize that dialogue and social interaction supports the development of literacy.

Recognize that boys, especially if they are reluctant readers, may enjoy listening to someone else read a book that they may not choose to read themselves. Reading a book is not the same as being read to. Some books a boy will enjoy reading by himself, while there are others he may enjoy when adults read to him. When someone else reads, the difficulty level and length does not deter a reluctant reader as long as it's a great story that engages their imagination. They benefit through hearing new words and sophisticated sentence structures because they infer the meaning of words

LITERACY IS NOT A SINGLE THING, AND IT DEVELOPS IN RELATIONSHIP.

from context and the adult reader's interpretation and inflections smooth the way for understanding. I also theorize that hearing complex sentences helps children internalize the deep structures of language, its rhythms, and cadences. Teachers and parents who can't recall a time when reading was anything other than pleasurable especially need to understand this difference.

GUIDELINE 53
AVOID MISREADING VIOLENCE   • • • • •

RECENTLY, I received a telephone call from a teacher concerned about a young boy's drawing of a decapitated person with plenty of reference to blood dripping. It contained the caption, "I'd rather be dead than live with you!" Upon exploration of his circumstances and history, we determined that he was not at personal risk but was only expressing what he sees around him reflected in the media. It is understandable that we are worried about violence, which seems so glorified today in television and the movies – not to mention gangster rap and video games. Fred Mathews' poignant article entitled, *The Forgotten Child*, gives these alarming facts about males and violence as reported by Statistics Canada:

- Males commit 99% of all violent crimes.

- Bullying happens once every 7 minutes on the playground and once every 25 minutes in class.

- The average age for men who "date" rape is 18.5 years old.

- The highest risk group for sexual assault are young women between 14 and 18 years old.

- 85% of teenagers who are sexually assaulted know their attacker.

- To be injured by a husband or boyfriend is the leading cause of injury women in Canada – higher than car accidents, stranger rapes and muggings combined.

- Women who are battered often stay in the abusive relationship because they are afraid to leave. Seventy-five percent of women who are killed by a husband or boyfriend were trying to leave when they died.

GUIDELINE 53
AVOID MISREADING VIOLENCE CONT'D

THUS it is not surprising that teachers and parents become concerned when they learn that boys are interested in books, or other forms of media, that contain violence.

• • • • •

Seeing

violence

does not

automatically

make a boy

become

violent.

However, it is easy to jump to conclusions and misread a boy's attraction to violence. With respect to the story about the boy's headless drawing, I learned the boy was attempting to be more expressive in his writing, which was the main criterion for the assignment. He chose his most current media experience – the video he watched the previous night was called *The Headless Horseman.*

Seeing violence does not automatically make a boy become violent. I have had numerous

EVEN GANDHI MIGHT BE TEMPTED TO THROW A FEW JABS.

discussions with fathers and sons about this matter and have learned that for many boys, it is the adventure and action associated with violent images that they find so attractive.

During my years as a sessional instructor at the University of British Columbia in the Department of Counselling Psychology, I frequently heard the argument that violent play on television causes boys to become violent. The research simply does not bear this out to be true. In Thomas Newkirk's book, *Misreading Masculinity: Boys, Literacy, and Popular Culture*, the author points out that researchers who record boys hitting a life size inflated Bobo doll after watching a violent movie are artificially instigated and the research is fraught with difficulties. Newkirk speculates that even Gandhi might be tempted to throw a few jabs.

When I talk with boys about their teachers' concern with violent language, as is often associated with televised wrestling, boys tell me that they understand gradients of nuance and boundaries of appropriateness. It is possible that boys who use this language are trying to connect socially with other boys within the conventions and constraints of the boy-code. According to Newkirk, boys are prevented by the boy-code from open displays of affection which might be interpreted as gay. Thus they bond through teasing and sometimes almost violent actions. Perhaps this roughness is not the ideal way of relating, but we must not read it as the certain sign of a sociopath either.

While acknowledging that we should all be concerned about actual violence inflicted by males, we do not want to over-react to the violence that takes place in the realm of the imagination – or call 911 when we see the macho posturing of an adolescent.

GUIDELINE 54
BRING THE OUTSIDE IN

SCHOOLS are not remote, utopian islands. They are touched by outside concerns, including corporate and commercial interests with a vested interest in heightening the contrasts between adult and youth culture – especially hyper masculinity and being *cool* – as a selling point. Exposure to media influences cannot be wished away. For many boys, knowledge about the outside world is a badge of power and status. If schools cannot get rid of the contaminating outside culture, is there a way that they can use it as a teaching tool?

It doesn't work to try to simply forbid exposure to media that is labeled *Parent Advisory*, for then parents are out of the loop while peers and the media are left to interpret and instruct. In parenting workshops I discourage parents from banning anything from their home initially. It is advantageous to listen with your child to degrading and violent music and discuss implications rather than try to forbid it. Typically, boys say, "Oh, I don't listen to the words, I just like the music. You don't have to worry." If boys are to develop literacy in the twenty-first century, we need to help them understand the media's influence along with its commercial interests. After a discussion, it is then certainly appropriate for a parent to set boundaries identifying limitations – which music they don't want others in the house to listen to, for example.

• • • • •

For many boys,

knowledge about

the outside world is

a badge of power

and status.

TO FACILITATE THE DEVELOPMENT OF BOYS' LITERACY IN SCHOOL, WE NEED TO TAP INTO THE MEDIA, CULTURAL, AND PRACTICAL INTERESTS THAT THEY BRING WITH THEM FROM THE OUTSIDE WORLD.

In the classroom, boys benefit when teachers can initiate discussion and critique of popular culture. Bringing in material from the world external to school can often draw boys into dialogue more successfully than traditional materials. I have overheard boys groan at the prospect of writing yet another paragraph identifying the advantages and disadvantages of something, but if you ask them to compare and contrast a topic that interests them from the world outside of the traditional classroom, their interest is captivated. They are interested to write about who should win the next wrestling match or why sucker punching in professional hockey is wrong – or right.

GUIDELINE 54
BRING THE OUTSIDE IN CONT'D

SCHOOLS can also promote literacy among boys by appealing to their practical interests. In their book, *Reading Don't Fix No Chevys,* Michael Smith and Jeffrey Wilhelm stress the importance of appreciating a boy's outside world, the reality principle as they call it, and its relationship to learning and literacy development. They say, "Figuring things out, fixing things, and making things all connected to the boys' desire for realism, was a theme expressed by every one of the boys in the study."

To facilitate the development of boys' literacy in school, we need to tap into the media, cultural, and practical interests of boys that they bring with them from the outside world.

• • • • •

GUIDELINE 55
GET BOYS HOOKED ON BOOKS THROUGH HUMOUR

GROWN-UPS may not always appreciate boys' uproarious laughter at certain vulgarities related to body functions. Sometimes women are particularly dismayed at the gales of laughter caused by indelicacies that contravene socially acceptable norms that invite connection and closeness among females. Making farting sounds with the underarm or even the real thing can bring gales of laughter to boys that even the media can't compete with. And a boy's affection for certain genres of literacy is no different. Some adults may recoil from books with titles such as *The Perilous Plot of Professor Poopie Pants, The Big, Bad Battle of the Bionic Booger Boy,* and *Walter the Farting Dog,* or magazines such as *MAD. Captain Underpants,* for another example, has endured as one of the biggest boons to child comedy since boys first learned that well-placed hand to the armpit trick. Sometimes boys can broaden their tastes in literacy through humour, moving from *Captain Underpants* to higher quality humorous books by Roald Dahl, or the Australian writer Paul Jennings. I have found that with children and adults alike, humour during the introductory phases of learning, creates engagement, and sustains motivation. Schools who prize quiet learners may have to alter their views if they are to tap into the power of humour in boys' literacy. Besides, boys often fidget or fight during *quiet learning* time. When classroom literacy permits a social tone, boys loosen up and motivation increases.

GUIDELINE 55
GET BOYS HOOKED ON BOOKS THROUGH HUMOUR *CONT'D*

• • • • •

Humour holds the

power to relax,

de-stress, and

even activate

the brain.

IN the book *Reading Don't Fix No Chevys,* the authors found that boys didn't have the opportunity to read funny books at school despite the scientific fact that humour holds the power to relax, de-stress, and even activate the brain. Discover what a boy finds hilarious and capture its power to develop a love of literacy. Laughter and the ensuing social interactions, when channeled, provide valuable frontloading oral literacy preparing boys for reading and especially writing about their experiences. Reading is a social act. We all love to talk about what we read, whether we are sharing our thoughts on the latest novel with a friend, reacting to an outrageous editorial with a colleague, or exploring a picture book with a child. Kids are no different – when they have opportunities to think and talk about their reading, they explode with thoughts, questions, and ideas. And sometimes with spontaneous laughter.

• • • • •

GUIDELINE 56
OFFER SHOW TIME

UNLESS boys learn to appreciate reading as a deep sustained pleasure, they are unlikely to develop strong literacy skills. Having fun with literacy in the classroom can extend to other pleasurable forms of drama such as *Reader's Theatre, Improv,* or *Role Drama.* These forms of drama provide a safe environment for boys to take their masks off or try on new ones, expressing a wider range of feelings than usual, and experimenting with new roles or behaviours.

I recall teaching students about persuasive writing while reading the story, *Rikki-Tiki-Tavi* by Rudyard Kipling, and utilizing role drama. For parents or teachers not familiar with the use of role drama in the classroom I wish to clarify that it is not acting. There are no scripted lines. In role drama, students become a character from a story according to their own interpretation. In this instance, they became snakes living in the forest watching the brave mongoose overcome the evil cobra with a single-minded devotion to duty, defending the safety of their human masters at any cost. Incidentally, the school principal played the role of the evil cobra, an element that enhanced their enjoyment whenever he would appear in the classroom. He also commented that he appreciated their playfulness as they responded with delight to his antics. Periodically, we would slow the drama down and deepen its intensity by pausing to reflect and write.

GUIDELINE 56
OFFER SHOW TIME *CONT'D*

DRAMA, which brings together multi-sensory integration, bodily movement, imagination, and cognitive understanding, helps to animate and engage students on multiple levels so that students are primed for the writing assignment that follows. In this case, a writing assignment that was particularly effective was one for persuasive letter writing. Still in the spirit of playful theatrics, I took on the role of town clerk – my alter ego – and we collaborated on developing criteria for effective writing. I then asked students to write a persuasive letter to the mayor about changing the forest bylaws. Students wrote prose that was rich and colourful – and which also met the criteria for the assignment. To this day I still have the collection of letters we wrote to the mayor – each demonstrating the power of drama to infuse passion, commitment, and depth into writing.

• • • • •

GUIDELINE 57
EMPLOY WRITING TEMPLATES

Boys time and again appreciate clear instructions and explicit criteria for evaluation of their writing.

NOT all forms of writing lend themselves to drama, and not all students like role-playing, especially if they are inhibited by the boy-code. Other springboards for writing can be useful. Some boys like efficient shortcuts that de-mystify the writing process. While using planning tools such as storyboards, writing frames, scaffolds, and templates, students can draw on their analytical skills. Boys time and again appreciate clear instructions and explicit criteria for evaluation of their writing. They often prefer structures such as heading titles and even the number of lines required for each section. I recollect one boy in my class who wanted to know the exact number of words required as it motivated him – the *one Smartie-at-a-time method*. To tell him to figure it out on his own or say, "When you grow up, no one will tell you the exact number of words that are required to pass an essay in university, so I won't either," would be discouraging and unhelpful. If a boy makes a special request to motivate him to write, I usually go with it. I have found that once boys become internally motivated to develop their literacy skills, they naturally shed these artificial structures and expand their writing as they proceed through school.

GUIDELINE 57
EMPLOY WRITING TEMPLATES *CONT'D*

I HAVE also found that when assignments ask for non-fiction writing, and boys are encouraged to use storyboards at the planning stage, writing quality increases, as does length. For boys who may not know where to even start writing, storyboards can provide a helpful structure. The formula approach frees them of the anxiety around the multi-tasking involved with larger writing assignments and permits them to focus on the writing process, one step at a time. But experts say the formula can inhibit creativity and the development of the writer's *authentic voice,* the five-paragraph format for essays has spread like wildfire nationwide. Although students should be aware that this formula or template is only one among many possibilities, it can provide a reassuring touchstone as boys build up their confidence.

• • • • •

GUIDELINE 58
WRITE LESS TO GET MORE

TYPICALLY, I find that too much homework results in avoidance, resentment, and decreased motivation. I discussed this issue on national radio when one of the mothers who joined me for the interview expressed her frustration with her son's teacher for assigning a project to be completed during Spring Break. Supposedly it was to be an *independent* project – even Shelagh Rogers, the CBC host, rolled her eyes at this prospect. Her son sat for hours of frustration that affected the whole family as he tried desperately to figure out what to write about. I advised the mother to sit at the computer and scribe for him, allowing him to use his oral literacy skills while she assumed the task of recording. Initially, she thought that she might be robbing him of the learning opportunity assigned, but I argued that she would alternatively be robbing him and herself of Spring Break. Shelagh reminded everyone that the title *Spring Break* did have the word *break* in it!

GUIDELINE 58
WRITE LESS TO GET MORE *CONT'D*

· · · · ·

Sometimes by

doing less we get

more, and that

more stays

with us longer.

THE homework task, which had already taken two days resulting in only a few sentences on paper and hours of groans in the air, was later completed in 20 minutes. In my capacity as a school counsellor, when working with boys who underachieve I often found that scribing helped them to get their ideas out. It helped them build writing confidence as they see their words in black and white and that they have said something of value. To presume that scribing provides too much help – or even cheating is simply misguided.

Before leaving this topic, there is one more story to relate about writing assignments which ask for too much writing, the wrong kind of writing, or even writing at the wrong time. All can be counterproductive, especially with boys. Bring to mind a school field trip that your son has been looking forward to for some time – perhaps to the local aquarium park where he has never been. You have gone online together exploring his options, perhaps planning how he will navigate the park to take in the sites that are most valued by him. You've even had a rich questioning dialogue about

"NO, DON'T LOOK AT IT. DON'T LOOK! IF YOU LOOK AT IT YOU WILL HAVE TO WRITE ABOUT IT!"

the ethics of marine life in captivity. Long before the actual event preparatory talk has been rewarding in itself.

Now, imagine him standing in front of the largest tank, the one he has been anticipating looking at for weeks, with arms outstretched and eyes closed—on the edge of frustrated tears. He is overheard yelling: "No, don't look at it. Don't look! If you look at it you will have to write about it!"

Sometimes writing at the wrong time, such as during a significant experience, can rob students of unadulterated pleasure, inquiry, and exploration. There will be of course a few field trips where it is appropriate for students to be recording written ideas – but mostly not. The majority of teachers know that learning can be expressed other ways, such as talking.

GUIDELINE 59
VALUE QUIET AND SOCIAL READING

• • • • •

Boys can be turned off literacy altogether by a doctrinaire approach to silent reading.

THE intent of SSR – sustained silent reading – is to provide students with regular time to read and develop their independent reading skills. It is worthy of pursuit, especially if you will allow me to add a *boy smarts* caveat. What many educators realize is that boys who struggle with text experience a tortuous isolation during silent reading, especially if they have other anxieties.

Boys can be turned off literacy altogether by a doctrinaire approach to silent reading. I recall a visit from an upset father who indicated that his son was sent home from school because he refused to follow the SSR rules. As it turns out the rules of SSR engagement in his classroom were fraught with rigid dogma and unsound teaching practice: 1) the student must read a novel; 2) it must be a reasonably thick novel; 3) the student may not change the novel – must stick with it; and, 4) the student's eyes must be on the pages throughout the 20 minutes. A monitor sat and recorded who broke the rules and would later report the offending student to the principal for discipline. Even I felt a little panicky imagining how I might respond.

I CAN BRING TO MIND ONE BOY WHO REGULARLY SAT WITH THE TELEPHONE BOOK DURING SUSTAINED SILENT READING SESSIONS.

I shall not expound on the obvious demerits of this particular interpretation of SSR use in the classroom; instead, I would like to review what does work – especially with boys. Permit boys to exchange material when they become bored. Loosen up the criteria of what reading material is allowed. As you will recall from an earlier chapter, boys' verbal abilities typically develop about a year and a half later than girls, so it stands to reason that reading capability mimics this developmental difference. It was the philosopher Rousseau who suggested that children learn best from short notes and letters related to their immediate interests. Over and over again, I have found that boys prefer to read magazines about fixing things, or enjoy the pleasure offered by fact books while skipping from one topic to the next. I can bring to mind one boy who regularly sat with the telephone book during SSR.

GUIDELINE 59
VALUE QUIET AND SOCIAL READING *CONT'D*

• • • • •

To read without

reflecting is like

eating without

digesting.

TO further build on literacy development, a useful classroom variation of SSR is STAR – sustained talk about reading. *Star* was born out of a classroom meeting decision with a group of students I taught. After the SSR allotted time, which varied according to students' age and abilities, the next ten to fifteen minutes were devoted to talk about what students had just read, or, for some reluctant readers, even about the illustrations or photos that interested them most.

The blend of focussed quiet reading followed by lively conversation, embeds literacy in a child's social world, preparing him for an adult career typically requiring more oral literacy than written.

Edmond Burke, Irish political philosopher, and statesman, said, "To read without reflecting is like eating without digesting." While doing comes easily to most boys, the capacity for reflective thought needs to be nurtured and encouraged. Boys need to talk about what intrigues them.

• • • • •

GUIDELINE 60
BECOME LITERATE ABOUT ADVERSITY

LITERACY can help people deal with adversity in a number of ways. Literacy gives people the knowledge needed to seek out resources, sift, sort, and evaluate selected information. It also helps people rehearse different responses to challenges in their imagination in writing, or in speaking. Finally, it helps people acquire the self-knowledge necessary to adapt to unanticipated changes and adversity.

While intelligence quotient (IQ), purportedly measures raw intelligence, and emotional quotient (EQ), measures emotional intelligence, adversity quotient (AQ) measures the ability to thrive in the face of adversity – to be resilient. While I have experienced difficulty advocating the notion of emotional intelligence with some educators and parents, AQ is more easily accepted.

GUIDELINE **60**
BECOME LITERATE ABOUT ADVERSITY *CONT'D*

• • • • •

Individuals with

high AQ

take greater

responsibility to

solve problems

and do not

blame others for

their setbacks.

AS adversity can take any form and magnitude, from major tragedies to minor annoyances, adversity quotient is a measure of how an individual perceives and deals with all kinds of challenges. Individuals with high AQ take greater responsibility to solve problems and do not blame others for their setbacks. They are more likely to believe that the problems they face are limited in scope and can be dealt with effectively. Those who can't handle adversity become emotionally overwhelmed more easily, are more likely to pull back and stop trying. A book called *Resilience: The Power to Bounce Back When the Going Gets Tough* argues that falling apart is sometimes a healthier response than a resolute all's well approach. That those who then re-integrate and re-organize after falling apart are more resilient than those who are more armoured.

Paul Stilts, the architect of AQ proposes that there are essentially three kinds of AQ - climbers, campers, and quitters. High AQ climbers are people who seek challenges and welcome change. Campers constitute the majority of the population and resist surrendering comfort, no matter what the cost of staying put. Quitters are those who are risk-averse and flee from challenges. Although the continuum of AQ is more nuanced and complicated than these three types, parents and teachers usually want boys to develop their abilities to tolerate adversity and to bounce back, even thrive at times of stress and disruption.

The ultimate goal of developing literacy in children is to ensure that they develop a lifelong love of learning and become happy

LITERACY GIVES PEOPLE THE KNOWLEDGE NEEDED TO SEEK OUT RESOURCES, SIFT, AND EVALUATE SELECTED INFORMATION.

and responsible contributing members of society. Instead of the engendered rules of stoicism in the boy-code, boys need guidance and the keys to communicate and write about their feelings and emotions as they learn about managing adversity. Although boys prefer to write in basic ways to communicate information and fact, expanding their literacy skills will help them to move further along the road toward resiliency and become better equipped to adapt to unwelcome change and respond to it creatively.

PROVIDING
ACTIVE **LEARNING** ·····

The great end of life is not knowledge, but action.
Aldous Huxley

There has been explosive growth in the availability of online instruction and virtual schools complementing traditional instruction.

The technology that has so dramatically changed the world outside of schools is now changing the learning and teaching environment within. Sometimes, the students themselves drive this, born and comfortable in the age of the Internet. There has been explosive growth in the availability of online instruction and virtual schools complementing traditional instruction. Tests can now be taken online, giving students, teachers and parents, almost instantaneous feedback.

Despite this growth in communication technology, many boys frequently tell me that their passion for learning seems to shrink – at school anyway. In a world where time can be measured in nanoseconds, the real challenge in schools isn't about morals and misbehaviour; it is about keeping up with students' ideas. This can be challenging when video games are networked over phone lines and boys talk to each other, and blow each other away onscreen. Some people wonder how schools can compete with that?

LEARNING IS NOT A **SPECTATOR SPORT**

• • • • •

Tell me,

I forget;

Show me,

I remember;

Involve me,

I understand.

ONE DAY, while I was sitting in the dentist chair I overheard a conversation between two women, who apparently had not seen each other for a while. They caught my attention as they chatted about schooling and their young boys who were running them ragged. In particular, I was struck by the comment, "My son used to like learning until he went to school." She went on to describe how restless he was, and how he found it boring and restrictive. While I silently felt for his circumstances, I also acknowledged that schools have come a long way since I was in Grade 1 and had my right leg tied to the desk to help me remain seated. Institutional change happens slowly over time but still the theme remains– boys need to move.

I too must acknowledge my preference for activity when I use the cordless telephone so that I may enjoy a saunter around the house or garden while talking with a friend or family member. The stationary phone seems so restrictive. As I consider the struggle that some boys have with a lack of activity in the classroom I recall the Chinese proverb – *Tell me, I forget; Show me, I remember; Involve me, I understand.* This brings to mind one particular 7 year-old boy, Pankajeet, who was exceptionally bright, verbal, and pleasant to converse with.

From his first day at school Pankajeet's parents were concerned. He had always been a busy boy and they wondered how he would accept the new rules of Kindergarten. Although he was excited about having other kids to play with at school, he had trouble sitting in circle-time or even at his group's table. When his parents had enrolled him in a karate class the previous year, hoping that it would help him socially and also channel some of his exuberant energy, he regularly broke rank and ran laps around the gym. He continued with his preference for laps around the class and resisted the teacher's efforts to rein him in. Around the third week he decided that Kindergarten was not for him although the teacher tried diligently to engage him in group activities. With coaxing he reluctantly gave it a shot, but persisted in being a handful. Grade 1 was no better as he found himself increasingly in trouble for disrupting the class. He was also having difficulty keeping friends, as his rambunctious behaviour was somewhat annoying even to them. Clearly something had to be done.

THANKFULLY Pankajeet's parents, teacher, and principal could all see that this bright boy had an expressed need for movement and they worked with him to develop a plan for frequent activity breaks every 10 minutes. In fact, that even included running laps. When Pankajeet understood that he was expected to get up and move every ten minutes it helped him settle into his work and sometimes he even decided to pass on the opportunity to run. Although this strategy might not work for every busy boy, it was tailored to Pankajeet's needs by giving him permission to be active and had the paradoxical effect of settling him.

· · · · ·

Boys need to utilize all their senses as they interact with the world.

Learning is not a spectator sport. Most educators acknowledge that the restless children are often boys; bright ones, quiet ones, boisterous ones, and misbehaving ones. We need to provide them with effective and affirming ways to use their energy.

To sit and listen just isn't engaging enough. Boys need to utilize all their senses as they interact with the world. Walking, talking, drawing, writing, laughing, singing, acting about what they are learning, relating it to past experiences, and applying it to their daily lives keeps learning alive and motivating. Movement strengthens the development of neurons and encapsulates information in the brain so it can be recalled more easily later. Active learning helps kids to take ownership for what they learn because

FIND A WAY TO MAKE LEARNING ACTIVE AND YOU'LL CAPTURE BOYS' MOTIVATION.

they put their whole self into it and as a result make it a part of themselves. For most boys this involves a lot of bustle and commotion – many preferring wide-open spaces. They want to walk, explore, see what their bodies can do, run, trip, fall, ride bikes, skateboard, get a job, learn to drive a car, and master their latest computer game which involves spatial activity despite holding their body relatively still.

ONE exuberant boy that I taught came up with his own active learning idea during a classroom meeting that grabbed everyone's excitement. While discussing how we might want to present our tall tales, which we were about to begin writing, we often identified the audience first as it gave the activity some authenticity. Reid suggested that we make the tall tales actually become tall, really tall. I smile as I recall the instant passion that erupted and ensuing design models for the physical lengthening of prose. For most of the boys, and a few girls, attention focussed on adding more to their story to make it taller. We negotiated criteria that slowed them down somewhat, but with such motivation to write tall tales they were unstoppable and engaged whole-heartedly in this writing adventure. The tallest tale ran eventually across the ceiling and down the wall to the baseboard. I can still see Reid's grin when he was announced the winner of the tall tale competition.

MOVEMENT AND ACTIVITIES JUST MAKE SENSE.
BRAIN SCIENTISTS SWEAR BY IT!

Even when doing something as benign as waiting for the bus I have witnessed boys creating a hullabaloo. I once observed some bus stop boys setting up a target on the sidewalk and then spitting coke to see who could reach the farthest. I have a cherished photo of a very bright boy named Mike who won the school district's Grade 4 chess championship. Imagine this, about 100 children – 90% boys – were competing in the gymnasium, with hardly a one sitting properly and many of them preferring to stand and shift weight foot to foot while playing. In the photo Mike is standing on his chair towering over the chessboard in a state of deep concentration – a trance – knees flexed, muscles engaged and every now and then shifting weight, anticipating future moves. When lessons in school are dynamic they capture a boys' interest and hold it there.

When lessons in school are dynamic they capture a boys' interest and hold it there.

GUIDELINE 61
GET ACTIVE!

• • • • •

More than 50% of

Canadian children

and youth aged

5 to 17 are not

active enough for

optimal growth.

AT the turn of the millennium the World Health Organization offered a disquieting study indicating that many of our children and youth are at risk for numerous health problems due to inactivity. It reported that less than one-third of young people from industrialized and developing nations are sufficiently active to benefit their present and future health and well-being. In Canada, a similar report called *Canada's Children and Youth: A Physical Activity Profile,* found that over half of Canadian children and youth aged 5 to 17 are not active enough for optimal growth. As the activity alarm bells ring we must acknowledge significant decreases in school physical education and increased time in which youth are sedentary. In an attempt to boost health everywhere, the World Health Organization encouraged countries to reverse these trends, with the school settings being identified as having the most promising impact on public health. The active schools movement has since swept across the globe, and in British Columbia, Action Schools were born. I invite you to visit their website, ***actionschoolsbc.ca***, for details on how to access material, ideas, and practical know-how.

IN order to help activate schools and increase physical activity, *Action Schools! BC* **has identified six zones of movement to promote diverse physical activities throughout the day. Their website identifies them as the following:**

• **School Environment** – makes healthy choices the easy choices for schools by creating safe, active, and inclusive environments

• **Scheduled Physical Education** – supports the curriculum goal to deliver 150 minutes of scheduled physical education per week

• **Classroom Action** – provides creative, alternative classroom physical activity ideas that complement scheduled physical education and support the curriculum

• **Family and Community** – fosters the development of partnerships with families and community practitioners to benefit from the wealth of resources available to promote and encourage active living

• **Extra-Curricular** – balances classroom action and physical education with a variety of opportunities for students, school staff and families to be physically active before and after school, and during lunch and recess

• **School Spirit** – cultivates school spirit by encouraging physical activity and celebrating the benefits of active living for the whole school

GUIDELINE 62
ACCOMMODATE LEARNING STYLES

• • • • •

The information

explosion of

modern times

necessitates so

much more from

students

these days.

IN the schools of days long ago, there was a standard set of facts that everybody should know and it was called *Normal School*. It offered a uniform assessment of all students using paper and pencil instruments, which yielded percentile ranks and stanines for all pupils nation-wide. Venturing off the explicit track set out by the *Normal School* inspectors was forbidden. It was a relatively straightforward affair as there was a certain amount of knowledge people had to learn. Learning one's ABC's and times-tables are examples of *Normal School* language still in existence today. The information explosion of modern times necessitates so much more from students these days. More information has been produced in the last 30 years than in the previous 5,000. Internet search engines have even catalogued one-sixth of the total information available and Internet traffic is doubling every 100 days. We are preparing boys for a world that we do not know. It's been a truism since Sputnik that we must continually raise educational standards because technological advances require ever-higher educational achievement by anyone hoping to be gainfully employed.

Fortunately, there are many roads to learning. Students bring different talents and styles of learning to the classroom. Brilliant students in the gym may be all thumbs in the art studio. If we give boys opportunities to show their talents and learn in ways that work for them, they can then be pushed to learn in new ways that do not come so easily. Because learning requires changes in beliefs and behaviour, it normally produces a mild level of anxiety. Movement facilitates the reduction in worry and angst.

> MORE INFORMATION HAS BEEN PRODUCED IN THE LAST 30 YEARS THAN IN THE PREVIOUS 5,000.

We each have a range of human intellectual potential which can be developed and give us more options. Much current teaching and assessment only takes into account linguistic and logical intelligence; thus school is very biased toward a certain kind of mind and against all of those who haven't developed that particular blend of intellectual strength.

GUIDELINE 62
ACCOMMODATE LEARNING STYLES *CONT'D*

• • • • •

Dr. Howard

Gardner forced

people to

re-evaluate the

definition of

intelligence and in

so doing, altered

our approach

to learning and

teaching.

THE concept of multiple intelligences, for example, started as a theory in the halls of Harvard University and has now grown to be one of the most influential movements in teaching effectiveness. Instead of seeing the mind as possessing finite quantities of a substance known as intelligence, Dr. Howard Gardner, the originator of the theory, rephrased the concept of intelligence, defining it as a person's ability to solve problems and create useful products. In doing so, he opened the door for not one but many intelligences, as we have many different ways of solving problems and learning. His work forced people to re-evaluate not only the definition of intelligence but also our approach to learning and teaching. The following is a brief summary of Gardner's eight intelligences:

- **Verbal/Linguistic** intelligence consists of the ability to think in words and to use language to express and appreciate complex meanings
- **Logical-mathematical** intelligence makes it possible to calculate, quantify, consider propositions and hypotheses, and carry out complex mathematical operations
- **Spatial** intelligence instills the capacity to think in three-dimensional ways, as do sailors, pilots, sculptors, painters, and architects
- **Bodily-kinesthetic** intelligence enables one to manipulate objects and fine-tune physical skills
- **Musical** intelligence is evident in those who possess a sensitivity to pitch, melody, rhythm, and tone
- **Interpersonal** intelligence is the capacity to understand and interact effectively with others
- **Intra-personal** intelligence refers to the ability to construct an accurate perception of one's self and to use such knowledge in planning and directing one's life
- **Naturalist** intelligence consists of observing patterns in nature, in identifying and classifying objects, and understanding natural and human-made systems.

You will notice that only two out of the eight intelligences are suited for the *Normal School,* the rest just don't fit. As you reflect on your son or the boys you teach you will be able to uncover many more intelligences and each boy with his own unique way of learning.

CHAPTER EIGHT

GUIDELINE 63
RESPECT GENDER LEARNING PREFERENCES

• • • • •

Children benefit

when we

understand what

their biases are so

that we may then

seek to provide

varied learning

experiences to

facilitate boys

and girls.

IN addition to considering multiple intelligences discussed in the previous chapter, *Boys and Girls Learn Differently,* authored by Michael Gurian, describes the typical learning biases that are most associated to each gender. While there are many exceptions to the rule, and children are like snowflakes with no two brains being alike, see if you can identify which gendered bias is typically attributed to boys or girls:

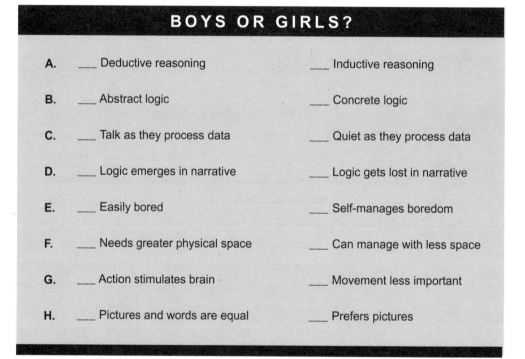

BOYS OR GIRLS?

A.	___ Deductive reasoning	___ Inductive reasoning
B.	___ Abstract logic	___ Concrete logic
C.	___ Talk as they process data	___ Quiet as they process data
D.	___ Logic emerges in narrative	___ Logic gets lost in narrative
E.	___ Easily bored	___ Self-manages boredom
F.	___ Needs greater physical space	___ Can manage with less space
G.	___ Action stimulates brain	___ Movement less important
H.	___ Pictures and words are equal	___ Prefers pictures

Remember that the answers on the next page may not apply to all boys, but certainly the bulk of them. Again, while some boys and girls may fit the descriptions, some may have learning preferences that are dissimilar.

GUIDELINE 63
RESPECT GENDER LEARNING PREFERENCES *CONT'D*

- - - - -

Boys require

more varied

stimulation to

keep them

attentive.

	ANSWERS

A. While boys process from a general principle to application, girls prefer examples and build on their conceptualization.

B. Boys tend to be better at not touching an object and still being able to calculate it –especially true with physics and advanced math.

C. Even in working groups, girls use more words than boys – except in boy groups where the higher status boys use more words.

D. Girls listen better and feel more secure in the complex flow of conversation and have less need to control conversation with dominance or logic.

E. Boys require more varied stimulation to keep them attentive.

F. Boy's need more physical space.

G. Movement seems to help boys not only stimulate their brains but also manage and relieve impulsive behaviour.

H. Pictures stimulate the right brain. In literature boys prefer imagining the movement while girls ponder the emotional workings of the character.

Children benefit when we understand what their biases are so that we may then seek to provide varied learning experiences that are both engaging and also honour their preferences. It also prevents us from misinterpreting their behaviour as is often the case with boys who appear rude but may be primarily expressing their need for more space to move and interact.

CHAPTER EIGHT

MAKE LEARNING RELEVANT

WHEN I consider the problems today's young people will have to face including global warming and other changes in climate, disastrous ups and downs in our interlinked financial markets, worldwide unemployment, more than a billion people living in deprivation, disappearing soils and forests, oppressive governments and corporations, and a stratified economic system that rewards the most wealthy among us, it seems that the least we could do is make school relevant.

The most powerful way to learn something is to use it.

Boys are more attentive to learning when relevant topics are taught along with suggestions for integration of new concepts into existing ones. If after a great deal of deliberation no relevance can be found avoid teaching that topic.

WHEN LEARNING IS RELEVANT INTERNAL MOTIVATION IS LONGER LASTING AND MORE SELF-DIRECTIVE.

The most powerful way to learn something is to use it. Boys have a tendency to be hands-on, as demonstrated when birthday gifts are opened, instructions ignored and a boy sets in to discover for himself how to make something work. When learning is relevant internal motivation is longer lasting and more self-directive than is external motivation, which must be repeatedly reinforced by praise or concrete rewards. I have often marveled at a boy's capacity to read complicated and lengthy *cheats* on the Internet to assist them to solve a computer game they are fascinated with. Make learning relevant and you will find that boys will not only become internally motivated but they will also grow to be better prepared for a world beyond school.

GUIDELINE 65
ENCOURAGE COOPERATIVE LEARNING

· · · · ·

Research

strongly

supports the

advantages

of cooperative

learning over

competition.

THE cooperation flag has been waving for some time, and for good reason. Both schools and the corporate world point to increased results with an emphasis on collaboration. Research strongly supports the advantages of cooperative learning over competition and individualized learning in a wide array of learning tasks. Compared to competitive or individual work, cooperation leads to higher group and individual achievement, higher-quality reasoning strategies, more frequent transfer of these from the group to individual members, and more new ideas and solutions to problems. In addition, students working in cooperative groups tend to be more intrinsically motivated, intellectually curious, caring of others, and psychologically healthy.

HUNDREDS OF STUDIES CONFIRM THAT WORKING TOGETHER TO ACHIEVE COMMON GOALS PRODUCES HIGHER ACHIEVEMENT AND GREATER PRODUCTIVITY THAN WORKING ALONE.

Students are linked with others so that the success of each depends on teamwork and teaches positive interdependence. Each student is held accountable through assessments that are shared with the student and the group. Students help, support, encourage, and praise others in their small groups as they learn and work together. Students also form strong personal relationships with their teammates applying skills such as leadership, decision-making, trust building, communication, and conflict management. Finally, students discuss their common learning goals, the procedures they follow to achieve the goals, and their progress, problems, and success as individuals and as a team.

GUIDELINE 65
ENCOURAGE COOPERATIVE LEARNING *CONT'D* • • • • •

THE number of possible cooperative and active learning tasks is limitless. *The Thinking Aloud Paired Problem Solving (TAPPS)* method is arguably one of the most powerful classroom instructional techniques for promoting understanding. It has four simple steps that make learning *hum* and supports learning through explaining and providing quiet time for introverted students:

- Teacher poses question and provides quiet time for students to think.

- Teacher designates the explainer and listener within each dyad.

- Explainers explain ideas to listeners. Listeners can ask questions of clarification, disagree, or provide hints when explainers becomes lost.

- Teacher critiques some explainers' answers and provides closure.

Hundreds of studies confirm that working together to achieve common goals produces higher achievement and greater productivity than working alone. Johnson and Johnson's research reports that students in cooperative classrooms, compared with those in competitive classrooms, have higher-level reasoning, more fluent and better ideas for solving problems, and greater transfer of learning from one situation to another.

GUIDELINE 66
UNDERSTAND COMPETITION

• • • • •

Boys argue

that they use

competition in

order to motivate

themselves.

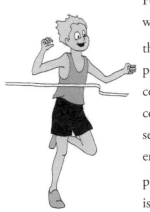

WITH the exception of sports, competition is unofficially forbidden in schools. This can be unsettling to many adults who know that the market economy is based on competition and their child will some day grow up and have to find his or her place in this world. The struggle between cooperating and competing is firmly rooted in gender roles. Women tend to value being sensitive and maintaining good relationships while men tend to value gaining status by following the rules. Since our society prizes individual success, women's orientation toward caring for others and/or cooperatively building a sense of community is often considered to be of lesser importance. These value differences are reflected in the gender roles established by our culture.

Is it possible that we need both – cooperation and competition?

Is it also probable that both cooperation and competition can be utilized in schools?

Polarization keeps the cooperation-competition argument going, but the main question is which approach helps boys and girls to learn and excel in school? While I have professed the merits of collaborative learning, boys' perspectives about competition warrant consideration. I have observed that competition between male friends is often seen as part and parcel of the classroom environment. To many boys it is a natural part of their everyday experience. Clearly, at times, there can be instances when competition is inappropriate, but mostly boys argue that they use competition in order to motivate themselves.

THE STRUGGLE BETWEEN COOPERATING AND COMPETING IS FIRMLY ROOTED IN GENDER ROLES.

GUIDELINE 66
UNDERSTAND COMPETITION *CONT'D*

• • • • •

Boys know that

competition is just

for fun and that

it provides them

with an opportunity

to celebrate their

achievement.

BOYS see competition between friends as casual and part of the learning environment rather than dominating the learning exclusively – and there is a sense of malarkey about competing. They know that it's just for fun and that it provides them with an opportunity to celebrate their achievement. One boy recently said to me, "It's good to have a race between friends 'cause they don't care if you beat them 'cause next time they'll beat you." From this standpoint, competition is understood as just part of the relationship, as a way of maintaining and promoting friendships. Boys have also told me that despite the notion that they aren't fast enough to be number one, they still like joining the race to be part of the group and enjoy the fun. It also stands to reason that if boys see their fathers as more competitive than their mothers they will interpret this as a blessing on masculine competition. You only have to sit for a little while in a room with a father and son who love watching hockey on television to understand this.

DESPITE THE STUDIES TOUTED BY COOPERATIVE LEARNING EXPERTS, I BELIEVE THAT BOYS BENEFIT WHEN WE UNDERSTAND AND RESPECT THEIR AFFILIATION FOR FRIENDLY COMPETITION.

I recently attended a spinning class – cycling with a group of people on a stationary bicycle – and appreciated that the young male instructor was using competitive phrases to try and get a sense of challenge going among us. At one point he teased us with a cocky grin, "Look up ahead there's another group – let's get them! Yea, we're bad to the bone," he exclaimed as four of us male riders smiled in return. The other eight female riders seemed oblivious to the jocularity. Perhaps they noticed but didn't feel comfortable to join in our exchange of grins.

GUIDELINE **66**
UNDERSTAND COMPETITION *CONT'D*

COMPETITION does not always have to be about sports. Last year, while presenting the keynote address at the Calgary Boys' Conference, I invited the Calgary Boys' Choir to be a part of my presentation. They sang beautifully. Afterwards, I interviewed this group of boys ranging in age from 4 to 24 about what exactly it was that inspired them to learn. They responded with most of the preferences I have mentioned thus far. When it came to the topic of competition their eyes lit up and they provided rich examples of how rivalry works in their choir practice, "Yea, when anyone hits a note wrong we keep track. I love singing and it's fun to do it with friends."

Despite the studies touted by cooperative learning experts, I believe that boys benefit when we understand and respect their affiliation for friendly competition and find a way to honour its presence in the classroom. After all, in the real world boys and girls have to negotiate both cooperation and competition. Our task is to make sense of which one is most appropriate for which learning experience. When the classroom imitates reality, boys and girls have a better chance of preparing themselves for their future.

• • • • •

GUIDELINE **67**
DEBATE

IN debating, the rules for engagement in the art of intellectual divergence are clearly defined. School debate programs are designed to teach public speaking, critical thinking, listening, and healthy dispute and are at the heart of classroom oral literacy initiatives. For boys in particular, debate can be an especially engaging, challenging, and exciting pursuit as it combines elements of competition with collaboration between individuals or teams. Debating requires creative thought, research, organizing of ideas, and practise – lots of it! Students learn to speak in front of audiences on a wide range of issues and also learn to think on their feet and utilize their skills to persuade, convince, and influence. Debate is a very challenging endeavour, but the skills learned will help boys to succeed in school, and beyond.

GUIDELINE 67
DEBATE *CONT'D*

• • • • •

Debate helps

students refine their

ideas and gives

them a structured

arena in which to

clash and disagree.

IT has often been said that, *if you don't stand up for anything, you'll fall for almost anything.* Debate helps students refine their ideas and gives them a structured arena in which to clash and disagree. Clark Moustakas, the popular psychologist, and advocate of play therapy for children, said, "Genuine learning always involves dialogue and encounter." Debate requires students to begin with a question, puzzle it out, develop their own perspective, and justify their conclusions. When their conclusions are challenged in thoughtful ways their thinking is pushed and expanded. Evaluation becomes more complicated than right or wrong and shades of grey become evident.

KIDS WHO DEBATE LEARN WHAT CHARLIE BROWN OFTEN STRUGGLED WITH, *IN THE BOOK OF LIFE,* THE ANSWERS AREN'T AT THE BACK.

While working with staff and students at the Calgary Science School, I learned that debate could make students' eyes light up in anticipation. Because they were taught a simple but well thought out structure, they learned to develop confidence in their abilities, beginning with opinion type debates such as which are better to have, cats or dogs? They later extended to more complicated questions such as, where should we send our garbage to be treated? At this school students begin by stating the pillars of their argument and then engage in respectful *clash*. Debates are relevant and extend inquiring minds. In debate, boys have the opportunity to get *all fired up* and channel their testosterone in useful ways that demands an element of rigor, sometimes missing for boys in many classrooms.

GUIDELINE **68**
ALLOW TIME TO FLOW

• • • • •

Jumping from

subject to subject

and worksheet

to worksheet

without relevance

or personal

commitment, only

trains our boys to

see the world in

sound bytes and

discourages their

engagement.

"TO pursue mental operations to any depth, a person has to learn to concentrate attention. Without focus, consciousness is in a state of chaos," says Mihaly Csikszenthmihalyi, author of *Finding Flow: The Psychology of Engagement with Everyday Life.* Without the ability to concentrate with absorbed focus we can walk through life unaware and out of touch with our deeper thoughts and emotions and are prone to bounce between extremes. During the day we can experience the anxiety and pressures of work, while during our leisure we can live in passive boredom. The key, according to Csikszenthmihalyi, is to challenge us with tasks that require a high degree of concentration and commitment. Instead of watching a video, play a musical instrument or take apart and fix a mechanical device.

It is in tunnels of passionate thought that students – and boys in particular as a result of their tendency toward singular contemplation – discover, investigate, and inquire from a deep place of internal motivation and feel truly content. Unfortunately, many boys will not find flow at school if they are not permitted time and reason to settle into profoundly relaxed and detailed exploration. Jumping from subject to subject and worksheet to worksheet without relevance or personal commitment only trains our boys to see the world in sound bytes and discourages their engagement.

I have often found in my recent work with boys who are at risk of dropping out of school, that their interests are rekindled when we provide them with time and coaching to concentrate and become absorbed in complete involvement, free of distraction. The key element for renewal in boys who are discouraged and unmotivated is to get them deeply involved in challenging but pleasurable activities. New research and insight on the role of inner-experience are destroying popular assumptions that emotions, such as passion, cloud logic. In their discussion of personal experience and emotion, Andy Hargreaves and Michael Fullan, authors of *Mentoring in the New Millennium*, indicate that feelings are actually indispensable to rational decision-making. I sometimes find that a boy's passion and intense engagement can be misread as anger. Passion is our mind and body's full flow of vitality; spiritual, mental, emotional, sensual, and physical. We were born to live passionately and to experience the highest forms of joy, love, and satisfaction.

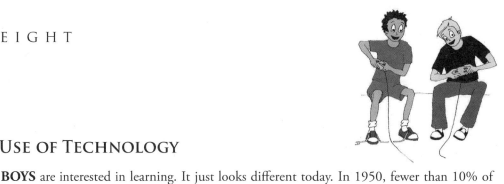

GUIDELINE 69
PROMOTE THE USE OF TECHNOLOGY

BOYS are interested in learning. It just looks different today. In 1950, fewer than 10% of American homes had television sets. Today, that figure has leveled off at around 97%. In the typical home at least one member is watching television more than six hours per day with the greatest amount of viewing being done by the very young. Drop into television culture, the Internet, video games, and other tools of technical wizardry and it is easy to understand why boys develop *two-second minds*. Do boys develop their fascination as a result of the technology, or does their penchant for technology result from a pre-disposition that is better addressed in this medium rather than others?

> ● ● ● ● ●
>
> Drop into television culture, the Internet, video games, and other tools of technical wizardry and it is easy to understand why boys develop *two-second* minds.

Many boys love some video games and not others because they find some challenging and yet attainable whereas others are boring – perhaps viewed as actual computer work.

> A GROUP OF BOYS USED MSN TO ARRANGE A FIGHT, UNBEKNOWNST TO THE TARGETED BOY!

Computers and the Internet are changing the way people learn. According to a report from the U.S. Education Department, 23% of preschoolers and 32% of kindergartners have gone online, primarily to visit interactive Web sites introducing letters and numbers. For older children, search engines and hyperlinks (those underlined words, phrases, or images that when clicked take you to a new Web page) have turned the online literary voyage into a kind of literary buffet – and futurists tell us that far more is yet to come. The range of technologies that encourage active learning is staggering. Many fall into one of three categories including tools and resources for learning-by-doing, time-delayed exchange, and real-time conversation. While many boys eat technology up, they often tell me that they know more than their parents and teachers.

GUIDELINE **69**
PROMOTE THE USE OF TECHNOLOGY *CONT'D*

· · · · ·

From digital

video, to digital

photography,

to the creation

of interactive

websites and

animations,

youth recognize

the power of

technology in

supporting their

right to be heard.

SOME boys use these tools for inappropriate reasons. At a colleague's high school, a group of boys used MSN to arrange a fight, unbeknownst to the targeted boy! The report, *Young Canadians In A Wired World,* found that, "most young people say they are not supervised regularly when they go online. Majorities say their parents never sit with them while they surf (68%), never use filters to block sites they don't want them to go to (65%), or never check to see which sites they've visited (54%). A majority of young people (55%) say their parents do check-in on them, sometimes or often, when they go online." When boys aggressively seek out computers and the world it opens, they need guidance to interpret – especially when the content is well beyond their years of understanding.

This age-gap in technological knowledge and comfort needs to be bridged if we are to tap into understanding a style of learning that many boys thrive on. Technology is not only an informational resource for our youth, but it gives them a hands-on method to voice their ideas and feelings. From digital video, to digital photograph, to the creation of interactive websites and animations, youth recognize the power of technology in supporting their right to be heard. In Vancouver, parents who are passionate about creating engaging and inquiring learning environments for their children are establishing an independent school called *Silbury School and Resource Centre,* and according to their website have attracted a lot of attention and inquiring minds – young and old. Rather than taking

WHEN BOYS AGGRESSIVELY SEEK OUT COMPUTERS AND THE WORLD IT OPENS, THEY NEED GUIDANCE.

boys to where we want them to learn, they are going to where learning is already thriving and abundant, like a robotics club for example – a meeting place for people who like building robots. Even the University of British Columbia's Engineering Department is getting in on the robot action and hosts an annual contest for students. This year they had to build a robot to rescue a doll. It entailed every aspect of mechanical design right down to writing the computer program. You might have guessed – all the voluntary participants were male. As technology widens its path in schools and more female teachers develop expertise, female students will follow. This can only benefit all students.

GUIDELINE 69
PROMOTE THE USE OF TECHNOLOGY *CONT'D*

IT is for these reasons and beyond that classroom practice should include more interactive teaching through the use of audio-visual instruction, CD-ROMs, electronic music studios, technical movie making, and the whole range of current multi-media tools, to name a few. It does not, however, automatically offer tonic to boys at the back of the room unless teachers are technologically literate or at least technologically facilitative. I've seen students with access to lots of technology, but I can't tell if the technology is being used to replicate workbooks or to develop the kinds of skills and practices needed to thrive in the future. The presence of technology by itself is no indicator of its effective use.

Let's face it, traditional teaching methods simply can't compete with the appeal of a media rich world of electronic games that makes children heroes or puts the fate of Harry Potter in their hands. Our challenge in education is to find a way to power up and meet boys half way so that they can do what they already like to do and girls can be encouraged to get on board too. It's not that our future depends on it, boys are simply unstoppable with it.

• • • • •

GUIDELINE 70
CONNECT WITH NATURE

THE introduction of *Nintendo 64* in 1996 was a seminal event in the recent history of boys' entertainment. It introduced 3-D graphics, the joystick and the ability to play *shoot 'em up* games that allowed competing against friends inside where weather was insignificant. Almost overnight, neighbourhood play shifted from outdoors to indoors.

With boys inside on computers, I wonder about what they are not doing? If delight deficiency disorder can result in stress and a loss of passion, what does nature deficiency disorder cause among males glued to their screens? It appears that kids have never before been so separate from nature and the cause may not be technology alone. Other possibilities include urbanization, parental fear about abduction, overly structured childhoods, and more. It is worth considering whether decreased opportunities to interact with nature may have far-reaching negative consequences.

GUIDELINE 70
CONNECT WITH NATURE *CONT'D*

• • • • •

Boys are more likely to be able to identify Pokemon characters than the trees and insects found in their front yards.

FOR many children, natural spaces where they can freely roam are nonexistent. I recall as a boy spending endless hours on my bike exploring the neighbourhood and weeks in pursuit of that gopher not to far away in a farmer's field. While *Who Has Seen the Wind*, by W.O. Mitchell, depicted the childhood reflection and rich boredom of bygone years, today's boys have more restrictions and some have never even played on a farm or in wide-open spaces. Making matters worse, playgrounds and even neighbourhoods follow sterile and structured designs often aimed at minimizing litigation. Corporate developers often win debates over open space and boys are more likely to be able to identify Pokemon characters than the trees and insects found in their front yards. Many schools have replaced recess with structured activity and after-school hours are filled with homework and adult-supervised activities. Indeed the folks, who at the turn of the last century complained of the decrease of outdoor exposure among children due to the decline in family farming, might be abhorred if they knew about the absence of fresh air activity for kids today.

NATURE CAN BE VERY THERAPEUTIC. THE GREAT OUTDOORS IS BILLED AS AN ANTIDOTE FOR EVERYTHING FROM STRESS TO LOW SELF-ESTEEM TO DEPRESSION.

Outdoor pursuits can also have a positive effect on *attention-deficit disorder* as well as confidence, critical thinking and decision-making. Fortunately, green urbanism (city designs that incorporate natural spaces), is one way to counteract the shrinking green space trend and is becoming prized by consumers looking for a place to call home. One easy to-do idea to encourage young boys to get outside is to leave a part of the back yard wild and free and messy and dirty so they can build forts and dig holes and hunt for bugs there. We can do the same at schools. We just have to have kids change from their designer clothing before they head outside for recess – maybe into overalls?

GUIDELINE 70
CONNECT WITH NATURE *CONT'D*

• • • • •

Boys need to

learn about

nature's cycles

and processes

and the

regenerative

power it holds.

THE great statesman and past president of the Czech Republic, Vaclav Havel, poet and playwright once remarked, "We must draw our standards from the natural world. We must honour with the humility of the wise the bounds of that natural world and the mystery which lies beyond them, admitting that there is something in the order of being which evidently exceeds our competence."

If our environment is in as much trouble as we think, it only stands to reason that we encourage boys to play out-of-doors so that they develop an appreciation and affinity for nature and its place in their hearts. Boys need to learn about nature's cycles and processes and the regenerative power it holds.

Boys, and girls for that matter, need to learn that a solar cell is inspired by the ways in which a leaf works, or that all our inventions have already appeared in nature in more elegant ways and at much less cost to the planet. Even the most clever architectural supports are already featured in lily pads and bamboo stems. A bat's multi-frequency transmission is far superior to our most advanced radar. Boys need encouragement and opportunity to connect with nature.

DISCIPLINE THAT
TEACHES RATHER THAN PUNISHES

In high school, I was the class comedian as opposed to the class clown. The difference is, the class clown is the guy who drops his pants at the football game, the class comedian is the guy who talked him into it.

Billy Crystal

● ● ● ● ●

Boys see many

examples of

rudeness

every day.

We see many models of misbehaviour on television, at sporting events, at work sites, in shopping malls, and even among our elected leaders. I recall a recent incident in my own neighbourhood when we took our small dogs for a walk. As we sauntered along, a large, unleashed dog came charging up to us. Since his male owner appeared around the corner, I politely asked him to call off his dog and casually reminded him that dogs were supposed to be leashed in this park. This middle-aged man swore at me, continued walking, ignoring my request to leash his dog so that we could walk in peace. Boys see many examples of this sort of rudeness every day.

The Vanier Institute of the Family reported Bjorkqvist and Niemela's extensive Scandinavian review of worldwide literature on aggression and concluded that culture, not gender, is the best predictor of aggression. In North America, the culture of masculinity among boys encourages boys to sharpen their maleness on the whetstone of the school's authority structure.

CHAPTER NINE

JONATHAN'S **STORY**

• • • • •

This story of

Jonathan illustrates

an imaginative

and empathic way

of transforming

a boy's restless,

unconstructive

energy into

something positive.

THE most experienced teachers struggle with how to discipline boys who are unruly. Is it possible that there is anything redeemable in a boy's aggression? Consider the following story.

Jonathan, a bright and active eight year-old, was at it again. Much to his teacher's dismay he was up wandering in the classroom for the third time during the lesson. While she kept trying to teach, other students were giggling, more focussed on Jonathan than on their math. The class was on the brink of chaos. She had tried asking Jonathan to return to his seat, but he would either ignore her request or say something rude. She had tried removing privileges and disallowing his participation in his favorite activities. Nothing ever worked.

Ms. Brown called an emergency meeting with Jonathan's parents, only to discover that they were having similar problems at home. Jonathan had recently been refusing to do his chores, instead busying himself with projects he preferred. Both parents had a no-nonsense authoritative parenting style and could not understand why their son was defying them. Even the eldest brother Tom had started pushing Jonathan to toe the line.

EVENTUALLY THE COUNSELLOR REALIZED THAT HE WANTED TO BE THE CLASSROOM BOOKMAKER!

A school-based team meeting was called and it was agreed that the school counsellor, Ms. Kari, would meet with Jonathan. "Sounds like you are a boy who is good at being in charge," Ms. Kari said during her first meeting with Jonathan. "Tell me about what you get to be the boss of here, at school?" "Nothin'—nobody lets me do nothin' 'round here," Jonathan barked. After some further exploration of how angry he felt with everyone at home and at school telling him what to do, Ms. Kari inquired about what he would like to be in charge of in the classroom. Jonathan thought for a moment then said that last week they had made some really cool books in the shape of rocket ships and that he would like to make more of those. Eventually the counsellor realized that he wanted to be the classroom bookmaker! "What do you need for materials?" Ms. Kari asked. Jonathan outlined a list that included grown-up scissors, special paper, string, and drawing tools. He agreed that he would complete his class work before going to the bookmaking center to ply his new found trade. He also agreed that he would leave all materials at the bookmaking desk and not spread them around the class.

• • • • •

After he had made

more than enough

books for possible

class projects,

he was given the

opportunity to

take orders from

other primary

classrooms.

Ms. Kari and Ms. Brown, who was very much onboard, gathered the materials and left them in a bookmaker's box outside the classroom door where Jonathan claimed them and took them to their designated spot the following morning. The teacher knew that there is nothing worse then being given a job and then being told exactly how to perform it.

Jonathan thrived as the classroom bookmaker. He appeared much happier as he attended to his schoolwork and spent every spare moment making books. After he had made more than enough books for possible class projects, he was given the opportunity to take orders from other primary classrooms. He especially appreciated the book order he received for an important diary that the principal required.

Of course, creative solutions are not forever. Around the third week into this venture, Ms. Brown noticed that Jonathan had begun to leave large scissors in other parts of the classroom. He was also not bee-lining to the book making center as he had been. She astutely guessed that he was becoming bored. She asked whether he wanted to continue as the classroom bookmaker or perhaps be in charge of something new. Jonathan identified another interesting project, but agreed to be in charge of training another student to take over the book making center. For his third week he became Head Bookmaker Trainer. His interest soared once again and held until he moved on to his next undertaking.

WHY ARE BOYS OVER-REPRESENTED **IN BEHAVIOUR PROGRAMS?**

THE over-representation of boys in behaviour support programs has been attributed to a number of possible causes. Unlike girls, who tend to keep their problems private and contain their emotions or show them in subtle ways, boys tend to put on performances. Girls tend more to present themselves as being sad or depressed but boys more commonly act-out. Their externalizing behaviour is more disturbing and difficult to manage especially in classrooms where teachers require lengthy periods of seatwork and attention to cognitive tasks.

Parents often tell me that they suspect boys' lower achievement results are linked with their misbehaviour. It's true that some adults resent children who are difficult to teach. If they expect these *hard to manage* children to do worse than others, they may even give them lower marks.

WHAT IS THE PURPOSE **OF DISCIPLINE?**

• • • • •

Conversation

Peace: Restorative

Action in

Secondary Schools

is a valuable

resource that

includes a student

workbook and a

trainer manual.

WHEN boys misbehave in schools, how do we teach them that they are directly accountable for their actions and help them to integrate their learning? We have come a long way from thinking that corporal punishment that involves not sparing the rod, the cane, or the paddle would ever be justified. We have come to understand that it increases the likelihood of antisocial behaviour and abuse further down the road.

One meaning of discipline is the teaching of appropriate behaviour. An approach to discipline that takes the idea of teaching this very seriously is *Restorative Action*. This approach prevents harm escalation, and strengthens students and their community. It invites full participation and consensus to work toward healing that which has been broken, seeking to repair relationships with people who have been hurt or harmed through another's actions.

School District # 35 in Langley, BC has recently published a program for implementing aspects of *Restorative Action* in both elementary and secondary school settings. *Conversation Peace: Restorative Action in Secondary Schools* is a valuable resource that includes a student workbook and a trainer manual. Additionally, for a more thorough discussion of a comprehensive approach to responding to

ONE MEANING OF DISCIPLINE IS THE TEACHING OF APPROPRIATE BEHAVIOUR.

misbehaviour, *Cooperative Discipline* by Linda Albert explores how the ideas in this chapter can be expanded to include the entire school community.

The following guidelines suggest constructive ways to discipline boys in schools.

GUIDELINE 71
SET A POSITIVE INTENTION

THE power of intention and thought sets a tone for what we experience. Our thoughts about others also have an effect on them too. As Candace Pert writes in her book *Molecules of Emotion,* thoughts trigger the release of peptides, which flood through the body and give rise to emotional responses that reinforce them. In other words, the more we think of something, the more we reinforce the likelihood of its occurrence. Our thoughts can pack a punch or give a hug.

· · · · ·

Our thoughts can

pack a punch or

give a hug.

When working with boys, I am aware that if I focus on what is wrong and come from a place of negativity and criticism, I will usually see more of the very behaviours that I am trying to change. Instead, when having difficulty with a particular student, I set my intention and choose to focus on potentially constructive aspects of their behaviour. When I taught in the public schools, at the end of challenging day I would make a point of walking with the troubled boy to the exit door and discuss everything else except the difficult day. Upon departure I'd say, "Tomorrow is another day.

BOYS HAVE THEIR RADAR DETECTORS FOR THE REAL THING SET ON HIGH.

We'll have another chance – I'm sure things will go better."

Consciously setting our intention to see where the strengths lie creates the possibility for something new to emerge. This does not mean that we ignore or sidestep issues. It means that even when we address concerns, we hold hope in our minds. This positive mind set sends an entirely different message to a student. He is better able to tap into his own thinking processes that give rise to faith in himself.

CHAPTER NINE

GUIDELINE 71
SET A POSITIVE INTENTION *CONT'D*

• • • • •

Negativity serves
to cloud and limit
possibilities, but
clarifying a positive
intent leads to
accomplishments.

REGRETTABLY, I have witnessed many behaviour support teams that appear supportive of a boy's success on the surface, but as soon as that behaviour contract is broken – look out! Boys need to know that when they mess up, they still have a place to go where people are willing to see beyond their poor choices driving behaviour. Sometimes, as parents and teachers, we have to look beyond our own discouragement to focus on underlying issues. Boys have their radar detectors for the real thing set on high. They know when adults are authentic and when they are merely placating or trying to control them or simply trying to establish a paper trail to appear responsible. When we set our clear intention that a boy is capable of being successful despite the odds, it greatly increases the likelihood that he will in fact succeed.

In my workshops for teachers, I call for the description of an extremely challenging situation with a boy. We then collectively look for a productive direction whereby we can begin to address underlying reasons for his misbehaviour. Negativity serves to cloud and limit possibilities, but clarifying a positive intent leads to accomplishments.

Another strategy that proved very successful for a modified Grade 6 class was to celebrate what we had learned every Friday afternoon with a party – yes, we called it a party because of the interest it generated. It began with a Wednesday afternoon classroom meeting to plan the event. The goal was to bring closure to the week with fun, and a sense of celebration and connection. Before the party could begin, we would look back on the week and identify the learning we had gleaned. Misbehaviour and conflict thus became cast into positive learning: 1) We learned to not put Lego down the toilet; 2) We learned to not leave the hamster home door open after we finished playing with him; and, 3) We learned how long it takes for the fire truck to arrive. I was forever amazed at the learning which boys valued. The end of week celebration proved especially valuable for those students who had struggled with misbehaviour that week as they felt included, respected, and hopeful about the new week ahead. Despite a history of low achievement, the group became tight knit. Each week we started fresh with a clean slate. Success was reflected in increased attendance levels and soaring grades.

SET AN INTENTION OF MUTUAL **RESPECT WITH PARENTS**

· · · · ·

If we're to bring boys

to a safe crossing,

we need all hands

on deck.

PARENTS struggle with all kinds of feelings when they have a boy who is bucking the system. When I was a classroom teacher, I met many parents who were trying their best to support high-spirited boys and noticed how often they apologized for their son's behaviour. They felt responsible and some feared they would be seen as bad or ineffective parents. The opposite was true, of course, as their concern and willingness to talk about their son offered the best support possible. I told them that I wasn't paid to teach cooperative kids but all kinds of kids, and that I expected to have challenging behaviours with some. We set the intention to work as a team. I also reminded them that Columbus would never have crossed an ocean if he had abandoned ship when a storm came up. If we're to bring boys to a safe crossing, we need all hands on deck.

GUIDELINE 72
HELP BOYS DEVELOP INTERNAL CONTROL

If we want to see boys

behave respectfully,

we must model

respectful behaviour

in all our interactions

with them.

DICTATORSHIP may yield a short-term sense of control, but this short-lived control comes at a price. Using threat to create fear leads to resentment and backlash over time. The goal of discipline is to help boys develop an inner sense of *response-ability*—that is, the ability to choose healthy responses, think for themselves, and responsibly mediate their interactions with others. Since boys place a high value on fairness, they are more likely to cooperate if they perceive that they are getting a fair deal.

One form of dictatorship that often has negative and far reaching consequences is interrogation. The adult may discover the culprit but at the high cost of breaking social alliance and increasing the snitch's vulnerability among peers. Some adults think they are teaching boys ethical behaviour by interrogating them to get to the truth. But if boys perceive the process as unjust and degrading, what are they really learning? When a boy is backed into a corner, shamefully confesses and comes out crying, he later may seek revenge in passive ways, further complicating the discipline process.

GUIDELINE 72
HELP BOYS DEVELOP INTERNAL CONTROL *CONT'D*

SETTING clear and consistent boundaries will help boys by creating safety and a rhythm and pattern for learning that is planned and predictable. Rules need to be simple, clear, and prioritized. As boys get older, the rules need to be adjusted in order to give them more age-appropriate responsibility so that they get practice doing for themselves – making mistakes, and learning from those mistakes. The ultimate goal is for boys to develop an internal control center, which can also lead to self-soothing and delay gratification behaviours. Effective discipline is marked by clear and caring limits, the use of humour, and power-sharing with boys so that they can take charge when appropriate.

• • • • •

GUIDELINE 73
CREATE STRUCTURE, SUPERVISION AND SUPPORT

Adults must actively seek out ways to support boys as they grow into manhood. There is no substitute for simply being present and putting time into the relationship.

THE three foundational elements of discipline are structure, supervision, and support. *Structure,* routines, and clear expectations provide boys with the opportunity to experience and explore their limits within a safe framework. When kids misbehave, we must first look at the environment they are interacting within to see how it is influencing their behaviour. Younger boys especially need their day structured so that they know what to expect. We have all seen kids having meltdowns when really they just needed some down time or a nap.

Supervision and actively watching and engaging with boys, communicates that we know what is going on, that we care, and that we take our responsibility as parents and teachers seriously. In addition, if boys know that there is someone who will consistently hold the line as they push up against it they are more likely to feel accountable for their behaviour.

Support is the glue that holds it all together. Kids don't care how much we know until they know how much we care. Support comes in many forms but it is truly the caring adult's ability to reflect back to the boy the good that they see which makes the biggest impact. Sometimes that means reframing how we see boys. How can we turn a seeming deficit into strength? Is that impulsive, loud and disruptive boy really a potential leader who needs a nudge in that direction?

GUIDELINE 74
LOOK BEYOND MASKS OF INDIFFERENCE

• • • • •

We have to look behind a boy's mask, observing clues such as his body language, hints, and silences.

THE protective mask of indifference which adolescent boys use to protect their vulnerability, must not fool teachers and parents. We have to appreciate that for boys, showing one's real self can be risky. The mask that boys wear covers fears of being shamed, bullied, or mocked. We have to look behind their mask, observing clues such as body language, hints, and silences.

Look behind a boy's mask to guess what underlying feelings are being expressed through his behaviour. Begin with a neutral consideration of what happened – the event. It is critical to avoid triggering defensiveness by describing behaviour with negatively charged, accusatory words. "Why were you so rude?" will not invite cooperation and will only get a boy's back up.

HAVING A LAUGH AT THE TEACHER'S EXPENSE IS OFTEN AN EFFORT TO RESIST AUTHORITY WHILE SIMULTANEOUSLY GAINING HIGH STATUS AMONG OTHER BOYS.

As you reflect about the boy's behaviour and the event, construct a tentative hypothesis about the nature of the boy's concerns. You may realize that he is trying not to advertise that he feels like a failure. Perhaps he feels overpowered and is attempting to compensate through bossy behaviour. Having a laugh at the teacher's expense is often an effort to resist authority while simultaneously gaining high status among other boys. Similarly, many boys control their behaviour by appearing indifferent to a teacher's public reprimand – a threat to their masculinity. Sometimes being the best at being the worst is a badge of honour for boys. Rudolf Dreikurs also reminds us "that a misbehaving child is a discouraged child." When we see past the behaviour to identify a boy's genuine striving for significance, we can help him claim his courage to do the right thing.

When possible, talk privately with boys about behaviour. They are more likely to drop the mask of unresponsiveness when there is no audience to judge the performance. The goal is to help boys develop emotional intelligence by naming and understanding the feelings that are driving their behaviours.

GUIDELINE 75
GUIDELINE 75
MAINTAIN CONNECTION WITHOUT SHAMING

· · · · ·

Effective discipline should address the behaviour directly without causing anger or bitterness.

WITH their competitive and oppositional style, boys are more likely to rebel against school authority, which they may experience as a *curriculum of control* (Knitzer, Steinberg, & Fleisch). Discipline that is rigid or humiliating inevitably erodes a boy's self-confidence. Unlike punishment, which tends to shame, effective discipline should address the behaviour directly without causing anger or bitterness. If, instead of trying to teach through discipline, the attempt is to control through punishment, boys feel resentment that leads them to exhibit a swaggering aggressiveness that the school does not reward – although society does. The challenge is to maintain connection through the discipline process without shaming or breaking the relationship bond.

Effective behaviour support separates the *deed from the doer,* and considers underlying patterns. It does not merely hold students accountable while adults abdicate responsibility for them. Assuming a position such as *zero tolerance, tough love* or *lock-step* discipline in response to non-constructive student behaviour is inappropriate and ineffective. The British Columbia Ministry of Education document *Focus on Suspension: A Resource for Schools* states "Suspension may in some situations have no effect or even increase the likelihood of the behaviour reoccurring.... out-of-school suspensions can contribute to a student's alienation from school and the likelihood of the student dropping out."

BOYS OFTEN QUICKLY DIG IN, REVERT TO TOUGH TALK, AND ATTEMPT TO DRAW ADULTS INTO POWER STRUGGLES OVER THEIR CONFLICT.

When confronted with a boy's indifference, adults often demand eye contact, "Look at me when I'm talking to you! Stop fidgeting and listen!" Yet, avoiding direct or intense eye contact often minimizes the perceived threat of anger that can occur during conflict while still maintaining focus. With minimal eye contact, look out the window and talk about the incident. The boy will likely perceive more personal space to reflect and be more likely to reflect thoughtfully on what occurred. You also will not have to see the boy rolling his eyes upwards.

GUIDELINE 75
MAINTAIN CONNECTION WITHOUT SHAMING *CONT'D*

· · · · ·

Sometimes

externalizing the

event can reduce

anxiety and can

help boys move

forward with taking

responsibility for

the harm they have

caused.

REPEATEDLY, I see adults severing connections while disciplining boys. Unfortunately boys often quickly *dig in*, revert to *tough talk*, and attempt to draw adults into power struggles over their conflict. They conclude that they are not appreciated for who they really are, and that no one really cares.

Recently, I witnessed an outstanding example of discipline. Jake, an impulsive Grade 11 boy who is an exceptional acrobatic, interrupted the conversation his teacher and I were having with a group of girls in the hallway by doing a handstand in front of us. The girls giggled in embarrassment as gravity pulled on his baggy clothing revealing more skin than necessary. Erin, the teacher, briefly commented with a smile and a good-natured voice that *Cirque de Soleil* would be lucky to have him, but that he needed to get back to his classroom. She paused, turned toward Jake, and said, "This would be a good time," then immediately looked away. She was authoritative and friendly, managing to keep her rapport with

AVOID INSISTING THAT BOYS STAND OR SIT STILL.

Jake while also making a point. As Jake headed back to class she added, "If you need a reference in your application for the Cirque – let me know, I'd be pleased to!"

Sometimes externalizing the event can reduce anxiety and help boys move forward with taking responsibility for the harm they have caused. One approach when meeting with a boy to discuss misbehaviour is to talk about the behaviour by writing it on the board - without other students present, of course – and then speak to the board when referring to the incident. This provides an indirect way of communicating that the behaviour written on the board is the problem, not the boy.

GUIDELINE 75
MAINTAIN CONNECTION WITHOUT SHAMING *CONT'D*

FIDGETING is frequently another way that boys speak with their body to let you know that they are feeling anxious and may need help to process the discussion – remember the corpus callosum and the need for bilateral stimulation! Avoid insisting that they stand or sit still and you most likely will observe that the fidgeting helps them to relax as you maintain connection while getting information about what has occurred.

A school principal recently told me that as a result of her growing awareness of boys' needs to move as they process information, whenever she has them come down for a potentially emotionally charged discipline conference, she no longer talks without doing some sort of activity. For instance, she walks and talks with them while looking around. Or she puts out paper and crayons for them. She reported that she even doodles at the same time to emulate a boys' style of relating and defusing potential conflict before it even has time to erupt.

When we want to teach through constructive discipline, we should strive to maintain emotional connectedness with boys—not shame them into behaving.

• • • • •

GUIDELINE 76
BE CURIOUS ABOUT AGGRESSION

BOYS possess a greater propensity for rebelling against and engaging in conflict with authority than girls who are more likely to try to avoid conflict and work to preserve harmony. For many boys, rejection of authority might be due to a developmental need although they are often very unskilled about how to accomplish this goal. Sam's story describes how aggression can unfold in a typical home.

GUIDELINE 76
BE CURIOUS ABOUT AGGRESSION *CONT'D*

SAM'S **STORY**

Dad has just woken up 5 year-old Sam and has asked him to dress for school. Five minutes later Dad discovers Sam playing with his Lego. In a stern voice Dad tells him it's time to get dressed. Ten minutes later Dad finds Sam in the kitchen in his pajamas looking for breakfast. Dad erupts! This might become the second time this week that he is late for work because of Sam.

• • • • •

While Dad may

have won this

particular battle,

Sam is winning

the war.

He marches Sam back to his room and orders him to get dressed. Dad stands at the door repeatedly barking at him to hurry up. Sam ever so slowly dresses and makes mistakes. Dad is furious and threatens to take away his favourite toy. Sam cries and gets dressed immediately.

While Dad may have won this particular battle, Sam is winning the war. Sam has discovered a special way to get power when he refuses to obey Dad's orders. Dad's repetition of his orders and demands makes Sam's refusal to cooperate useful for showing Dad who's in charge. Sam doesn't like being ordered and reminded about what to do, so deciding what he will do in his own time makes Sam feel a cut above Dad. Until Dad is ready to step outside of the power struggle and teach Sam to be cooperative, he'd better not expect to get to work any earlier. When we understand how we inadvertently feed undesirable behaviours, we can reassess our approach to discipline.

INCREASED TESTOSTERONE LEVELS CAN PROPEL A BOY WITH MISGUIDED POWER TO BECOME OVERLY AGGRESSIVE.

At puberty, misguided bossiness, or *lawyer's syndrome* – where boys convincingly argue to prove who's boss – only become more challenging. Increased testosterone levels can propel a boy with misguided power to become overly aggressive and potentially violent unless taught more socially harmonious ways of living. Youth violence, explains Garbarino in his popular book, *Lost Boys: Why Our Sons Turn Violent and How We Can Save Them,* "is often a boy's attempt to achieve justice as he perceives it." The warning signs, he says, are a lack of connection, masking of emotions, withdrawal, silence, rage, trouble with friends, hyper-vigilance, and cruelty toward other children and even animals.

GUIDELINE 76
BE CURIOUS ABOUT AGGRESSION *CONT'D*

HOWEVER, we should be careful not to label all aggression as anti-social and recall that often among men aggression can be highly valued and prized behaviour as expressed in the following comment, "He's really aggressive with that account and getting great results!" Aggression is also part of curiosity, exploring the world and trying new things – in short, asserting oneself in potentially positive ways. For many boys, the challenge is learning how to express themselves in acceptable ways that don't infringe on the rights of others. For parents and teachers, it's learning how to co-opt the aggression for constructive purposes.

• • • • •

GUIDELINE 77
ALLOW BOYS TO SAVE FACE

SOME boys may know that they are transgressing and that they will get caught eventually, but they want to appear as if they are in control. When *heels are dug in*, adults need to pull back to avoid escalating the situation. *Cooperative Discipline* says, "By insisting that students do things our way, we risk provoking a new confrontation, one that is often more unpleasant than the original. Is it worth it?" Insisting on doing things his own way can be the boy's method of showing he is the boss of himself, which can be productive for him on one level. When we get ensnared in counterproductive arguments and power struggles, we have to ask ourselves what the boy is really learning. Eye rolling, muttering, and smiling at inopportune moments are meant to provoke us and also to save face. Don't get hooked.

Adults must look also beyond boys' unconstructive behaviour to teach a vocabulary for emotions. For many boys and men, anger is one acceptable emotion – the funnel through which all feelings are channeled. Once a boy gets comfortable using words for what he is experiencing such as hurt, anxiety, frustration, disappointment, and shame, he can begin to deal with it, and help himself. Say something like, "Sounds like you may be frustrated," when boys bark, "This assignment is stupid!" When he hits another person, rather that automatically assume the worst, help him to find words, "Hitting is not okay, so I suspect that something must be really upsetting you to react in this way. What's going on?" As you try to guide boys toward more socially positive choices, remember to let them save face and maintain their integrity.

GUIDELINE 78
STAY OUTSIDE OF A BOY'S CONFLICT CYCLE

SOMETIMES a memory, perception, or event can trigger a classic *fight or flight* reactivity in boys. The body responds to the real or perceived threat by preparing itself for battle, and as adrenalin is released, breathing, heart rate, and blood pressure increase dramatically. Quality of judgment is impaired as blood shifts from the higher cortical functions of the frontal lobe to the survival responses of the back brain. There is also a temporary shift in blood volume away from vital organs and into the extremities to fuel the classic *fight or flight* response. The boy is now ready to punch or run. Some boys are triggered more easily than others – frequently their fathers will comment that they reacted similarly as boys.

· · · · ·

Quality of judgment is impaired as blood shifts from the higher cortical functions of the frontal lobe to the survival responses of the back brain.

When a rush of feelings overwhelms boys and their emotional volcano is about to blow, they need support, guidance, and leadership. Helping a boy develop more emotional coping skills and become less reactive to perceived threats is no easy task. It requires a low-key approach that is sensitive to timing. Once a boy's biological defense system kicks in, the boy will be too agitated to hear what you have to say. If the boy is in a state of intense agitation, your very best response in that case is to make a graceful or controlled exit.

REMEMBER: IT CAN TAKE ONE FOOL TO START BACKTALK
BUT TWO FOOLS TO MAKE A CONVERSATION OF IT.

Right after a crisis, boys are typically not too keen to talk either, as they need a cool-down period to shake off the emotion before they can discuss the event in a rational way. Have you ever noticed that in nature animals also shake off a potential threat by literally shaking their entire body? Boys need time to release the charged-up emotion and allow it to drain off. Adults who step in prematurely to try and have a sensible talk soon find that they have stepped right into conflict. When they hear boys spit out irrational statements such as, "Leave me alone. I hate you! I don't need you!" or "If I wanted help I would have called 911!" adults can find their own temperature rising, matching the boy's aggressiveness with their own counter-aggressiveness. Everyone loses when adults become thermometers rather than thermostats, which can help regulate emotional intensity.

GUIDELINE 78
STAY OUTSIDE OF A BOY'S CONFLICT CYCLE *CONT'D*

• • • • •

When a boy starts

to talk about the

incident, use

simple prompts

to encourage his

story to unfold.

UNLESS a boy begins to talk and seems to want to connect, avoid too much focus on his emotions as it will be perceived as insincere and he will likely attempt to pull you into his conflict. Nothing can be gained if a boy is not ready to use words. To help a boy discharge the intense emotions, you might say something like, "Walk with me to get the supplies for the other class – you don't need any more problems." While walking or waiting, convey calm support. Avoid the temptation to leave the boy alone, but remain nearby, communicating concern. Often this can be communicated non-verbally through your body language or your intention. Sometimes a few simple words work best, "When you're ready, we'll figure this out," or "It's understandable that you're upset if you believe that you've been cheated."

IN NATURE ANIMALS SHAKE OFF A POTENTIAL THREAT BY LITERALLY SHAKING THEIR ENTIRE BODY.

When a boy starts to talk about the incident, use simple prompts to encourage his story to unfold. Encouragements such as "I really want to hear what happened from your point of view," or "It's important for me to understand what caused you to become so upset," keeps you outside of his conflict while drawing him out. If the retelling triggers more emotions, allow them to wash through. Teach him that he can handle strong emotions and learn strategies of self-soothing – maybe something physical such as going for a run. Modelling calmness yourself is important. Only when he is willing to converse can you start to explore what happened and how to rectify the situation.

GUIDELINE 79
GENERATE CONSEQUENCES THAT ARE RESTORATIVE · · · · ·

• Respectful

• Related

• Reasonable

• Reliably enforced

• Restorative

WHEN boys transgress, restorative or cooperative action discipline is far more constructive than punishment. Boys who are punished often have revenge fantasies that interrupt the learning process. Boys who are not given the opportunity to make amends for what they have done tend to view the punishment as a clearing of the ledger, which allows boys to re-offend in the future without attending to the harm they have done or to their own feelings of guilt or remorse. For many boys consequence is a codeword for punishment.

Measures to address boy's unruly behaviour in ways that that teach responsibility ideally will be: respectful, related, reasonable, reliably enforced, and restorative. The purpose of a consequence is to change the future, not punish the past.

STEVEN'S **STORY**

The following example illustrates a response that fits these criteria.

A creative young boy, Steven, accidentally discovered that he was able to withdraw $20.00 a day from the local bank machine without having any money in his account. Banks have since corrected this glitch, but you can imagine his parents' stunned dismay when the bank manager called to explain what had happened. At first the father reproached himself for not having questioned some of the recent purchases his son had made.

After taking some time to consider options for responding, the father decided to invite Steven out to walk the dogs – which typically meant you are about to be held responsible and it will be okay. Remembering that movement helps keep the discussion relaxed and non-confrontational by making it easier for boys to process charged emotions, you'll appreciate the father's wisdom here.

STEVEN'S **STORY** *CONT'D*

* * * * *

The father and son
explored options
calmly and no one
lost their temper.

About two blocks down the way the father gave him the straight goods – a brief description of what he had learned. Wisely, he avoided using the entrapment approach, which goes something like this, "The bank manager called and left a message. Do you know of any reason why the bank manager might call me to speak about you?" Most boys, and especially teenagers, are going to hedge their bets and respond with a resounding, "No!" This brazen denial usually gets the parents worked up as they start an accounting ledger to keep track of exactly how many lies their son tells them. The resulting frustration defeats the discipline process.

Steven was quiet for the remaining twenty minutes of the walk. His father commented, "You must really understand the gravity of this incident and are thinking it over carefully." Steven avoided eye contact and said he needed more time to figure things out. His father agreed that they could discuss it after dinner or early the next morning before school. Steven decided that he would talk that evening after he went 'blading' – which gave him more process time through the action of bilateral stimulation and movement.

THE RESTORATIVE APPROACH
ALLOWED STEVEN TO REPAIR
THE DAMAGE HE HAD CAUSED
AND RECLAIM HIS INTEGRITY
AND HONOUR.

The father and son explored options calmly and no one lost their temper. Steven decided his consequence would be to cash in a savings bond to return the $300 that he had stolen. It was reasonable that he would pay back only what he took. While his father did not sit in on the meeting between Steven and the bank manager to discuss restitution, he did walk with him to the bank, waited for him in the lobby, and met briefly with Steven and the manager when they were through. The manager came out with a big smile because Steven not only paid back the money, but also had offered, nudged by Dad's coaching the previous night, to clean the parking lot of debris for the next two weeks to restore his relationship with the manager and the bank.

His father reports that Steven continues to be a loyal customer at that bank and will likely remain so for years to come as a result of his positive experience.

A restorative approach lets everyone win.

GUIDELINE 80
RESPOND – DON'T REACT

I OFTEN joke with parents who feel backed into a corner by their kids, usually adolescents, to resist the temptation to argue – and duck out. They can leave the scene, maybe going to the bathroom. Their exit stops the negative momentum from building into further conflict. Once safely in the bathroom, parents have the chance to regain balance and focus while they avoid getting drawn further into a conflict. I also add that parents of boundary-pushing adolescents can benefit by storing a number of photos of their boy when he was a baby or toddler beneath the sink so while in the bathroom they can be reminded about why they had him in the first place. Brief time away helps parents to regain composure enabling them to hold firm yet compassionate boundaries so that boys can calm down too.

> A temporary exit stops the negative momentum from building into further conflict.

RESPONDING, RATHER THAN REACTING, DOESN'T LET BOYS OFF THE HOOK, BUT TEACHES THEM MUTUAL RESPECT.

Teachers can do the same by psychologically removing themselves and withdrawing from the conflict – but only for the moment. When a boy says, "I'm not going to do this homework, you've not given us enough time – you expect too much and well, whatever…" a teacher can respond with, "You have a point. Let's have a conversation about reasonable expectations. I'll write it on the board so I won't forget. Meanwhile, I have another student that needs my help. I'll check back with you in a moment." Responding, rather than reacting, doesn't let boys off the hook, but teaches them mutual respect.

I can think back to an experience I once had with a boy named Brad who was exceptionally angry – with everybody. Upon returning to the classroom I overheard him speak inappropriately. When I turned toward him, he haphazardly offered his middle finger and announced to the hallway crowd that he had no intention of completing his homework. That moment is firmly planted in my memory. Everybody was waiting for me to do something. I must tell you that a tremendous *fight or flight* reaction emerged within.

RESPOND – DON'T REACT *CONT'D*

• • • • •

It's common for

boys to try to

draw adults into

an argument to

scuttle a discipline

discussion.

A QUICK glance at a colleague, who offered a gentle and all-knowing smile, reminded me that the issue was not maintaining control of Brad but control of myself. I also heard a childhood voice: *Ignore it and walk away. If it is a problem deal with it later, not in the heat of the moment.* Later, I had an opportunity to touch base with Brad and learned that he was struggling in my math class and felt as though I was embarrassing him by more frequently asking him if he needed help than other students. I apologized and we set about planning a tutoring schedule. He didn't apologize directly to me for his behaviour in the hallway earlier, but he thanked me afterwards, paused, and smiled as if he wanted to say more but couldn't–not yet. I assumed his reflective pause to be a non-verbal apology.

It's common for boys to try to draw adults into an argument to scuttle a discipline discussion. Teachers and parents may become sidetracked from their calm response and find themselves reacting instead. During these times it's important to remember that it is the certainty of the response – not the severity that makes the impact. It is adult responsiveness and calm follow-through, not the strength of your response, that speaks of commitment and care. I recall a boy who said, "Well, if you'd only teach it properly, maybe there wouldn't be a problem

DON'T FIGHT AND DON'T GIVE IN!

here!" to which his teacher replied, "You have an interesting point. I'd be pleased to consider alternative approaches, but meanwhile, please come in for a tutorial so that I can assist you to get the grade you want and deserve." Sometimes we can think that if the consequence is stronger – such as sending a boy to the office or suspending him – that boys will learn more, but usually the result is only resentment and distance between you and him.

I remember talking to a wise and experienced teacher Bronia Grunwald, coauthor of *Maintaining Sanity in the Classroom*, several years ago. At over 80 years-old, she didn't mince words. "Don't Fight and Don't Give In!" she advised. She understood that we discipline students best when we discipline ourselves.

No matter how boys push our buttons, we have to get to know those buttons so we can cultivate the habit of responding, not reacting.

ASSESSING
BOYS' LEARNING

When dealing with people, let us remember that we are not dealing with creatures of logic. We are dealing with creatures of emotion.

Dale Carnegie

• • • • •

Boys often

express their

learning in ways

that typical school

assessment

procedures do not

validate or reward.

Assessment and evaluation are integral components of the teaching-learning cycle. Assessment implies the act of gathering information on a regular or even daily basis in order to understand individual students' current learning needs, competencies, and progress. Evaluation is the culminating act of interpreting the information gathered for the purpose of making summative decisions or judgments about students' learning and needs, and the quality of their performance according to certain pre-determined criteria, often at reporting time. The main purposes of assessment are to guide and improve learning and instruction by monitoring progress. Effectively planned assessment and evaluation can promote learning, build confidence, and develop students' understanding of themselves as learners.

Sometimes boys can express their learning in ways that typical school assessment procedures do not validate or reward. Boys' preference for activity, spatial perception, abstract reasoning, and dialogue – previously referred to as *report talk*, may not be measured adequately by standard testing.

CHAPTER TEN

SIMON'S **STORY**

• • • • •

Thinking his son

was very

intelligent and

creative, the

father began

to wonder how

this passion for

volcanoes could

be developed

further.

I remember a boy in Grade 4 who was very excited about the science theme his teacher had introduced and looked forward to the upcoming lesson and even the test on volcanoes. Since watching a TV special about active volcanoes some time ago, Simon had become fascinated with them. He especially loved how they blew their stacks, releasing the pent–up force of molten lava skyward with a spectacular display of force.

Simon spent much of one weekend working on the home study activity. His father helped him design his own volcano and even added special effects of sound and moving parts. Simon's father genuinely delighted in sharing his son's enthusiasm. Thinking his son was very intelligent and creative, the father began to wonder how this passion for volcanoes could be developed further – perhaps even leading to a sustained interest in science.

Simon went to bed full of ideas, eager to tell his friends at school the next day all about the weekend volcano project with his dad – especially what a mess it made in the garage when it erupted. Since there was nothing that he didn't know about volcanoes, he was even looking forward to the test.

Later that week Simon's father came home to find his son storming around the house. After a few false starts, Simon finally blurted out that his teacher was unfair and stupid and so was her test on volcanoes. The test questions were straight out of the textbook and Simon was frustrated that he couldn't show the teacher all that he knew about volcanoes. His frustration had turned to anger at the teacher who had no idea that Simon now felt cheated, unhappy about school, and about the idea of future tests.

• • • • •

The problem is

not the standards

themselves, but

rather the process

by which the

standards are

compared.

IN the 1990's, educational reformers who sought to measure how well students were learning found that changing assessment methods is more difficult than changing instructional or curriculum designs. Ultimately examinations are externally set, and students have to prepare for assessments.

However, throughout the elementary school years and some of the middle grades, we can use alternative formats for assessing and evaluating. Visual and oral assessment are particularly helpful for boys.

Through close observation of boys in the process of learning, the collection of frequent feedback on their learning, and the design of modest classroom experiments, teachers can learn much about how boys learn and, more specifically, how they respond to particular teaching approaches. Classroom assessment can be designed which provides useful feedback on what, how much, and how well boys are learning. Teachers can then use this information to refocus their teaching to help boys make their learning more effective.

SUCCESS AND FAILURE ARE OVERLAID WITH MORAL SIGNIFICANCE IN OUR CULTURE.

There is a lot of talk about standards in education as comparisons are made between grades, gender, schools, countries, and so forth, as if these grades were an accurate picture of reality. No one can argue the benefits of raising school achievement and that standards help to eliminate redundancy, clarify what we mean by high expectations, and assess student learning in relation to clear benchmarks. The problem is not the standards themselves, but rather the process by which the standards are compared. Success and failure are overlaid with moral significance in our culture. It is good to succeed and shameful to fail. Public shaming of the bottom half of the class or list of aggregate school achievement and accolades for the top ignores how motivation really operates. The emphasis on external scorecards and ranking for kids–and for their schools – that are summative rather than formative leads to inequity. Educators are naturally more motivated to spend time where it is easiest to reap rewards by encouraging those who are the easiest to motivate and who are already doing well. However, the students who are doing less well get left even further behind.

CHAPTER TEN

SCHOOL **ASSESSMENTS**

• • • • •

There is probably

no such thing as

a fair test.

GIVEN that classroom teachers have no control over school grades printed in newspapers, or higher political directives forcing emphasis away from the process of learning and instead on to standardized testing, it's hard to see what individual teachers can do in classrooms to influence the inequitable nature of public tests and examinations. Given that there is probably no such thing as a fair test anyway, it would seem to be more prudent for teachers to do what they can do to raise the achievement of all pupils by working as effectively as possible within the current system.

How might three main types of school assessments be modified to give a more fair and accurate reflection of boys' learning needs and achievement?

• **Diagnostic assessment** typically occurs at the beginning of the school year and before each unit of study. The purposes are to determine students' knowledge and skills, their learning needs, and their motivational and interest levels. By examining the results of diagnostic assessment, teachers can determine where to begin instruction and what concepts or skills to emphasize.

• **Formative assessment** and evaluation focus on the processes and products of learning. Formative assessment is continuous and is meant to inform the student, the parent/guardian, and the teacher of the student's progress toward the curriculum objectives. This type of assessment and evaluation provides information upon which instructional decisions and adaptations can be made and provides students with directions for future learning.

• **Summative assessment** and evaluation occur most often at the end of a unit of instruction and at term or year-end when students are ready to demonstrate achievement of curriculum objectives. The main purposes are to determine knowledge, skills, abilities, and attitudes that have developed over a given period of time, to summarize student progress, and to report this progress to students, parents/guardians, and teachers.

The guidelines in this chapter are designed to help teachers apply their knowledge of gender differences and preferences to their assessment methods.

GUIDELINE 81
USE A RANGE OF ASSESSMENTS THAT REFLECT GENDER PREFERENCES

WHILE there are many exceptions to generalizations about gender preferences and strengths, the following short exercise can help you identify the most likely preference and tendencies for males and females. You might even consider whether these inclinations fit your own learning style.

LEARNING STYLES

a. __	loves rules	__	is flexible
b. __	thrives on relationships	__	thrives on action
c. __	great spatial abilities	__	great multi-tasking and sensoral abilities
d. __	quick to forgive	__	works to establish alliances
e. __	prefers cooperative activities	__	prefers competitive activities
f. __	relational problem-solvers	__	abstract problem-solvers
g. __	respects authority	__	respects feelings
h. __	quick impulses	__	responds to needs
i. __	ready for action	__	ready to adapt
j. __	process-oriented	__	product-oriented
k. __	communication is direct	__	communication is indirect

GUIDELINE 81
USE ASSESSMENTS THAT REFLECT GENDER PREFERENCES *CONT'D*

ANSWERS

THE research concludes that boys: a) love rules; b) thrive on action; c) have great spatial abilities; d) are quick to forgive – which is why boys are often ready to play a minute after an argument; e) prefer competitive activities; f) are abstract problem-solvers; g) respect authority; h) are ready for action; i) are product-oriented – the *let's just get there and we'll talk later* approach; and, j) communication is usually more direct.

In order to accurately assess learning, evaluation and assessment methods should be gender-sensitive. For example, too many multiple choice exams will be more allied with a masculine style of memory and may not adequately represent girls' learning preferences and styles. In contrast, too many long-winded essays will be much easier for girls than for boys, who, if they must write, tend to prefer short structured exam questions, preferably with clearly outlined expectations for length of response.

Boys also prefer short regular quizzes. They may see tests as an unequal contest between teacher and student, whereas quizzes seem more to pit student against student and hence appeal to their peer competitiveness. Predetermined, structured quizzes help boys feel more in control of the outcome. Boys are also much more likely to study for a quiz than a test. This is especially true if they can work in teams so that individuals can play a quiz as they might play hockey – each one chooses a position that plays from their strength.

> • • • • •
>
> In order to accurately assess learning, evaluation and assessment methods should be gender-sensitive.

GUIDELINE 82
BEWARE OF HARSH RANKINGS THAT DISCOURAGE AND SHAME BOYS

TEACHERS trained to teach in the *Normal School* were encouraged to arm students against the harshness of the world by toughening them up in childhood. When teachers openly rank students according to test scores, grades, or some other competitive criteria, only those at the top feel good. For students who strive to be at the top, and who care about their

· · · · ·

Failure is an

inevitable

part of

learning.

class rank, ratings might be an incentive to improve their performance, but rankings and ratings often detract boys from the real purpose of assessment, which is to identify what has been learned and what still needs to

SOMETIMES THE ASSESSMENT DOES NOT MEASURE WHAT BOYS KNOW.

be learned. Rankings and ratings often serve only to entrench those students in the bottom half or bottom quarter of the class in a place of discouragement.

We do not want to equate underachievement or failure with character deficiencies. Failure is an inevitable part of learning. Poor achievement is not necessarily a reflection of laziness or conscious choice. Sometimes boys have poor work habits or study skills. Sometimes the assessment does not measure what boys know. Sometimes boys are unable to concentrate for reasons that have little to do with school. Pushing too hard with these boys can backfire, sending them further underground where they resent school learning.

We should work to reduce student stress around assessment. Some boys who are naturally anxious can do much better when they have a positive connection with the teacher. When a teacher has a close relationship with a student, they can read them better and sense when, and how, to give feedback and information about learning.

GUIDELINE 83
KEEP EXPECTATIONS POSITIVE AND REALISTIC

RESEARCH consistently shows that high expectations produce good results, and low expectations produce poor ones. If you ask a boy to do something in a way that assumes and expects that he will – mainly because you believe it is possible – he is most likely to succeed. If you assume that if he won't be successful, then he more probably won't.

When boys feel trusted by their teacher or parent, they in turn feel proud and work to maintain the trust.

· · · · ·

When boys feel trusted by their teacher or parent, they in turn feel proud and work to maintain the trust.

With assessment of student performance, we need appropriate and realistic expectations that are high enough so that students have to reach but not so high as to discourage them. Be sure that grading focusses on criteria identified when the assignment is given and look beyond sloppiness. Remember that boys

LOOK BEYOND SLOPPINESS, REMEMBERING THAT BOYS TYPICALLY DEVELOP THE FINE MOTOR SKILLS NEEDED FOR NEAT HANDWRITING ABOUT A YEAR AND A HALF BEHIND GIRLS.

typically develop the fine motor skills needed for neat handwriting about a year and a half behind girls.

Adjust the scope of expectations for boys who need to improve behaviour. It is also worth mentioning that the expectations may need to be reduced accordingly for boys who need to make behavioural improvements. If too much is demanded at one time, or the bar is too high, boys often regress or give up altogether.

GUIDELINE 84
USE RUBRICS TO INCREASE LEARNING

RUBRICS are schematized, objective assessment tools that use a grid to measure clearly stated objectives. They specify a range of criteria that indicate the degree to which a student has met those objectives on a rating scale. Rubrics chart progress in comparison to stated benchmarks and provide consistency and clarity of expectations for students about what is expected, and how performance will be evaluated according to a full range of criteria rather than a single number or grade. Teachers can also weight their criteria in order to show which elements of an assignment are most important. With some rubrics, students can decide on a particular mark beforehand by seeing clear guidelines about what criteria they need to meet in order to get 20 points, say, or 15 points. By making criteria for evaluation explicit, rubrics can help students understand what teachers are looking for.

• • • • •

By making criteria
for evaluation
explicit, rubrics
can help students
understand what
teachers are
looking for.

In making rubics:

- Determine the criteria from curriculum, unit, and lesson objectives.
- Review specific criteria with students before beginning the assignment.
- Involve students in developing some or all of the criteria.
- Choose criteria that are easily observed to prevent vagueness and increase objectivity.
- Use jargon-free language to describe criteria so that data can be used in interviews with students and parents.
- Make the observation manageable by keeping the number of criteria to less than eight and by limiting the number of students observed to a few at one time.

GUIDELINE 85
STIMULATE GRADE TARGETING

STUDENTS may be given many choices within the classroom, but those choices are contained within parameters, as determined by the teacher. Rubrics help students in targeting their efforts and in the end it also helps the teacher save time. Once you know what each point along the scale will look like grading is much easier. Rubrics developed for one level or one assignment can be modified for others.

When students help to create rubrics, and define the criteria within prescribed variables by which an assignment will be assessed, they can better understand the assignment and how it will be evaluated. When boys help develop a rubric which specifies what criteria need to be met for certain grades, they are more likely to work toward getting the grade they decide upon. Instead of using assessment as a means of control, teachers who give boys responsibility by involving them in the assessment process, encourage their feelings of competence, control, and autonomy – ultimately ownership for school success.

• • • • •

GUIDELINE 86
FACILITATE ORAL ASSESSMENT

BOYS need to practise expressing their thoughts and ideas out loud. Lack of oral communication skills, or oracy skills, will hinder a boy's ability to explain his thinking in school and elsewhere. According to Geoff Hannan, a researcher from the UK, at age 11, boys are 11 months behind girls in oracy, 12 months behind in literacy and 6 months behind in numeracy. The difference in language development is reflected and perhaps reinforced in play. A girl plays with her dolls, following a narrative structure practising her advanced language skills while she moves about her playhouse – multitasking – building on the ability to think in a non-linear way.

GUIDELINE 86
FACILITATE ORAL ASSESSMENT *CONT'D*

A BOY playing with an action figure makes grunting, wham, and bam noises and is more interested in movement engrossed in a single-minded way. My choice of toys in this example reflects social stereotyping, but give a girl a car to play with and she will give it a name, a character, and personality. Give a boy a doll and he will likely use it as a weapon and commence with play shooting. Perhaps we should give him his action figure back and play alongside him as we encourage him to explain what is happening as he makes up stories to accompany his game to build up his narrative skills.

• • • • •

At age 11, boys are 11 months behind girls in oracy, 12 months behind in literacy and 6 months behind in numeracy.

Fathers and adult males could make explicit attempts to listen especially to younger boys and also *talk out loud* the dialogue that is often referred to as *inner speak*, for example: "I am thinking about whether we should stop on the way and get some milk. Oh, perhaps there is enough. I am not sure. I sometimes get annoyed with myself when I don't pay attention to these details. I guess I shouldn't be so hard on myself. It won't hurt if we have some extra milk in the house. What do you think, Johnny?" Listening to adult males explore ideas and weigh options in this dialogic way can significantly influence young boys.

GIVE A BOY A DOLL AND HE WILL LIKELY USE IT AS A WEAPON.

Within lessons, encourage boys to articulate their thoughts. Unlike girls, who are generally more active participants in any question/answer session, boys need to be prompted with questions that help them to speak through problems.

Develop boys' skills of reflection and evaluation. It helps to do this regularly at the end of each lesson in the form of a routine discussion.

GUIDELINE 86
FACILITATE ORAL ASSESSMENT *CONT'D*

SOME effective techniques for monitoring boys' progress in the areas of oracy include the following:

> - Make video and audio recordings of a variety of formal and informal oral language experiences, and then assess these according to pre-determined criteria, based upon student needs and curriculum objectives.
> - Use checklists as concise methods of collecting information and rating scales or rubrics to assess student achievement.
> - Record anecdotal comments to provide useful data based upon observation of oral activities.
> - Interview boys to determine what they believe they do well or areas in which they need to improve.
> - Confer with boys during the writing and readings process and observe them.

• • • • •

GUIDELINE 87
DRAW ON SPATIAL STRENGTHS

SPATIAL ability, or mental rotation, is the ability to rotate quickly and accurately two- or three-dimensional figures in imagination, and to interpret the graphic representation of changes in the position of the sides of the object. Although not all boys have this strength, (such as some boys with special needs) many have spatial abilities that contribute to their love of video games, skateboards, and sports.

Try assessment methods that allow boys to draw on this strength. Instead of consistently relying on assessment through talking or writing, on occasion use visual means of assessment – for example, graphic flow diagrams which they have to fill in, or puzzles they re-organize in order to convey understanding of chronology or arrangement of ideas. Boys can also use diagrams in presentations.

GUIDELINE 87
DRAW ON SPATIAL STRENGTHS *CONT'D*

• • • • •

We need visual

assessments

as well as oral

assessments.

A FEW months ago I was interviewing a boy in Grade 11 who had stopped attending school. He looked away from me while tugging at the tear in his jeans. His answers to my questions were monosyllabic. However, when I stopped trying to talk with him, and turned toward a visual mode of interaction on the computer, he perked up. When I asked him to show me his favourite site, he said little, but took me on a journey into what he valued.

As he endeavoured to locate a site he'd forgotten, our conversation turned to cars as I had learned from his mother that he got the highest grade in auto-mechanics and welding in the school. Despite these two high grades, he had been labeled low functioning.

HE WAS LABELLED LOW FUNCTIONING BUT GOT THE HIGHEST GRADE IN AUTO-MECHANICS.

Although this boy struggled with words, he possessed a spatial intelligence that did not show up in typical school assessments.

When he couldn't locate the site to show me how a piston operated in a car, he drew it. I marveled at his careful attention to detail. Silently he drew arrows and labels for me.

We need visual assessments for boys, especially ones like him. I can't help but think that if he had received more opportunities to demonstrate his learning through visual means that he might have found the confidence to develop his oracy skills.

COLLABORATIVE LEARNING NEEDS COLLABORATIVE ASSESSMENT

IN our culture, collaborative learning and collaborative assessment are sometimes hard sells. Provincial and national standardized achievement tests stress individual performance, competition, and content mastery over the process mastery used in collaborative learning. Some worry that individual accountability will get lost in collaborative learning and group grading, or that one student will dominate the group or do all the work for the group.

• • • • •

Cooperative learning experts specifically call for individual accountability as one of five major assessment components.

Johnson and Johnson, renowned cooperative learning experts, specifically call for individual accountability as one of five major assessment components. Another is interdependence, which includes group grading and a reward system for group improvement. The two ideas are complementary, not contradictory.

Some of the techniques available for assessing groups include:

- teacher observations during group work

- group grading for projects

- students grading each other or evaluating the level of contribution made by each member to a team project

- extra credit given when groups exceed their previous average or when individuals within a group exceed their previous performance by a specified amount

- use of a mastery approach whereby students may retake tests after receiving extra help from their groups or the teacher; and the use of individual quizzes, exams or assignments

Collaborative assessment techniques mirror what happens in the adult world or work when groups of successful men and women collaborate to achieve desired ends.

GUIDELINE 89
GIVE FREQUENT AND REGULAR FEEDBACK WHILE MODELING ACCEPTANCE OF MISTAKES

WHEN adults take time to talk about their own mistakes, boys learn that it's okay to make mistakes themselves. As a classroom teacher, every Monday morning I would begin my week with students in a conversation called, *What Was Your BIGGEST BLUNDER of The Weekend?* We would laugh and tease each other while also providing feedback by contributing our opinions. Sometimes in the hallway after school, we would take time to hear about how things worked out. Students especially loved it when I selectively disclosed appropriate aspects of my personal life and invited their opinions. I recall once telling about trying a little bleach in the wash without taking time to check the washer basin properly and ended up bleaching my wife's favourite red blouse. For weeks the kids in the schoolyard would ask me about how my washing was going. The girls, incidentally, advised me to give my wife whatever she wanted as a consequence for my careless mistake. By modelling how to look at and learn from our mistakes–something women generally find easier than men do – we can prepare boys to receive feedback that can help them grow.

• • • • •

Boys need appropriate feedback on their school performance at frequent points along the way.

To capitalize on time spent with learning assessment and motivate boys to become actively involved in their learning, teachers can close the feedback loop by letting boys know what they have learned from the assessment and how this information can be used to improve future learning. Boys need appropriate feedback on their school performance at frequent points along the way. As they begin an assignment, boys will likely need help to assess their existing knowledge and competence. In class they need frequent opportunities to perform and receive suggestions for improvement. Assessing a book report at various junctures helps boys get their bearing and figure out where they are in the overall assignment. They may decide to work harder or slack off a bit, depending on their needs.

Feedback should be targeted and specific to the content being learned. It must also be timely and involve the student so that boys feel empowered. Students generally appreciate feedback at least every 10 to 30 minutes, and younger students like it even more often. Sometimes rituals around feedback that are built into the structure of the day can ensure that it will be given. Feedback may also come from other students, or even from the entire group to a specific individual.

GUIDELINE 90
LET BOYS LEAD WITH STUDENT-LED CONFERENCES

THERE are many innovative ways to assess and report learning, but the parent-teacher interviews, which were standard fare in the *Normal School* still have a place. Teachers prepare carefully for them in order to make the best use of limited time. They report on a student's progress, give ideas and suggestions about how the student and teacher are going to work towards improvement and invite parents to provide their perspective. Teachers may also provide suggestions about how parents can help their child at home to boost his or her academic performance.

• • • • •

Boys are the key people in determining a plan of action for their improvement.

Conferences provide a wonderful opportunity for parents to ask their questions and gather information that will help them encourage their kids to achieve. Sometimes teachers can share student portfolios–collections of

BECAUSE STUDENTS FACILITATE THEM, STUDENT-LED CONFERENCES SHIFT TRADITIONAL ROLES.

relevant work that reflect a boy's efforts and development – to give a snapshot of the boy's progress. Inevitably, the time allotted for the interview ends too soon. Ideally, parents and teachers commit to continue the school-home partnership to generate the best results for the student.

It is best when boys are also involved so that they can hear exactly what is being said, but mostly so that they become the key person to determine their plan of action with the support of adults. If Simon had been involved in a discussion about his poor showing on the volcano quiz, he would have had the opportunity to indicate his frustrations with how the experience of studying the volcano didn't match the quiz questions and perhaps he could have shown his passion for the topic in another way.

GUIDELINE 90
LET BOYS LEAD WITH STUDENT-LED CONFERENCES *CONT'D*

EDNA Nash, a graduate school professor and encouraging mentor, introduced me to student-led conferences, which originated from a teacher study group in Arizona. Because students facilitate them, these conferences shift traditional roles. I originally started using them in the classroom in the mid 1980's, and while interest in this approach has waned somewhat, I would argue that these conferences could encourage student motivation and engagement in a powerful way.

• • • • •

Typically students run the meeting and show participants their portfolios. They formally introduce parent and teacher and take charge of the agenda. They allot time for adults to ask questions and field the questions themselves.

> Typically students
> run the meeting
> and show
> participants their
> portfolios.

By deciding what to present to their parents, and by reflecting on what they have already accomplished and what they plan to accomplish in the future, students have an opportunity to internalize and consolidate the gains they have made in learning. They also engage in a metacognitive task that is especially helpful for boys–thinking about thinking and learning. The experience gives students ownership of their learning through planning, organizing, directing, reflecting and celebrating their accomplishments.

I have fond memories of one class, which decided to set up activity stations around the classroom in order to have their parents experiment with the same hands-on activities they'd had in the class. One boy was thrilled when his father didn't know an answer to a question about how much metric volume his mouth would hold. So he led the father to the sink and insisted that he make an estimate. I can still hear him: "Dad, you have to estimate first. Otherwise you won't be able to tell if you are getting better at estimating with the metric system." The father smiled knowingly – his estimate didn't even come close.

In student-led conferences, students get to make choices about whom to invite. They might ask grandparents, neighbours, a Big Brother, as well as parents. One boy even insisted on having his dog present.

Children who have the opportunity to take charge, to lead their parents or others, can experience a healthy pride in their own school performance. With an interested and attentive audience from outside the school, supportive learning is born, and students themselves become stars of their show.

SCHOOL-WIDE **PLANNING**

Never doubt that a small group of thoughtful, committed people can change the world. Indeed, it is the only thing that ever has. **Margaret Mead**

· · · · ·

All efforts to raise the achievement of boys must be made without threatening the gains made by girls in recent years.

Experts who have been taking a hard look at boys' achievement are rediscovering differences between boys and girls that go far beyond obvious biological differences. Understanding the uniqueness of boys and making room for them to be themselves is crucial for their school success. Boys need love, discipline, respect, moral guidance, and understanding. They do not need to be excused for their behaviour, nor do they need to be rescued from their masculinity.

All efforts to raise the achievement of boys must be made without threatening the gains made by girls in recent years. We need to be careful not to initiate changes that will pit boys against girls, or ignore those who are truly disadvantaged. As we discuss the development of school-wide plans to raise boys' achievement and each school's adaptation to its particular needs, let us keep in mind the central mandate of public education: the fostering of critical inquiry within inclusive community.

Each community of learners is diverse. What works in a small farming community where children may be bused to school is different than the needs in a larger urban setting. What works for one school or community might not work in another. We need to steer clear of one-size-fits-all bandwagon oratory.

TOM'S **STORY**

AS you examine ways your particular school can mobilize in order to introduce and implement ways to raise boys' achievement, you need to invite collaboration from all stakeholders – including the boys themselves. You will also need to examine objective data and consolidate it with your qualitative input.

The following story about a boy named Tom characterizes the importance of school-wide collaboration to meet boys where they are.

• • • • •

Everyone was stymied by his propensity to choose failure and conflict despite an abundance of available support.

Tom's personal school file was as thick as they come. The resource teacher took a long time to read it, marveling at Tom's ingenuity and his ability to stay true to his guiding principle of being in charge at all costs. As an only child of professional parents, he had received the most intervention and assessment she had ever read about in all her years of teaching. However, his academic underachievement had persisted, and now, as an adolescent, he became either passive – or belligerent and aggressive when challenged. Police involvement procured placement in a part-time drug treatment program that he had attended daily after school and on Saturdays for the past three months. Everyone was stymied by his propensity to choose failure and conflict despite an abundance of available support.

INVITE COLLABORATION FROM ALL STAKEHOLDERS.

After the completion of his program, he and his parents were to meet with a team of school and community professionals to determine his future – a future that to some looked bleak and without hope. I met him around a table with over a dozen people, each bringing their own expertise and perspective. I hoped someone would be able to get to the heart of the matter. Tom's face was set with a look of indifference and anger. As one of the more recent members of the team, I didn't know him well and found the historical particulars rather daunting.

TOM'S **STORY** *CONT'D*

• • • • •

The room

had become

saturated with the

problem of Tom

as the detailed

shortcomings and

unproductive years

spewed forth.

The list of professionals in attendance was long – school principal, resource teacher, behaviour teacher, school counsellor, school psychologist, social worker, addictions counsellor, police officer, the family therapist, his youth worker from the community and also from the school, a district coordinator, and a district administrator. One by one each person offered comments from their background of expertise or experience with Tom. After the first few people spoke, a look of discouragement spread over the faces of Tom's parents – it must have been overwhelming for them to hear this summary of their son's life so far – layer after layer of failure, discouragement, and uncooperative behaviour. The room had become saturated with the problem of Tom as the detailed shortcomings and unproductive years spewed forth. When another professional offered in a very friendly and upbeat tone, Tom's psychometric testing results, the litany of unfamiliar terms and standard deviations caused eyes to glaze over around the table. The room was charged with negativity and spiraling downward.

NOT ALL KIDS ARE SUITED FOR THE INSTITUTION OF SCHOOLING, AT LEAST AS IT PRESENTLY STANDS.

Something had to be done quickly to transform the tone for Tom and his parents.

I commented that we had reviewed lengthy details about Tom's lack of success and now it would be helpful to hear about what was going well in his life – his strengths. You could have heard a pin drop.

After what felt like a lengthy silence, a brave youth worker stated that she had a different perspective on Tom's Grade 7 year and proceeded to distribute photos of him and a project team he had worked with. She told stories about Tom's gifts, to be spontaneous, funny, creative – and a leader. She described his final elementary school year when she facilitated the school's Anti-Violence Consultant Team and Tom was the captain. Tom's previous sitting position at the table had slipped toward a horizontal daze and now he was sitting up, alert, and holding back a slight grin. The lines on his youthful forehead cleared. The youth worker's story was brief, poignant, and uplifting. It shifted the focus to what was right about Tom. Here new possibilities and plans emerged that greatly helped Tom shift to more constructive behaviours.

TOM'S **STORY** *CONT'D*

• • • • •

A school-wide

approach to raising

boys' achievement

requires a conceptual

framework with

guiding principles

that are sowed in a

philosophy of hope

and optimism.

It is often at a very extreme point of discouragement that parents and school staff begin to put school grades in their proper perspective. Not all kids are suited for the institution of schooling, at least as it presently stands. The upshot was that Tom agreed to return to his acting school one evening per week and on weekends, and instead of taking a taxi, his father drove him and sat in on the Wednesday evening classes. Acting was at the heart of Tom's passion and distinctive talents. The school supported this plan and Tom re-engaged in learning. With further encouragement he even agreed to return to school part-time. The principal's creative suggestions for modifications to his schedule underscored the staff's willingness to be flexible and work with Tom.

A school-wide approach to raising boys' achievement requires a conceptual framework with guiding principles that are sowed in a philosophy of hope and optimism. The emphasis must not be on grades, but on developing strengths – gifts, talents, and capacities.

Albert Einstein said, "You cannot solve the problem with the same kind of thinking that created the problem." Boys benefit when we drop our preconceived notions of schooling and try fresh approaches. More than ever before, we need to work together in a collaborative way and with strong resolve to make a difference for boys.

• • • • •

GUIDELINE 91
TAKE TIME TO ASSESS COMMUNITY READINESS

NOT all schools are at the same stage of readiness to implement a comprehensive approach to gender achievement disparity. Each school community needs to assess the degree of teacher and community receptiveness before any meaningful change can be implemented.

GUIDELINE 91

TAKE TIME TO ASSESS COMMUNITY READINESS *CONT'D*

TAKE time to consider whether boys' achievement warrants further discussion at your school. Talk with teachers and other interested parties from the community, including boys' family members. A community of teachers-as-students can engage in a reciprocal learning process around the topic of gender and achievement. What do you, colleagues, friends, and boys' family members, know about boys' underachievement in school, home, or elsewhere? It is only after assessing how boys are faring at your school, and how other school staff regard the issue of boys' achievement, that you can determine whether more comprehensive exploration and discussion is warranted.

• • • • •

An increased

population of boys

can greatly affect

classroom climate,

behaviour, and

learning.

Remember that teachers will have varied perspectives on boys' needs. Guard against becoming discouraged if you discover that only a few teachers in your circle share a concern about boys. Although each school is unique, so is each department, grade level, teacher, and parent. Teachers who attend my workshops report that they often have a greater percentage of boys in their classrooms and notice how an increased population of boys can greatly affect classroom climate, behaviour, and learning. These teachers, some of whom are also parents struggling with raising sons at home, want to help boys channel their energy constructively. Sometimes it can be helpful to find at least one other person to discuss ideas and share resources. If only a small group of educators are concerned, they can still establish a discussion group and report back to the entire staff as needed. If there is not enough interest, you may end up deciding to delay action for the time being. However, if your school staff and parents decide to proceed with making a plan to raise boys' achievement, be prepared for the challenging process involved with change. As this topic taps into wide ranging cultural and political issues, achievement and gender is anything but straightforward. Remember, if everyone is not involved in the discussion they may later feel forced into putting their time and effort into a project that their heart is not invested in. Mandated change usually backfires – leaving teachers and others confused and annoyed. Consulting from the ground up is necessary not only to gather information but also to create buy-in. What really matters is how people make decisions and take action – how collective thought comes together for a greater purpose.

GUIDELINE 92
RAISE AWARENESS

• • • • •

Even if something

that was tried

previously didn't

work, it could

later take on a

new meaning in

a new context

with a broader

commitment.

SINCE teaching is mostly a very autonomous act, there is often little time for teachers to talk with each other about possible school-wide initiatives. I have observed the rich ideas that come out, however, when teachers have the time and opportunity to engage in dialogue with each other. At this generative stage of open-ended discussion, protect against discouragement by shutting down ideas with the attitude of *been there and done that* thinking. Even if something that was tried previously didn't work, it could later take on a new meaning in a new context with a broader commitment. As a team, consider the following list of widely held perceptions in the community and media about boys' under-achievement as a stimulus from which to begin discussion:

- Boys get more attention because they are more rambunctious.
- Girls get more attention because they are more compliant.
- Girls are better at school than boys.
- Girls are better suited for the cooperative and structured nature of school.
- Boys have few role models for learning and appropriate social behaviour.
- Boys pay less attention to homework than girls.
- The women's rights movement has worked against boys.
- Boys don't read as well as girls.
- Boys are anti-authority and just more independent than girls.
- The adolescent years affect boys' achievement more that girls' achievement.
- Boys' hormones make them more distracted than girls in the upper grades.

Much of the debate about boys' achievement has concentrated on cultural and political issues outside the school's domain. Research into school effectiveness suggests that it is inside the classroom where individual teachers can make real differences to their success. Avoid the *blame game*–a tempting but distracting byway.

The studies from other schools, educational theorists, and researchers can provide ideas and hint at strategies that have worked in various contexts. But it is critical that educators consider what will work in their unique school.

GUIDELINE 93
TALK WITH BOYS TO DIG DEEPER

BOYS do not always find their way to expression of ideas easily. *The Inner World of the School* suggests that student views "…deserve to be taken into account because they know, better than anyone, which teaching styles are successful, which techniques of learning bring the best out of them." Teachers can gain insight into the complexity of under-achievement by talking directly with boys – both those who fare well in school and those who are not making the grade. Through reflective dialogue, you will become better acquainted with boys' needs, perspectives, and design approaches that are best suited for them and your school community.

• • • • •

Teachers can gain

insight into the

complexity of any

underachievement

by talking directly

with boys.

Involve boys in the program development process from the beginning. Don't let adults make all the decisions and then ask boys to help. Including boys and girls of all ages in the process of decision-making, implementation of programs, assessment and evaluation increases the chances of success.

At home and at school, boys need opportunities to reflect on schooling, boyhood, and on life in general. Discussion groups, debates, classroom posters, icons around the school, and other ideas that give *cause for pause* are helpful. Interviewing boys gives insight into the importance of the relational aspects in teaching as well as method and content. It's not too surprising that boys tend to work for teachers they believe understand, like, and respect them as individuals. When I talked to boys about the kinds of teachers they prefer, boys' comments, while varied, suggested that they learn teachers – not subjects.

- "Teachers who let you have the entire recess help me to learn the mostest."

- "Teachers who let their guard down and have a little fun teach better."

- "If a teacher isn't fair with the rules I won't listen or learn."

- "I can handle a lot – just not shouting."

- "My favourite teacher still liked me, even when I was bad."

- "I like teachers who switch it up – offer varied activities – and turn learning into something new everyday."

GUIDELINE 93
TALK WITH BOYS TO DIG DEEPER *CONT'D*

I HAVE found that boys consistently report to me that they learn best from teachers who are fair, fun, and provide varied and stimulating learning activities. Consider making available to all students – boys and girls – the list of following items that typically describe a good teacher. Notice if there exists any gender differences or if a particular subgroup of boys value one teacher behaviour or approach significantly over another:

• • • • •

When listening to boys, be sure to consider if history and present grades affect attitudes toward learning.

• doesn't shout	• is friendly
• is firm	• respects students
• listens	• provides interesting assignments
• has fun	• provides appealing activities
• is fair to all	• has high standards

Also have boys and girls rate their favourite school subjects and notice any gender variance that may exist. Many studies show that while English is the most popular subject in secondary school, more boys like technical and science coursework than girls. Are there unique preferences in your school community?

When listening to boys, be sure to consider if history and present grades affect attitudes toward learning. Do boys who are receiving lower grades and behaviour support have differing views? How might different groups of boys have varying needs?

GUIDELINE 93
TALK WITH BOYS TO DIG DEEPER *CONT'D*

AFTER completing your surveys and focus group discussions with boys, reflect on your experience of listening to boys:

- Was it difficult? Why or why not, what do you think?
- To what extent did it seem useful? How?
- How difficult or easy did the boys seem to find this experience?
- . What conclusions did you draw about possible causes of boys' underachievement?
- How do these conclusions compare to your original hypotheses?
- How do your theories and conclusions compare to those of colleagues?
- . What possible directions or solutions arose naturally in discussion with boys and your subsequent reflection and discussions? What are they?

• • • • •

GUIDELINE 94
COLLABORATE WITH PARENTS

MORE than any other group in our society, it is parents who care about making schools, classrooms, and learning work for their boys. When boys are striking out, it is essential that parents be consulted as partners. Parents and teachers may look at young children's learning from different perspectives, but they share a common goal – making sure that children receive the best education possible. Mutual respect and communication between home and school takes advantage of both perspectives to provide children with the kind of care and education that will help them thrive.

Peter Senge, who was named a 'Strategist of the Century' by the *Journal of Business Strategy,* (September 1999) said that: "Schools may be the starkest example in modern society of an entire institution modeled after the assembly line. This has dramatically increased educational capability in our time, but it has also created many of the most intractable problems with which students, teachers, and parents struggle to this day." Challenges with boys at school more often than not reflect the challenges parents face at home. Through dialogue parents and teachers can recognize these shared problems and figure out how best to meet the needs of boys – together. Involving parents is typically not a hard sell when parents view teachers as approachable and receptive to their perceptions and concerns.

GUIDELINE 94
COLLABORATE WITH PARENTS *CONT'D*

I HAVE noticed over recent years that parents are much more vocal about their concerns regarding schooling and boys. At a presentation to over 300 parents last fall, an articulate parent who wanted her voice to be heard asked if there was a school trustee in the audience. She then publicly expressed her dissatisfaction about what she saw as the school's inflexibility toward boys' learning.

Cooperative Discipline, a highly successful guide to supporting student behaviour and learning, offers practical advice when partnering with parents. "When listening to parents' concerns avoid the temptation to take their defensiveness personally, for when we understand how parents feel we're better able to respond empathetically…To win parental cooperation, it's critical that we talk about behaviour in non-judgmental terms," says author Linda Albert. It's not surprising that some parents will blame the school for the plight of their son, just as some teachers blame the parents or community. In an atmosphere of mutual respect, however, we can discuss highly charged issues around boys and learning and work together for success.

• • • • •

To win parental cooperation, it's critical that we talk about behaviour in non-judgmental terms.

PARENTS HAVE A RIGHT TO PARTICIPATE IN THEIR CHILD'S EDUCATION AND EVERYONE BENEFITS WHEN THE EDUCATION SYSTEM IS HELD ACCOUNTABLE.

GUIDELINE 95
AVOID RUSHING INTO QUICK-FIX BANDWAGON SOLUTIONS

IMPLEMENTING haphazard solutions before examining the current state of boys' achievement in your school and best practice from other learning communities may bring about some quick success with perhaps a story in your school newsletter, but this change will not be lasting or deep. Like any structure or building constructed on a shaky foundation, the results may be initially impressive, but will soon start to show the cracks. Although it's useful to review studies and the approaches that other schools have used, you need to think carefully about how these approaches could be transferred to your school community. In light of this forewarning, I offer two trendy debates for your consideration – just remember, action without understanding often leads to bandwagon thinking.

• • • • •

Action without

understanding

often leads to

bandwagon

thinking.

SINGLE-GENDER **CLASSES**

SINGLE gender classrooms are being eyed across North America as a possible solution to raising achievement. *The Globe and Mail* summarized the research supporting gender separation and offered the following benefits of segregating girls and boys in schools: 1) Students can break free of gender stereotypes. Boys feel freer to pursue interests in music, art, drama, and foreign languages while girls are more likely to take advanced math, physics, and information technology; 2) Boys are freer to express enthusiasm and bullying will be reduced; 3) A curriculum can be tailored to different learning styles as girls seem to do better with a collaborative approach while boys respond to a louder and more lively style, even confrontational; and, 4) In a coed setting, receiving an "A" lowers a boy's status with other boys (February 1, 2003).

At a Montreal high school the experimentation with separating males and females classes appears to have been a success, according to the principal. In separate classes, students are reported to be more attentive. Girls explore ideas more fully while boys appear to have less need to posture. It is hard to argue with proven results, but we should avoid the assumption that separating genders for learning will automatically lead to increased achievement in all school communities. Besides, are girls the only reason boys posture? Don't *roosters strut their stuff* for other boys in masculine activities, including certain sports?

GUIDELINE 95
AVOID RUSHING INTO QUICK-FIX BANDWAGON SOLUTIONS *CONT'D*

• • • • •

Rather than ponder

whether groups

should be mixed

or not, we need

to challenge the

prevalence of

sexist attitudes

and practices

in our schooling

communities.

THE National Association for the Advancement of Single Sex Public Education has become the vocal champion for separating boys and girls at school. Although I applaud their chief advocate's concern for the plight of boys in public schools, I question some of his speculations – for example, his complaint that some female teachers are barely audible to boys at the back of the class, or that boys need to be yelled at to get their attention. Blaming female teachers? Yelling at boys? How will that teach boys the valuable lessons about balancing conflicting needs and cooperation between the genders?

Is separating boys and girls really the answer? It all depends on the needs of each community. While some critics say that separation shelters students at an impressionable age from social tensions, others claim that it actually plays into gender stereotyping and only makes the problem worse. It has also been suggested that it isn't the gender separate classes that make the difference, but it is often the extra attention from teachers that comes with it.

A one-size fits all approach is appealing in some ways, but we must be careful not to grab hold of something just because it seems expedient. A growing body of research has indicated that gender inequalities are interwoven with social class, ethnicity, sexuality, and a variety of individual differences. Rather than ponder whether groups should be mixed or not, we need to challenge the prevalence of sexist attitudes and practices in our schooling communities.

Despite Australian school administrators publicly denouncing the introduction of a separate education for boys they confirmed their commitment to focus on gender equity: "…to address the differing concerns and educational experiences of boys and girls it is necessary to acknowledge that gender is a central issue for both girls and boys. It is clear that boys have needs that are not being met effectively by schools. Narrow versions of masculinity and obsolete views of men's and women's roles restrict boys' opportunities in relation to their educational and social development, vocational experiences, and therefore their subsequent life chances." On the matter of separating boys they were particularly forceful and indicated that a "gender apartheid approach would fail to recognize the complex nature of gender" and would further exacerbate the already divisive and destructive environment that has surrounded discussion of gender issues in education.

CHAPTER ELEVEN

ATTRACTING MEN **TO TEACHING**

THROUGHOUT the western world efforts are being made to get more males into teaching. According to the National Education Association's research in 2002, just 21% of the 3 million U.S. teachers are men. Over the last two decades, the ratio of males to females in teaching has steadily declined. The number of male teachers now stands at a forty year low. I worry that we are giving children the message that nurturing and teaching among males must not be important because there are few men around.

The rationale behind trying to bring more men into the teaching profession rests on the notion that boys need male role models in our schools and benefit from seeing men in an educator's role, just as aboriginal children benefit when they are taught by aboriginal teachers. It is hard to argue against gender-balance among teachers.

• • • • •

Over the last two decades, the ratio of males to females in teaching has steadily declined.

MEN IN SCHOOLS CAN BE ANCHORS IN THE STORM, ESPECIALLY FOR MALE STUDENTS.

However, the tone of this discourse becomes critical of female elementary school teachers, who are accused of feminizing boys, making them dependent and working against the development of positive manhood (Sexton, 1969). Michael Gurian, author of *Boys and Girls Learn Differently*, also claims that female teachers want to see behaviour that is more natural for girls than boys. I would argue that while female teachers have likely been socialized differently than the boys they teach, this does not necessarily mean that they will not be able to accept or understand male behaviour.

The Ontario government has recently released its report *Narrowing the Gender Gap: Attracting Men to Teaching,* which outlines its plan to attract males to careers in teaching over the next three years. The report covers international views concerning gender and achievement and explores barriers to men becoming teachers. These include perceptions that men are less nurturing, and the impressions that teachers are overworked, underpaid, and have low status. The report also courageously addresses the taboo subject of men touching children, and the fear of false accusations of sexual misconduct. The report claims, finally, "…men in schools can be anchors in the storm, especially for male students.

ATTRACTING MEN **TO TEACHING** *CONT'D*

LAST year the Australian Senate Committee report into the *Sex Discrimination Amendment* (Teaching Profession Bill, 2004) commented that: "…it is quality of teaching and learning provision and not teacher gender that has the most profound impact on the scholastic educational outcomes of boys and girls." I could not agree more. While it's understandable that we might want to attract more male teachers, we have to be careful that we don't attract men at the expense of female teachers, who often are wonderful mentors to boys. Over the past two decades I have been impressed by the level of care and leadership offered by women in our schools.

• • • • •

GUIDELINE **96**
PROVIDE PROFESSIONAL DEVELOPMENT

SCHOOLS are learning organizations for teachers as well as students. Teachers and other educational leaders need to continually update their knowledge of various teaching practices including the ways in which gender differences at different developmental stages come into play in the classroom. Because of the very limited information teachers receive about gender in their preparation to become teachers, they need in-service training about gender-based differences in communication and behaviour and their cultural/socio-economic variations.

In-service training can help teachers understand boys' school-based needs. They can also learn how to modify instructional and behaviour management procedures to address dominant and less dominant styles of learning, behaving, and communicating. Teachers who understand that it is the quality of student-teacher rapport that has the greatest effect on boys' achievement will be especially receptive to cultivating the kind of emotional intelligence and interpersonal skills needed to communicate well with all students – including boys.

GUIDELINE 96
PROVIDE PROFESSIONAL DEVELOPMENT *CONT'D*

GIVE teachers time for reflection and engagement with issues related to boys' achievement. Seek both internal and external supports to acquire the necessary tools. The entire school community can change, as I have seen. Over the years I have had the opportunity to be a part of some great learning teams. Participating in a process that is bigger than myself and beyond my immediate responsibilities has given rise to an experience of deep connection and community. Some of my best experiences in schools have occurred at the most challenging times, when people pulled together as a team. Of course, not everyone will embrace change – at least 10% of your learning community will probably resist – but in-service opportunities can provide fresh and stimulating ideas. Weigh the input of those who wish to participate – then move ahead.

• • • • •

GUIDELINE 97
DEVELOP A PLAN OF ACTION

BEGIN by establishing a framework of understanding that provides the structure for action. Within this framework will be the components, which reflect the values of the school community, and reflect awareness of differing needs of males and females. The framework may also include relevant and promising bits of programs and strategies that have been tried elsewhere.

Throwing financial resources toward increasing boys' achievement is not enough. It is likely that your school already has examples of where such initiatives have been unsuccessful. Sometimes the funding was invested at the wrong time, often too early and well before the initiative had been thoroughly explored. Typically, when funding suddenly becomes available, everybody rallies, wanting to get in on the action. Using initial funding to focus on creating dialogue centered on building capacity is most useful and will lead to a thoughtful plan of action.

CORE COMPONENTS

MANY educators and parents have spent countless hours participating in discussion teams to create amazing plans only to have them gather dust on the shelf. Thus it is essential to take time to ensure that everyone shares a common vision and is committed to the successful implementation of the plan for improving boys' achievement. Think big as short-term initiatives produce limited benefits at best, whereas multi-year planning is more likely to produce enduring benefits. Remember that sustainable funding has to be guaranteed for long range planning. Do not be satisfied with one-time events; such as a father-son reading day or bring your dad to school day. Strive to make raising boys' achievement an integral part of the school culture.

According to Michael Fullan, author of *Leading in a Culture of Change,* before embarking on any project involving change or developing an effective plan of action, you should ensure that four components are in place. These are vision, skills, incentives, and resources. Essentially, your team will need to reflect on the following questions with respect to gender and achievement:

- What is our vision of where we want to be?

- Where are we now?

- How will we get to where we would like to be?

- What skills do we need?

- What incentives do we need to sustain motivation?

- What resources are available to assist?

Fullan cautions that any missing component will lead to breakdown, bewilderment, and false starts. When we embark on school-wide change, we throw ourselves into temporary imbalance and discomfort and wobble with uncertainty. Just like core body strength training, we develop new responsive muscles when we accept imbalance. For more information about this approach read, *The Human Side of School Change,* by Robert Evans, who offers a penetrating analysis of educational metamorphosis, and views resistance as constructively transformative.

• • • • •

When we embark

on school-wide

change, we

throw ourselves

into temporary

imbalance and

discomfort as

we wobble with

uncertainty.

CORE COMPONENTS *CONT'D*

• • • • •

Just like core body

strength training,

we develop new

responsive muscles

when we accept

imbalance.

The Association for Supervision and Curriculum Development suggests that a school plan contain the following elements:

- Objective
- Purpose
- How it supports district goals
- How it supports the school improvement plan
- How it supports teacher performance/student data analysis
- Participants
- Timeline

  - workshops
  - peer coaching and informal peer observation
  - action research
  - collaborative teacher planning
  - faculty/team meetings
  - study groups
  - off site visitation
- Strategies used to implement the objective

- Narrative of results
- Evidence of improvement

GUIDELINE 98
PURSUE ACTION RESEARCH AND COLLECT DATA

ONCE your school has established a reasonable plan of action, appoint a research and evaluation regime to assess the effectiveness of intervention strategies and programs introduced. Keep in mind that males and females are biologically and behaviourally much more similar than different and that the differences that do exist don't imply that one strategy is necessarily better than another. In addition, we need to be careful about drawing conclusions about measurable differences that compare group scores on human capabilities and behaviours.

· · · · ·

Beware of

projects that

leave girls out.

IN THE NAME OF OBJECTIVE DATA AND RESEARCH, THE CLAIM OF EDUCATIONAL GENDER BIAS HAS CREATED CONFUSION.

Beware of projects that leave girls out. I recall one school that embarked on a literacy project for boys that excluded girls. They reported confusion about why they couldn't be included in the new library team that was reviewing new books. Whatever you do, make it fair and inclusive for both boys and girls.

Be attentive and cautious when interpreting data and especially when reporting it to the wider community. In the name of objective data and research, the claim of educational gender bias has created more confusion than solidarity. Numbers and newspaper headlines can be used out of context in ways that produce unconstructive buzz. The American Association of University Women's (1992) assertion that girls were being short-changed in the classroom and boys were favoured was eventually proven unreliable and refuted by their own statistics (*Twenty-Twenty*, March 22, 1996). An American Assistant Secretary of Education was even reported to say that the misrepresented gender data led to "a feeding frenzy of victimization based on a lot of hype" (Bushweller, 1994).

Conventional school research has potential pitfalls. It can be difficult to reach agreement about how boys can best be served. If the dialogue is cut short, dissent can be suppressed or ignored. If inappropriate questions are asked, the resulting data will be irrelevant. Conflict over interpretations of data can make teachers decide to opt out of the boys' project.

PURSUE ACTION RESEARCH AND COLLECT DATA *CONT'D*

FOR these reasons and more, the conventional research approach – commencing with a hypothesis and proceeding to a conclusion – is best replaced by action research. Action research is a form of collaborative inquiry that provides teachers with new opportunities to reflect on and assess their teaching with boys, to share feedback with fellow team members and to make decisions about which new approaches to include in the team's curriculum, instruction, and assessment plans.

• • • • •

There is no one

approach that

works for all

schools.

Possible topics related to boys' under achievement that schools could focus on include:

> • limited language and social skills
>
> • absenteeism
>
> • disruptive behaviour
>
> • street values
>
> • low expectations

There is no one approach that works for all schools. Cultural sensitivity awareness training may benefit one community. Another community might choose to try specific strategies such as writing frames or storyboards to promote more active writing.

DATA COLLECTION

MEANINGFUL and effective data collection tools that can demonstrate shifts in student achievement are crucial to the credibility and success of your project.

• • • • •

Data do not

drive decisions;

people do.

DATA COLLECTION TOOLS

- Be clear as to why you are collecting data. Formulate good questions that relate to the specific information needs of the project.

- Be certain about how you are going to use the data you collect.

- Design a process to collect data. Our beliefs and values affect this selection process.

- Use the appropriate data analysis tools and be certain the necessary data are being collected. Ensure that the data is accurate, useful, and not too time consuming to collect. It must also be reliable enough to allow you to formulate hypotheses and develop strategies with confidence.

- Identify an accurate sample size.

- Use multiple sources of data to increase the believability of the findings. Collect data from more than two sources or points of view, each which provides a unique justification with respect to relevant information about the situation.

- Data should indicate the answer to the original questions asked.

- Do not make inferences from the data that the data will not support.

- Visually display the data in a format that can reveal underlying patterns.

- The key issue is not how we collect data, but how we generate useful information.

- Data cannot stand alone. It is the meaning we apply to the data that is critical.

GUIDELINE 99
ASSESS AND REPORT ACTION RESEARCH • • • • •

BE sure to build into your plan enough time and resources to adequately assess, summarize, and report your action research results. The following list of suggestions will assist you in reporting your findings:

- Describe what drew your school community to your questions about boys.

- Explain why your question is important to your school.

- Identify instruments used to collect data (surveys, questionnaires, etc.).

- Provide student and adult samples, quotes, and observations.

- Identify the literature reviewed and other sources of information.

- Outline how you organized your data by themes, chronologically, or by questions.

- Describe any struggles encountered devising questions, collecting data, or intrepreting findings.

- Reflect on the experience of participating in a collaborative action research inquiry.

- Communicate the changes you've gone through including insights & inconsistencies.

- Offer conclusions and findings about what your school community learned.

- Consider future directions and ideas for additional growth.

- Include photos demonstrating the process of collaboration of boys visibly achieving at school.

A PROJECT INVOLVING BOYS FROM **A VISIBLE MINORITY**   • • • • •

The Te Roopu Tautoko Committee was formed with the intention of discussing, reviewing, and producing new policies and developmental plans to enhance the learning environment for Maori students.

AN example of one exceptionally comprehensive school project that set about to address achievement and attitudes took place at Tauranga Boys' College in New Zealand. The Te Roopu Tautoko Committee was formed with the intention of discussing, reviewing, and producing new policies and developmental plans to enhance the learning environment for Maori students. This initiative, which aimed to raise the reading levels of 400 Maori boys who comprised 25% of the total school population, had a wide reaching effect. It involved teachers, parents, and students and centered upon four key initiatives: 1) teacher

THE AIM OF THE MENTORING PROGRAM WAS TO EXPLORE POSITIVE WAYS OF ENCOURAGING MAORI STUDENT PARTICIPATION.

effectiveness professional development for the science department staff; 2) a mentoring program for referred 9-13 year-old Maori students; 3) a reading program (*Pause, Prompt, Praise*) – for sixty-nine year 9 and 10 Maori students; and, 4) the formation of a Te Roopu Tautoko Committee to work with the Maori community.

The focus of the professional development activities was to develop positive relationships between teachers and students in science, a subject area in which Maori students were underachieving. The aim of the mentoring program was to explore positive ways of encouraging Maori student participation, building confidence, and increasing engagement and subsequent success in school. The goal of the reading program was to increase the reading level of students reading below their chronological age to foster positive confidence and attitudes.

A PROJECT INVOLVING BOYS FROM **A VISIBLE MINORITY** *CONT'D*

• • • • •

53 of the 69 Maori

students who were

involved in the

program improved

their reading level

and 39 of these

students had

surpassed their

chronological

reading age.

AFTER two years the summary of key results revealed limited evidential data of shifts in Maori student achievement as a result of the project. However, the following outcomes were reported:

- an increase in the percentage of Maori teachers on the staff from 6.5% to 15.2%;

- an increase in the number of Maori parents on the Board of Trustees, from one, to two;

- heightened awareness amongst staff of the critical importance of developing positive relationships as a key to increasing Maori student achievement;

- increased teacher consciousness and sensitivity toward the notion of a culturally located school;

- staff commitment to professional reading to improve their practice;

- increased reading resources available in the school; and

- significant gains in the reading ages of Maori students involved in the reading program. For example, 53 of the 69 students who were involved in the program improved their reading level and 39 of these students surpassed their chronological reading age.

Other boys, like those in this Maori community who are from non-dominant ethno-cultural traditions, are not simply struggling with changing and inconsistent messages about masculinity. They are also grappling with wider and more profound issues associated with racism, poverty, and degradation. We must respond to their needs.

GUIDELINE 100
DEVELOP A COLLABORATIVE SUPPORT TEAM FOR BOYS

I ONCE worked at a school that created a *Guardian Angel Team* in which each teacher identified a boy or girl who was struggling and became their school guardian angel. I have fond memories of one of my younger recipient students inviting me to attend his student-parent-teacher meeting claiming, "The more people you have on your side the better!"

• • • • •

The more people

you have on your

side the better!

Traditional *School Based Teams*, which often include a teacher, administrator, counsellor, and other professionals, have experience addressing the educational needs of students. The team of professionals that met to discuss Tom, the boy introduced at the beginning of this chapter, were part of a *School Based Team* that invited several specialists to discuss his predicament. Such a discussion can, in the worst cases, become simply a team decision about where to allocate resources. Without meaningful understanding of the issues, it may unwittingly contribute to a boy's further discouragement. Our boys need more.

A *STRENGTHENING* TEAM CAN HELP BOYS BECOME MORE RESPONSIVE BECAUSE THEY BEGIN BY FOCUSSING ON WHAT'S RIGHT RATHER THAN WHAT'S WRONG.

A *Strengthening Team* for boys, or girls for that matter, is less formal. It consists of the boy who is struggling and desires growth, a close friend or two, along with an adult facilitator and significant adults directly involved in the boy's life who invited by the boy. Sometimes boys will invite a Big Brother, cousin, or a neighbour to the meeting. The focus is on resiliency, capacity building, and identifying strengths and talents to overcome current challenges.

GUIDELINE 100
DEVELOP A COLLABORATIVE SUPPORT TEAM FOR BOYS *CONT'D*

• • • • •

Focussing on

what's right lets us

move ahead into

a healthier, more

positive direction.

BOYS who typically abhor meetings with parents and professionals and prefer to remain at home and abdicate their opportunity for input will respond favourably to a more relaxed discussion about how to reclaim, recover, or redeem a part of their life that has gone awry. *A Strengthening Team* can help boys become more responsive because they begin by focussing on what's right rather than what's wrong. Rehashing the past keeps us stuck, but focussing on what's right lets us move ahead into a healthier, more positive direction.

I have been invited to sit in on many *Strengthening Teams* with boys of all ages, and even with adult males who have lost their confidence or hope as a result of violence, addiction, marital breakup, or a corporate makeover. Over the years I have discovered that it does not require special training to participate in a team which builds hope – only an open mind, along with a willingness to see past the presenting problem and speak to the innate resiliency and creative genius within each person. In fact, before I arrive at a *Strengthening Team* meeting, I resolve not to leave before I have a sense of the boy's uniqueness.

WHEN BOYS KNOW THAT WE VALUE THEIR AUTHENTIC SELVES AND SEE BEYOND THEIR IRRESPONSIBLE BEHAVIOUR, THEY CAN LEARN TO TAKE RESPONSIBILITY.

When speaking to boys or men who have been seriously damaged or degraded by others through violent or abusive behaviour, I sometimes notice my own initial fearful reactions. As I peek beyond their mask of anger I can see their hurt and then their deeper purpose and potential to contribute their talents. With multi-layered histories of discouragement, it sometimes takes a while to develop a plan of action because often during this process the boy or man is skirmishing with his own negativity. Through the uplifting support of the *Strengthening Team's* affirmative care, they can begin to incubate possibilities.

GUIDELINE 100
DEVELOP A COLLABORATIVE SUPPORT TEAM FOR BOYS *CONT'D*

I RECALL one particularly complex story. A father had been incarcerated for sexually molesting his biological son. The son wanted to re-establish a relationship with his father who had been in jail for a year. The professionals preferred that the boy receive play therapy and were resistant to the idea of father/son contact. I too was understandably cautious, but the father agreed to be a part of a *Strengthening Team* via his only permitted weekly telephone call on Wednesday mornings. Over time we considered various possibilities. Obviously the details associated with this particular case are beyond the scope of our current discussion. However, I can report that two months later I found myself supervising speakerphone telephone contacts between this father who was himself recovering from a history of abuse and his very pleased 10 year-old son. The judge commented that the plan was highly unusual but granted approval under strict conditions.

This is an extreme example. But all circumstances can present challenges, and all require a commitment to heal and address the basic human needs to feel capable, connect in socially meaningful ways, and contribute to others. I recall a boy in Grade 5 whose giftedness led to much peer ridicule. He became the Captain of the Lego Robotics Team and with his leadership, dozens of boys and parents attended after school competitions. Once a boy in Grade 10 struggling with a marijuana addiction became the *right-hand* assistant to a community police officer when she offered drug-proofing education programs. I was amazed at her ability to maintain connection with him even when he would briefly return to drug misuse.

When boys know that we value their authentic selves and see beyond their irresponsible behaviour, they can learn to take responsibility, reclaim their courage, and their self-respect. It can test our own maturity when we struggle with underachieving boys who defy our efforts and the rules of the school. It's easier to focus on their behaviour than to think about meaningful learning they will be able to take with them into the world. When we collaborate, gathering our resources and intentions to help boys meet their potential, we participate in something that is bigger than ourselves. Collaboration will help us to leave a lasting legacy—a contribution that may or may not be recognized at the time.

• • • • •

There are no easy or quick answers, but we who are educators love to be challenged and there's no better place for a challenge than working with boys in schools.

THE
CONCLUSION

Education is not the filling of a pail, but the lighting of a fire.

William Butler Yeats

The institution of public schooling is one of the most stable and enduring establishments of our democracy. This stability is both a blessing and a curse. We have an enduring tradition of helping large numbers of students with varying abilities develop their inquiring minds. However, the school system is also so large and unwieldy – and, like any institution, essentially conservative – that it can be slow to respond to socio-cultural changes. Unless we respond to the pressing needs of students, our educational institutions may become irrelevant to the education of our youth – boys especially. How do we transform education to meet the needs of today's students?

Many people have assumed that teaching and learning are gender-neutral and free of bias, but we have recently become uncomfortably aware of how much differences in the cultures of masculinity and femininity influence our attitudes toward teaching and learning. Within the stability of the school structure gender biases are expressed in the power structure – how people work together and treat each other – all of which send important messages about gender expectations to both boys and girls.

• • • • •

Classrooms

inculcate particular

versions of

masculinity and

femininity that

become part

of a student's

experience.

WE are all influenced by gender bias in one way or another as a result of our lived experiences, and schools represent a microcosm where these biases play out. In the classroom for example, kindergarten boys get more frequent attention from the teacher when engaged in block-building activities as compared to when they play stereotypical females games such as house. Classrooms inculcate particular versions of masculinity and femininity that become part of a student's experience.

We have recently become rightly concerned about boys' lagging academic achievement. Sometimes we notice boys' apathy and disengagement with learning at school. Other times alarming headlines blare at us: *"Boys are Flailing and Failing in Schools."* Then again, we may read carefully documented reports such as a 2004 report from Statistics Canada called *The Gap In Achievement Between Boys and Girls* that underline ways in which boys' achievement has fallen behind that of girls, particularly in literacy. The report concludes, "On a number of counts, the evidence suggests that more young men than women are experiencing difficulties with school. Young men, particularly male dropouts, appear to be less engaged in school and they continue to

ALL PEOPLE ARE EXCEPTIONAL AT SOMETHING – SCHOOL IS A PLACE TO HONE TALENTS.

drop out of high school before completing the requirements for graduation at a higher rate than girls." Serious issues such as truancy, discipline, substance misuse, and poor learning attitudes are often viewed as the chief problems with boys in schools, but these are only symptoms of a much larger underlying malaise where capable boys are disengaged.

I recently heard the heartbreaking story of a Grade 2 boy who refused to get down from the tree during recess. Billy pretended to not hear the playground supervisor who got the principal to intervene. Once the principal confirmed that Billy was indeed safe and unusually agile, he listened to his predicament. Billy courageously said that he wouldn't stop climbing the tree because, "it's the only thing that I'm good at." All people are exceptional at something – school is a place to hone talents.

CONCLUSION

· · · · ·

Many examples

of male behaviour

that boys witness

today are

inconsistent with

community values

and boys need

help to make sense

of the conflicting

messages.

IF we accept phrases like *boys will be boys,* we buy into a view that does not help prepare young men to grow up and survive in an increasingly competitive and violent world. While men of my generation used to emulate John Wayne or James Dean, today's boys see much more exaggerated images of masculinity such as sports heroes who are ready to drop their hockey sticks at the slightest provocation and pummel an opponent, or multimillionaire professional athletes in trouble with the law – demanding rights without accepting responsibilities. These examples of male behaviour are inconsistent with many community values and boys need help to make sense of the conflicting messages.

What can we do?

My foremost intention in writing this book was to encourage a more positive focus about boys' strengths in school. There is no quick-fix solution to the complex matter of boys' declining school achievement. It will take sustained and systematic work to build on strengths and envision new possibilities so that all students, including underachieving boys, can thrive.

IF WE BUY INTO PHRASES LIKE *BOYS WILL BE BOYS,* IT IS NOT VERY HELPFUL.

Admitting that there is a problem is an important place to begin. During the last five decades of social change, schools have been asked to shoulder more and more of the burden of responsibility. Despite schools being the focal point in children's lives, they cannot be a panacea for all social problems, or address every developmental need that children bring with them to school. We need the meaningful involvement of the larger community. Children learn best when the significant adults in their lives – teachers, parents, family, and community members – work together to encourage and support them. This basic premise should act as a guiding principle in how we structure our response to boys' needs.

SENIOR school district administrators, school trustees, and school principals need to believe in and support boys' initiatives to enable success. Encouraging fathers and men to spend more time with their sons and listening to the voices of concern of mothers and female teachers is essential. Frontline teachers need support for exploring innovative ways to expand their practice to benefit both boys and girls. Support and resource sharing from the corporate community to explore ways for boys to channel testosterone and creativity in productive and enjoyable ways would be helpful. The media can begin to promote healthier images of masculinity that convey respect, compassion, and empathy among males and females, young and old, advantaged and disadvantaged.

We need to respond across the community in ways that do not pit boys' educational needs against the needs of girls. To address the underachievement of boys and girls, we need a holistic approach. We need to bring all of ourselves to the critical work of mentoring the next generation. Yes, we need practical strategies and knowledge about best teaching practices. We also need imagination, and the courage that comes from the heart.

• • • • •

Ackerman, D. (2004). *An alchemy of mind: The marvel and mystery of the brain.* NY: Scribner.

Adler, A. (1998). *Understanding human nature.* Center City, MN: Hazelden Books.

Albert, L. (2003). *Cooperative discipline. Circle Pines,* MN: American Guidance Service.

Alloway, N. (1995). *Foundation stones: The construction of gender in early childhood.* Carlton, Victoria: Curriculum Corporation.

American Association of University Women. (1992). *"How schools shortchange girls."* Washington, DC: AAUW Educational Foundation and National Education Association.

Arnold, R. (1997). *Raising levels of achievement in boys.* Slough: Nfer, Emie.

Bailey, D., & McCristall, M. (1991). *Cool solutions: A complete guide to peer counselling in the elementary school.* Vancouver, BC: Pathways Press.

Barrett, B., Annis, A., & Riffey, D. (2004). *Little moments big magic: Inspirational stories of big brothers and big sisters and the magic they create.* Gilbert, AZ: Magical Moments Publishing.

Berk, L.S., Tan, S.A., Fry W.F., et al. (1989). *"Neuroendocrine and stress hormone changes during mirthful laughter."* Am J Med Sci.;298:390-396.

Biddulph, S. (1997). *Raising boys.* Sydney: Finch.

Bjorkqvist, K., & Niemela, P. (1992). *Of mice and women: Aspects of female aggression.* San Diego, CA: Academic Press.

Bleach, K. (1988). *Raising boys' achievement in schools.* Stoke on Trent: Trentham Books.

Bly, R. (1990). *Iron John.* Reading: Addison-Wesley.

Braden, W. (1999). *Homies: Peer mentoring among African-American males.* Dekalb, Ill.: Leps Press

Bray, R., Gardner, C., & Parsons, N. (1997). *Can boys do better?* Leicester: Sha.

British Columbia Ministry of Education. (1999). *Focus on suspension: A resource for schools.* Victoria: Crown Publications.

Burgess, S., McConnell, B., Propper, C., & Wilson, D. (2003). *"Girls rock, boys roll: An analysis of the age 14-16 gender gap in English schools."* CMPO Working Paper Series No 03/084. Bristol: University of Bristol, CMPO.

Bushweller, K. (1994). *"Turning our backs on boys."* The American School Board Journal, 181(5), 20-25.

Chinn, P.C., & Harris, K.C. (1990). *"Variables affecting the disproportionate placement of ethnic minority children in special education programs."* Multicultural Leader, 3(1), 1-3.

Chopra, D. (1989). *Quamtum healing: Exploring the frontiers of mind body medicine.* NY: Bantam.

Clark, A., & Millard, E. (Eds) (1998). *Gender in the Secondary Curriculum: Balancing the Books.* London: Routledge.

Crabb, L . (1991). *Men and women: Enjoying the difference.* Grand Rapids, Michigan: Zondervan Publishing House.

Cragg, S., Cameron, C., Craig, C., & Russell, S. (1999). *Canada's children and youth: A physical activity profile.* Ottawa: Canadian Fitness and Lifestyle Research Institute.

Cullingford, C. (1991). *The inner world of the school.* London: Cassell.

Csikszintmihalyi, M. (1990). *Flow: The psychology of optimal experience.* NY: Harper Perennial.

Davidson, R. (1992). *"Anterior cerebral asymmetry and the nature of emotion."* Brain Cognition: 20 (1), 125–151.

Dennison, P., & Dennison, G. (1994). *Brain Gym: Teachers' edition revised.* Ventura, CA: Edu-Kinesthetics.

Dreikurs, R., Grunwald, B., & Pepper, F. (1982). *Maintaining sanity in the classroom.* NY: Harper and Row.

Epstein, D., Elwood, J., Hey, V., & Maw, J. (Eds) (1998). *Failing boys? – Issues in gender and achievement.* Buckingham: Open University Press.

Evans, R. (1996). *The human side of school change.* San Francisco: Jossey-Bass.

Fausto-Sterling, A. (2000). *Sexing the body: Gender politics and the construction of sexuality.* NY: Basic Books.

Flach, F. (1997). *Resiliency: The power to bounce back when the going gets tough.* NY: Hatherleigh.

Forness, S. R., & Kavale, K, A. (1996). *"Treating social skill deficits in children with learning disabilities: A meta-analysis of the research."* Learning Disability Quarterly, 19, 2-13.

Fromm, E. (1956). *The art of loving.* NY: HarperCollins.

BIBLIOGRAPHY

Fullan, M. (2001). *Leading in a culture of change.* San Francisco: Jossey-Bass

Garbarino, J. (1999). *Lost boys: Why our sons turn violent and how we can save them.* NY: Anchor.

Gardner, H., Csikszentmihalyi, M., & Damon, W. (2001). *Good work: Where excellence and ethics meet.* NY: Basic Books.

Glasser, W. (2002). *Unhappy teenagers: A way for parents and teachers to reach them.* NY: HarperCollins.

Glasser, W. (1986). *Control theory in the classroom.* NY: Harper & Row.

Goleman, D. (1995). *Emotional intelligence: Why it can matter more than IQ.* NY: Ballantine.

Gur, R.C., Mozley, L.H., Mozley, P.D., Resnick, S.M., Karp, J.S., Alavi, A., Arnold, S.E., & Gur, R.E. (1995). *"Sex differences in regional cerebral glucose metabolism during a resting state."* Science; 267 (5197), 528–531.

Gur, R.C., Skolnick, B.E., & Gur, R.E. (1994). *"Effects of emotional discrimination tasks on cerebral blood flow: regional activation and its relation to performance."* Brain Cognition; 25 (2), 271–286.

Gurian, M. (1996). *The wonder of boys.* NY: Putnam.

Gurian, M. (2001). *Boys and girls learn differently!* San Francisco: Jossey-Bass.

Hagan, K. (1992). *Women respond to the men's movement.* San Francisco: HarperCollins.

Halberstam, D. (1983). *The best and the brightest.* NY: Penguin Books.

Hannaford, C. (1995). *Smart moves: Why learning is not all in your head.* Alexander, NC: Great Ocean.

Hargreaves, A., & Fullan, M. (2000). *Mentoring in the new millennium: Theory into practice.* Toronto: Ontario College of Teachers.

Hoff Sommers, C. (2001). *The war against boys.* NY: Simon & Schuster.

Hutshinson, D. (2004). *"A critical evaluation of raising boys' attainment."* Educational Psychology in Practice, 20, 1, 15.

Jensen, E. (1998). *Brain-based learning* (Rev. ed.). San Diego: The Brain Store.

Johnson, D., & Johnson, R. (1989). *Cooperation and competition: Theory and research.* Edina,MN: Interaction Book Company.

Johnson, D., & Johnson, R. (1996). *Meaningful and manageable assessment through cooperative learning.* Edina,MN: Interaction Book Company.

Keirsey, D., & Bates, M. (1984). *Please understand me: Character and temperament types.* Del Mar, CA: Prometheus Nemesis.

Kelly, G. A. (1955). *The psychology of personal constructs.* NY: Norton. Reprinted by Routledge (London), 1991.

Kindlon, D., & Thompson, M. (2000). *Raising Cain: Protecting the emotional life of boys.* NY: Ballantine.

Knitzer, J., Steinberg, Z., & Fleisch, B. (1990). *At the schoolhouse door: An examination of programs and policies for children with behavioral and emotional problems.* NY: Bank Street College of Education.

Kohn, A. (1993). *Punished by rewards: The trouble with gold stars, incentive plans, A's, praise, and other bribes.* Boston: Houghton Mifflin.

Kronberg, R., & York-Barr, J. (Eds.). (1998). *Differentiated teaching and learning in heterogeneous classrooms.* Minneapolis, MN: University of Minnesota, Institute on Community Integration.

Langley School District #35. (2003). *Stand together: Student anti-harassment curriculum.* Langley, BC.

Lew, A., & Bettner, B. (1992). *Raising kids who can.* NY: HarperCollins.

Liedloff, J. (1975). *The continuum concept: In search of happiness lost.* Cambridge: Perseus.

Lipton, B. (2005). *The biology of belief: Unleashing the power of consciousness matter and miracles.* Santa Rosa, CA: Mountain of Love/Elite Books.

Lynn, K. (2003). *Who's in charge anyway: How parents can teach children to do the right thing.* Vancouver: Whitecap.

Mathews, F. (2003), *"The forgotten child: The declining status of boys in Canada."* Transition Magazine, Vanier Institute of the Family; 33(1).

Moir, A., & Jessel, D. (1992). *Brain sex: The real differences between men and women.* NY: RandomHouse

Maltz, W. (1991). *The sexual healing journey: A guide for survivors of sexual abuse.* NY: Harper Collins Publishers.

Martino, W., & Pallotta-Chiarolli, M. (2001). *Boys' stuff: Boys talking about what matters.* Sydney: Allen & Unwin.

McIntyre, T. (1996). *"Earning the respect of streetwise youngsters."*

Reclaiming at-risk youth; 4(4), 38-41.

Meckler, L. (1999). *"Drop in teen crime reported."* Boston Globe, 9 July, p. A3.

Miedzian, M. (1988). *Boys will be boys: Breaking the link between masculinity and violence.* NY: Doubleday.

Millar, T. (1997) *"Medicating boys: The little diagnosis that could."* Vancouver Sun, December 4, (pg. A21).

Nelson, J. (1994). *Positive discipline.* Rocklin, CA: Prima Publishing.

Newkirk, T. (2002). *Misreading masculinity: Boys, literacy, and popular culture.* Portsmouth, NH: Heinemann.

Office for Standards in Education, (2003). *Boys' achievement in secondary schools.* (HMI 1659). London: OFSTED.

Pagels, H. (1982). *The cosmic code: Quantum physics as the language of nature.* NY: Oxford University Press.

Peritz, I. (2003). *"Where the boys are."* The Globe and Mail; p. F8.

Pert, C. (1997). *Molecules of emotion.* NY: Touchstone.

Piaget, J. (1977). *"The stages of intellectual development in childhood and adolescence."* In Gruber, H. E., & Vonéche, J. J. (Eds.), *The essential Piaget* (pp. 814–819). NY: Basic Books.

Pittman, F. (1993). *Man enough: Fathers, sons, and the search for masculinity.* NY: Perigee.

Pollack, W. (1998). *Real boys: Rescuing our sons from the myths of boyhood.* NY: Holt.

Postman, N. (1995). *The end of education.* NY: Vintage.

Project Resiliency: Youth overcoming addiction (documentary, DVD). (2005). Langley: School District #35.

Restak, R. (2001). *The secret life of the brain.* Washington, DC: Joseph Henry Press.

Rising to the challenge: Are high school graduates prepared for college and work? (2005). Washington, DC: Achieve, Inc.

Senge, P., Cambron-McCabe, N., Lucas, T., Smith, B., Dutton, J., & Kleiner, A. (2000). *Schools that learn: A fifth discipline fieldbook for educators, parents, and everyone who cares about education.* NY: Doubleday/Currency.

Sexton, P. (1969). *The feminized male: Classrooms, white collars, and the decline of manliness.* NY: Random House.

Scarce, M. (1991). *Male on male rape: The hidden toll of stigma and shame.* NY: Perseus Books.

Schaefer, A. (2000). *G. I. Joe meets Barbie, Software engineer meets caregiver.* Vancouver: British Columbia Teachers' Federation.

Shapiro, F., & Forrest, M. (1997). EMDR: *Eye movement desensitization and reprocessing.* NY: Basic.

Smith, M., & Wilhelm, J. (2002). *"Reading don't fix no chevys".* Portsmouth, NH: Heinemann.

Tannen, D. (1997). *You just don't understand.* NY: Ballantine.

Terry, B., & Terry, L. (2000). *"Boys' underachievement is a problem, but it is not their fault! – Current perceptions and practical strategies."* Topic; 23, 3.

Tomlinson, C. (1999). *The differentiated classroom: Responding to the needs of all learners.* Alexandria.VA: ASCD.

Vorrath, H., & Brendtro, L. (1985). *Positive peer culture.* NY: Aldine Publishing Company.

Wiggins, G., & McTighe, J. (1998). *Understanding by design.* Alexandria, VA: ASCD.

Wolin, S., & Solin, S. (1993). *The resilient self: How survivors of troubled families rise above adversity.* NY: Villard.

Zimmer, C. (2004). *Soul made flesh: The discovery of the brain—and how it changed the world.* NY: Free Press.

Web sites

Canadian:
Responding to boys' needs at home and school. http://www.MentoringBoys.com

G.I. Joe meets Barbie, software engineer meets caregiver: Males and females in B.C.'s public schools and beyond. http://www.bctf.ca/Publications/ResearchReports/2000sd03/

Ontario study – *Narrowing the gender gap: Attracting men to teaching.* http://www.oct.ca/en/CollegePublications/ PDF/Men_In_Teaching_e.pdf

McCreary Centre Society: *Adolescent Health Survey.* http://www.mcs.bc.ca

Male teachers in Canada. http://www.maleteachers.com

BIBLIOGRAPHY

The boys' and girls' literacy project at St. Thomas University, NB. http://people.stu.ca/~edresearch/boysngirls.html

Canadian adolescent boys and literacy home page. Research through the University of Alberta and University of Victoria. http://www.education.ualberta.ca/boysandliteracy/

Big Brothers Big Sisters of Canada. http://www.bbbsc.ca/

Young Canadians in a wired world. http://www.cfc-efc.ca/docs/mnet/00002_en.htm#active

Statistics Canada: International student assessment results. http://www.statcan.ca/english/freepub/81-004-XIE/200412/pisa.htm

Government of Canada. School achievement of Canadian boys and girls in early adolescence, 1998. http://www11.sdc.gc.ca/en/cs/sp/arb/publications/research/1998-002344/page06.shtml

Canadian boys: Growing up male. Vanier Institute of the Family. http://www.vifamily.ca/library/transition/331/331.html

Fitter International Inc. distributes active discs – inflatable air cushions that permit movement at a desk. Telephone contact: 1 800 348 8371 http://www.fitter1.com/balls.html?mtcPromotion=header%3Eactive_sitting

United States:
http://www.guysread.com/ *Trends in international mathematics study* – National Center for Education Statistics. http://nces.ed.gov/pubs2005/timss03/science5.asp

Differences in educational achievement for low income black males and females. Article in Harvard Newsletter by Christopher Wheat, May 27, 1997. http://www.wjh.harvard.edu/~cwheat/malefemale.html

NASSPE: National Association for Single Sex Public Schools. http://www.singlesexschools.org/advantages-forboys.htm

American Association of University Women – Equity education reports. http://www.aauw.org/research/girls_education/hssg.cfm

Positive masculinity - Michael Obsatz. http://angeresources.com/shamebased.html

United Kingdom:
Raising achievement of boys. http://www.simonmidgley.co.uk/achieving/gender.htm

Raising boys' achievement toolkit. The Department for Education and Skills and the National Healthy Schools Standard booklet on raising boys' achievement. http://www.standards.dfee.gov.uk/genderandachievement/nhss_boys_achievement2.pdf?version=1

OFSTED (Office of Standards in Education). *Yes he can: Schools where boys write well.* http://www.ofsted.gov.uk/publications/index.cfm?fuseaction=pubs.summary&id=3317 .

Girls rock, boys roll: An analysis of the age 14-16 gender gap in English schools. http://www.bris.ac.uk/Depts/CMPO/workingpapers/wp84.pdf

Australia:
A variety of research reports on the topic of boys and schooling offered by The Commonwealth Department of Education, Science, and Training. http://www.dest.gov.au/schools/boyseducation/

Homophobia: The fear behind the hatred. http://www.bidstrup.com/phobia.htm

Gender education – The Victoria Department of Education and Training site. Search under *boys education and working with boys* for some useful reports and information. http://www.sofweb.vic.edu.au/gender/index.htm

Improving the Educational Outcomes for Boys. Search under General Publications: Education of Boys. http://www.decs.act.gov.au

Boys: Getting it right. The Education and Training Committee tabled its report on the education of boys (contains over 200 submissions), October 2002. http://www.aph.gov.au/house/committee/edt/eofb/report.htm

Australian bibliography: *Boys and schooling.* http://www.education.qld.gov.au

New Zealand:
Tauranga Boys' College. http://www.tbc.school.nz/
Report on raising boys' achievement project. http://www.tki.org.nz/r/maori_mainstream/tekauhua_case_rotorua_e.php

AUTHOR INDEX

SUBJECT INDEX

"MacDonald has a unique perspective and sets a new standard for exceptional teaching and parenting of boys, regardless of their behaviour or achievement levels. *Boy Smarts* is an engaging and much-needed primer that is packed with commanding and constructive leadership." – *Kathy Dodd, Parent and Teacher, Hazelton*

· · · · ·

"Wow! This book is fresh, exciting, and of vital importance. Barry offers skillful and open-hearted originality to create a highly applicable and cutting-edge resource. It actually shows you how to harness testosterone, talents, creativity, and mentor boys for a lifetime of success!" – *Judy McBeth and Barbara Scott, Executive Directors, Big Brothers Big Sisters of Langley*

· · · · ·

"The genius of boys is often the proverbial square peg of schooling. Throughout this book MacDonald shows us how to effectively meet boys where they are at through genuine understanding and rigorous inquiry-based learning." – *Ron Sweet, Principal, Calgary Science School*

· · · · ·

"This book is brimming over with collective wisdom to help boys become successful team players through the development of their own uniqueness and exceptionality." – *Leo Ezerins, 1986 Grey Cup Champion and CFL All Star, Financial Consultant*

· · · · ·

"*Boy Smarts* is a fascinating read and makes the complex reality of teaching and mentoring boys straightforward. It reaches far beyond the National Curriculum and gets to the very heart of teaching and communicating with boys. MacDonald inspires us to move beyond a boys will be boys mentality and to a healthier model of masculinity." – *Julie Ashton, Parent and Teacher, Cheshire, England*

"Boy Smarts is a landmark book with wide appeal! Written with clear direction and a heartfelt understanding for the plight of young boy's today, MacDonald combines his extensive theoretical expertise and practical know-how to provide an illuminating guide that every parent and teacher should read. His ideas respect the nature of boys, while also showing how to nurture them."
– *Karen Elkins, Vancouver Gifted Association, and President – Silbury School*

• • • • •

"This book is remarkable! MacDonald masterfully captures how a community can significantly improve schooling for boys and awaken their passion for learning."
– *Adeline Nychuk-Jensen, Parent, Winnipeg*

• • • • •

"MacDonald combines brain research, our toughest cultural realities (MSN, X-Box, and Grand Theft Auto), and the ancient wisdom of respect and humour to understand each boys' motivation to learn and excel." – *Sarah Forward, Teacher, West Vancouver*

• • • • •

"When it comes to knowing how to work with boys, families, and schools, nobody does it better. Barry has written a brilliant book that is highly relevant for families and schools today."
– *Dr. James Robert Bitter, East Tennessee State University*

• • • • •

"We must help boys to use their time, energy, and talents in positive and contributory ways – it's that simple. MacDonald provides perceptive and proven strategies to accomplish this goal with boys of all ages and from all walks of life. He lays the foundation for constructive and positive futures." – *Marilyn McGuire, International Consultant, Author, Gangs and Violence: School-wide Strategies for Prevention and Intervention*

"Barry has marvelously assembled current research, theory, and practice to create a comprehensive and enlightening resource for school staff, community professionals, and families (aunts, uncles, and grandparents too)! Boy Smarts weaves new gender understandings into an optimistic framework that shows us all how to bring out the best in boys."
– *Edna Nash, Psychologist, ICASSI Board and Faculty*

• • • • •

"*Boy Smarts* is a sharp and illuminating book that challenges everyone to make powerful changes to schools and how we communicate with boys." – *Don Smart, Adler Workshops NZ, New Zealand*

• • • • •

"*Boy Smarts* has given me hope that our interactions with boys are more influential than the powerfully negative messages culture bombards on them." – *Brandon Hawes, Teacher, Victoria*

• • • • •

"*Boy Smarts* carefully guides you through the corridors of boyhood and schooling and documents wise observations about boys' interactions with their peers and adults to help you gain their confidence and lead them to success." – *Mark Ely, Executive Director, Big Brothers of Greater Vancouver*

• • • • •

"MacDonald is a gifted educator and counsellor who shows us how wonderful, intelligent, and caring boys really are. The fantastic guidance offered by him will make considerable impact in the schooling of boys." – *Jennie Monahan, School Psychologist, Australia*

• • • • •

"MacDonald provides concrete direction that doesn't preach, but inspires!"
– *Anne MacLeod, Teacher, Gitwinksihlkw*

For my mother and my father,
who took me on a train ride across America when I was a girl,
and for Uncle B, who was waiting when we got there—B.Y.

For Lesly and Clare—S.S.

KATHARINE LEE BATES LOVED WORDS.
Stories, rhymes, and clever ways of saying things came quickly to her mind. In 1868, when she was nine years old, her mother gave her a red leather diary. After inscribing her name, she began, "I am writing, scribbling, rather, just for fun. Not that I have anything to say. There is a charm in bright, clean, unfilled pages, which I, for one, cannot resist." In truth Katharine had lots to say. She filled those blank pages with her jottings about growing up in the seaside town of Falmouth, Massachusetts.

KATHARINE'S FATHER HAD DIED WHEN SHE WAS A BABY, AND THE FAMILY

did not have much money. As her older brothers and sister went to work, Katharine, the youngest, helped out at home and kept on writing. In one story of hers, a character mused: "I would study and study. I would know what makes the beautiful colors around you, dear old setting sun, and I would learn all about the nations on the other side of the globe. I would find out why some poetry is poetry and some isn't…and how my head thinks."

Probably Katharine herself felt this way, for she was a witty, imaginative student. With a loan from her brother Arthur, she was able to attend a new college for women called Wellesley. By the time she graduated, she had sold some poems and stories. Later she returned to Wellesley to teach English literature. She wrote poetry all her life. And she did travel—to the British Isles, Europe, Egypt, and the Middle East.

In 1893, when Katharine was thirty-four, she was invited to lecture out west for three weeks in July at a college in Colorado Springs. She accepted eagerly. The extra money would be useful, for by now Katharine was helping to support her mother and sister. And she was glad for the chance to see more of her own country. Of course, she took along her diary and her writing notebooks.

As she settled herself in the train, she must have wondered what adventures the trip would bring. "Left Boston on Fitchburg road at 3 P.M.," she wrote in her diary. She surely did not guess all that lay in store.

THE FOLLOWING DAY THE TRAIN stopped at Niagara Falls. Katharine watched and listened as rivers of water roared and pounded and plunged. On the train that night, she noted, "The glory and music of Niagara Falls." She also wrote a poem about the falls, ending with the lines, *Columnar mist and glistening rainbow play,/A splendid thrill of glory and of peril.*

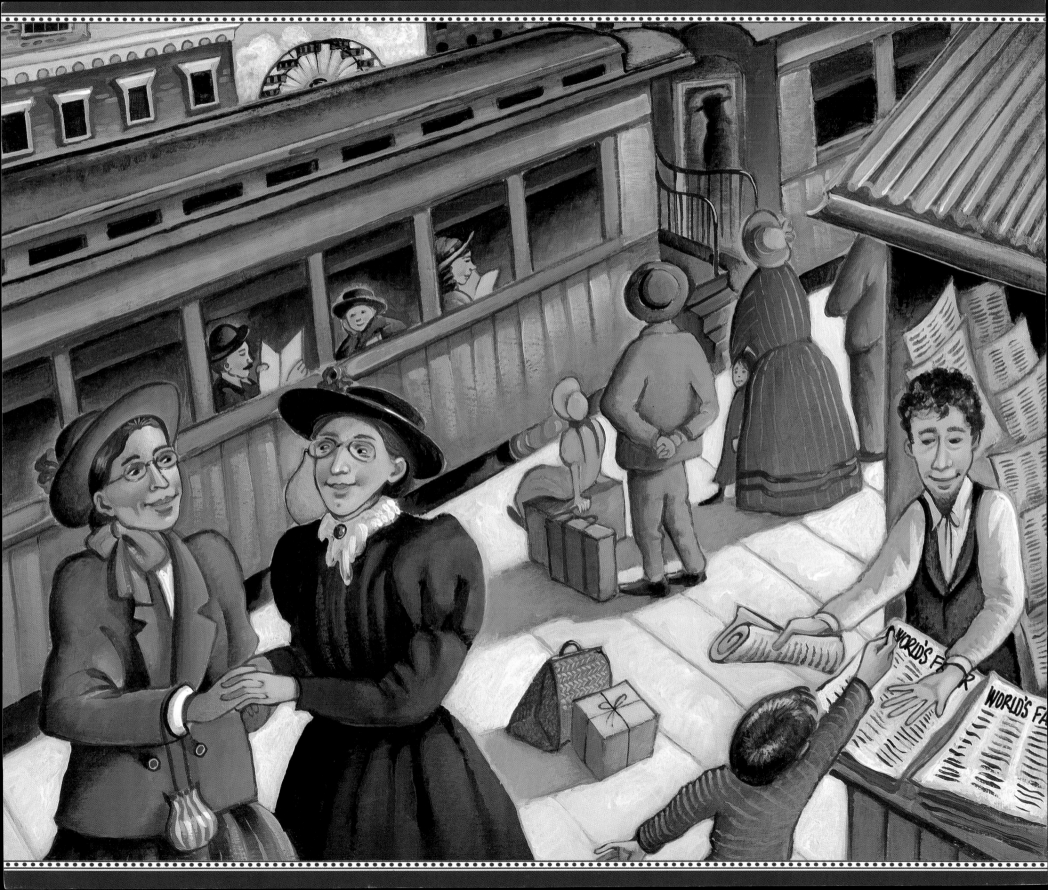

WHEN THE TRAIN REACHED CHICAGO, KATHARINE
was able to spend the weekend with her good friend Katharine
Coman, whose family lived in nearby Oak Park. The two women
had met at Wellesley, where Miss Coman taught history and eco-
nomics. Firmly committed to women's education, they were to
become close lifelong friends and traveling companions. "We were
merry together," Katharine once said.

Katharine respected the social activism of Miss Coman, who
came from an Ohio abolitionist family and who wrote, spoke, and
organized to improve the conditions of immigrant women laboring
in factories and sweatshops. Her friend had a "Westering heart,"
Katharine wrote, "a vigorous and adventurous personality."

Miss Coman appreciated Katharine's poetry, her devotion to
her students, and her vision for a better world. Katharine believed
that each person's life held great possibilities. *Dare to dream/Spirit
outsoars space*, she urged in one of her poems. Also blessed with a
sense of whimsy, Katharine named her bicycle "Lucifer"; often
hummed to herself; penned stories and poems for children; read
dog books to her own dog; and even hosted a party for parrots on
her back steps.

Miss Coman also planned to teach in Colorado Springs that
summer. But for now, the two caught up on each other's news and
visited friends. Then they went to a fair.

THE FAIR WASN'T JUST ANY FAIR.

It was the World's Columbian Exposition, celebrating the four hundred years that had passed since Christopher Columbus's voyage to the New World. Once the fair was over, the grand-looking buildings, which were made of only thin white plaster, would be taken down. But for now it all gleamed like a magnificent alabaster city. Katharine never forgot it.

THE PURPOSE OF THE FAIR WAS TO SHOW WHAT A GREAT NATION

had grown up in America. Each state had created a display of its own special industries and foods. The California Building featured a knight made entirely of prunes. There were also buildings boasting new machinery, new transportation vehicles, and new inventions such as the zipper. At the Palace of Electricity, many felt the glow of their first electric lamp. In the Anthropological Building, a life-size model of the Great Siberian Mammoth stared down at visitors. The nations of the world set up exhibits, too. The two Katharines admired the dress of people from distant lands.

Impressive though it all was, sadly the fair also reflected the prejudices of the times. African-Americans were provided refreshments and rest rooms only in the Haiti Building. Native Americans appeared in a side show. And no women had been invited to participate in planning the fair. After considerable protest, they were allowed to erect their own building, which they did splendidly with the help of an architect from Boston named Sophia Hayden.

In the distance towered the Wheel, designed by the young engineer George Washington Ferris. Some folks were afraid to ride it, but not the two friends. Time was short, however, so the ride would have to wait until they returned. "The Fair. A thing of beauty. Off again at 6 P.M.," Katharine noted.

THE NEXT DAY, WHICH WAS THE FOURTH OF JULY,

Katharine's New England eyes delighted in the rich amber wheat fields of the Great Plains rolling by her window. "Hot sirocco run across Western Kansas," she wrote in her diary, calling herself, "A better American for such a Fourth." As the train sped west, she also turned to her notebooks. Her busy schedule had taught her to write in bits and snatches, her poems often coming "by accident" in spare moments.

BALANCED ROCK

CATHEDRAL SPIRES

KATHARINE ARRIVED IN COLORADO

Springs tired and a bit homesick, but after a few days' rest she was ready to teach. In her free time, her hosts took her sightseeing in the canyons, valleys, and bluffs of the Rocky Mountains. She explored the Garden of the Gods, where huge red rock formations jutted out of the earth in intriguing shapes. People had given them fanciful names: Kissing Camels, Sleeping Giant, Seal and Bear, Cathedral Spires, and Balanced Rock. She saw shimmering lakes, plummeting waterfalls, and heard coyotes howl by moonlight. Once, when a mountain road collapsed just as her wagon passed, she had to spend the night in a gold-mining boom town called Cripple Creek—with no baggage along except a book of poetry. She also visited the grave of Helen Hunt Jackson, who had written about the government's injustice toward Native Americans.

ONE DAY, KATHARINE AND A GROUP OF
teachers set out for the top of Pikes Peak, a famous mountain that reached over two and a half miles into the clouds. The rough dirt road did not go straight up but followed a long and twisty route with frightening hairpin turns. Now and then a wagon did tip over, despite the driver's skill. Local people liked to joke that the drivers didn't need their monthly salaries—relieved tourists, grateful to be back down safely, made such generous tippers!

The teachers took a train to the base of the mountain. Then the merry group piled into prairie wagons emblazoned with the slogan "Pikes Peak or Bust." Halfway up, the drivers stopped at a place called the Halfway House and exchanged the tired horses for sturdy mules. The wagons trundled on, up and up, as the pinewoods gave way to spare "dead white stems, a ghostly forest," then rocky land, and finally the summit.

KATHARINE STOOD AND GAZED OUT
at the sea-like expanse of fertile plains below her. She felt the giant arc of the ample skies above. In the distance the Rockies shone purple in the sun. At that moment, the opening lines of a poem floated into her mind.

But no sooner had the words come to her than two teachers began to faint from the altitude. "Quick, into the wagons," the drivers called. So Katharine had only "one brief ecstatic" glimpse from the top of Pikes Peak.

"PIKES PEAK OR BUST," KATHARINE NOTED

in her diary that evening. "Most glorious scenery I ever beheld." Into her notebook she penciled the lines of poetry that had come to her that day. *O beautiful for halcyon skies/For amber waves of grain./ For purple mountain majesties/Above the enameled plain! America! America! God shed his grace on thee…*

Katharine sat working on more verses. As she wrote, she remembered her train ride across the country. She thought about the glory of the land and about the courageous pioneers who had struggled west in covered wagons to make new lives. She thought about her own forebears who had crossed the rough Atlantic. She remembered the Civil War, which had been fought during her childhood, to end slavery and keep the nation whole. She recalled the progress and ingenuity exhibited at the fair. But Katharine knew that beyond that gleaming white city was another city, a Chicago crowded with hunger and gloom. She had seen that, too. America was in an economic depression that year. Banks had closed. Workers were striking. People needed help.

Katharine wrote about a time when "selfish gain" would "no longer stain" her country. One of her verses went: *O beautiful for patriot dream/That sees beyond the years/Thine alabaster cities gleam/Undimmed by human tears!* She knew that it was not always easy to be fair and loving and to share with others. But her poem envisioned a country where people would join together out of their best selves to make life better for everyone.

AFTER SUMMER SCHOOL WAS FINISHED,
Katharine headed east, stopping once more in Chicago. Again she and Katharine Coman visited the fair. This time, they rode Mr. Ferris's wheel.

IN EARLY AUGUST KATHARINE ARRIVED BACK IN
Wellesley. "Reached home for tea," she jotted. Soon she was busy teaching and laid aside her notebooks from the trip. She wasn't particularly pleased with the poetry she had written that summer. "Consider my verses. Disheartening," she noted in her diary.

Two summers later she came across the Pikes Peak poem and decided to send it to a magazine called *The Congregationalist*. The editor liked it and printed it in the July Fourth issue. Lots of other people liked the poem, too. Almost immediately it was set to many different tunes, even to a march. Soon schools, churches, synagogues, scout troops, and clubs throughout the land were singing Katharine's poem, which was now known as "America the Beautiful." It was even translated so that immigrants new to America could sing it in their own language.

Katharine revised her hymn, as she called it, several times, to make some phrases "more simple and direct" and "a bit more musical." After many years, a contest was held to choose the perfect music, but none of the nine hundred entries seemed just right to the judges. A hymn composed by Samuel Ward is the music we sing today.

AS THE SONG GAINED POPULARITY, PEOPLE
from far and near came to Wellesley to meet Katharine Lee Bates.
Over and over she was asked to tell the story of the bumpy ride up
the mountain and her moment's glimpse from the top of Pikes
Peak. She often invited visitors to stay for tea and to meet her col-
lie dog and parrot. And she showed children treasures from her
travels.

WHEN CONGRESS SET OUT TO SELECT A NATIONAL ANTHEM,

many citizens wanted "America the Beautiful" instead of "The Star-Spangled Banner." Even now, many Americans would vote for Katharine's song.

Over the years, Katharine received hundreds of letters about "A the B," as her family nicknamed it. She did her best to answer them, even writing the words out in longhand for a grandfather who wanted copies for each of his ten grandchildren. Reporters often asked for interviews. One commented that Katharine seemed to want to talk more about her pets than about her celebrated song.

People were forever suggesting small changes to Katharine's verses. One common request was that she add a stanza expressing international brotherhood, or unity among all nations on earth. Saying her song was long enough, Katharine had an interesting solution: "When you sing…think of 'From sea to shining sea,' as applying from the Pacific to the Atlantic, around the other way…and that will include all the nations and all the people."

Aside from the money she received when the poem was first published, Katharine never requested payment for its use. She once told a group of teachers, "It is not work to write a song, it is great joy."